Routledge Revivals

Language, Gender and Childhood

First published in 1985, this book brings together recent work on women and children from the nineteenth-century to the present. The contributors explore in different ways, and from different points of view, the way in which issues of language have been — and are still — central to the history of women and their relation to domestic and educational practices. A crucial issue is the contrast between what it spoken about girls and women, and what girls and women can speak about. The contributors relate this theme specifically to women's position as mothers and the education of girls and women.

I0882762

Language, Gender and Childhood

Edited by
Carolyn Steedman, Cathy Urwin and Valerie Walkerdine

Routledge
Taylor & Francis Group

First published in 1985
by Routledge & Kegan Paul

This edition first published in 2017 by Routledge
2 Park Square, Milton Park, Abingdon, Oxon, OX14 4RN
and by Routledge
711 Third Avenue, New York, NY 10017

Routledge is an imprint of the Taylor & Francis Group, an informa business

A Library of Congress record exists under LC control number: 852446

ISBN 13: 978-1-138-21418-7 (hbk)
ISBN 13: 978-1-315-44640-0 (ebk)
ISBN 13: 978-1-138-21425-5 (pbk)

edited by

Carolyn Steedman
University of Warwick and
University of London, Institute of Education

Cathy Urwin
Child Care and Development Group, Cambridge

and

Valerie Walkerdine
University of London, Institute of Education

Language, Gender and Childhood

First published in 1985
by Routledge & Kegan Paul plc

14 Leicester Square, London WC2H 7PH, England

9 Park Street, Boston, Mass. 02108, USA and

Broadway House, Newtown Road,
Henley on Thames, Oxon RG9 1EN, England

Typeset in 11 on 12 pt Linotron Bembo
by Inforum Ltd, Portsmouth
and printed in Great Britain
by T.J. Press (Padstow) Ltd,
Padstow, Cornwall

Library of Congress Cataloging in Publication Data

Language, gender, and childhood.
(History workshop series)
Summaries of papers presented at History workshop
HW13, 'People's history and socialist theory' in
Oxford in 1980
Bibliography: p.
Includes index.
1. Sociolinguistics—Great Britain—History—19th century—Addresses, essays, lectures. 2. Women—Language—Addresses, essays, lectures. 3. Children—Language—Addresses, essays, lectures. 4. Women—Great Britain—Social conditions—Addresses, essays, lectures. 5. Child rearing—Great Britain—History—19th century—Addresses, essays, lectures. 6. Educational sociology—Great Britain—History—19th century—Addresses, essays, lectures. I. Walkerdine, Valerie. II. Urwin, Cathy. III. Steedman, Carolyn. IV. Title. V. Series.
P40.45.G7L35 1985 401'.9'0941 85–2446

ISBN 0–7100–9977–0 (pbk.)

Contents

Contributors

Karen Clark	Equal Opportunities Commission and Department of History, Birkbeck College, University of London
Gill Frith	Department of English, University of Warwick
Catherine Hall	Department of Cultural Studies, North East London Polytechnic
Alex Owen	School of Communication and Cultural Studies, University of Sussex
Jacqueline Rose	School of Communication and Cultural Studies, University of Sussex
Carolyn Steedman	Arts Education Department, University of Warwick
Cathy Urwin	Child Care and Development Group, Cambridge
Valerie Walkerdine	University of London, Institute of Education

Acknowledgments

The ideas explored in this book were first raised when the History Workshop 14 collective met between January and November 1980. Thanks to them and to Cora Kaplan, who took over the convening of 'Language and Learning', the sub-plenary for which most of the chapters in this book were originally written. Her intervention at this stage helped shape many of these contributions. Thanks as well to Raphael Samuel for delivering to the editors his own oral history of History Workshop.

1
Introduction

This collection of essays is concerned with the way in which modern women and children have been historically constructed. As a collection, it examines both speaking and silence, what could be spoken, where and when; and how words, language and texts were formative in producing taken-for-granted conceptions of childhood, femininity and motherhood. In seeking to understand these formations, it looks particularly at people interacting with written language, as one way of exploring the complex relations between social regulation, the circumscription of action, and subjective experience in both past and present.

The theme of speaking and silence, of finding a voice, has been an important one in the recent history of feminism.[1] The theme has been foreshadowed, perhaps, by the concern of social historians with the language and experience of working people and minority groups, and with making the formerly invisible visible. Until recently however, women and children have been comparatively neglected by this process of rescue. Grand histories and grand theories chart the struggle of 'the people', and any social practice in which women or children dominate, like schooling or nursing, or work situations associated with the provision of care, has been treated as marginal or of extremely low status. This neglect of women and children is not of course confined to history. Within sociology, for instance, children only seem to become interesting at adolescence when, if masculine, they can display the magic quality of resistance.[2] Women and children are denied resistance and we seem to have nothing very interesting to say about the positions they occupy.

But since the late 1970s the study of women and children, the places they occupy and their power to speak from those positions, has received new impetus. The imperative now is to move beyond an uncovering of fragmented sites of resistance.[3] This approach requires a form of analysis which does not simply point to the existence of either alternative forms of language or lacunae of silence as expressions of social inequality. Rather, it demands that we understand the possibilities for change by examining how forms of speaking and forms of truth have been produced, and how these regulate or circumscribe what can be said about what, when and where. In this process, we are also forced to re-analyse what constitutes subversion and resistance, and how the subjective and the political intersect.[4]

The aim, then, is not simply to put the study of women and children on the map as objects whose existence can be taken for granted, but rather to uncover how modern conceptions of women and children have been produced. This enterprise results in a reading of the past in which the current concerns of feminists are centrally implicated, and which offers a challenge to the categories of power and resistance, change and fixity. Women and children are not fixed and unchanging entities, but change in status and position through personal and historical time. Beyond this, the collection is intended to demonstrate the value to historians of discovering new subjects for historical analysis and to show particularly how, over a specific historical period, an analysis of the position of children and women is central to understanding it.

These essays cover a period from the early nineteenth century to the present day. Crucial to this period are not only the historical typicalities it usually presents – the consequences of industrialisation, the birth of the modern nation state, imperial expansion and colonialism – but also certain shifts in regulation and government and in the structure and distribution of power. Overt regulation, exerted through coercion, shifted towards forms of covert regulation through the production of particular social apparatuses and technologies. These themselves depended on the development of scientific knowledge, in particular on the control over the body through medicine, and the development of the scientific study of populations, in which Malthusian economics and social Darwinism were central. These apparatuses incorporating the notion of the norm (evidenced most obviously in the modern idea of the intelligence quotient) supported the practices which produced, and continue to produce, the individual who is the target for social regulation. This individual is universal, natural or pathological, and the social practices which regulate it have brought with them particular conceptualisations of women and children. For example, as women, particularly bourgeois women, were systematically excluded from the public sphere of politics and administration and confined to the private world of the home, their confinement was supported by the emergence of discourses particularly associated with medicine and education, which stressed the 'naturalness' of this position, and constructed the feminine as irrational, emotional, and psychologically formed for the bearing and rearing of children. Over the same period, working-class women, having to engage in paid employment, surrendered their children to family surrogates of the correct form, who, through the practices of schooling, would produce them in a normal image. At the same time, class differences were submerged as the category 'child' was produced – a child whose development was defined in relation to a universal norm.

An understanding of the regulatory apparatuses of nineteenth-century society is thus integral to understanding how women have been defined primarily in terms of their capacities for bearing and rearing children. This definition not only curtails their opportunities for finding an alternative language, but permeates their desires: women want to be what they have been made to be.

> We sometimes forget, in the animosity of our contentions, that differ as we will, we are still of the same kind and of the same country, kith and kin of one another, united by one common bond of mutual dependence and mutual interest. We often forget this. Woman's gentle nature never forgets it. She knows no hatred, nor will let us know any, if we but appeal to her . . . whose province and whose dearest task it is to soften, to bless and to purify our imperfect nature. . . .

Catherine Hall quotes here (page 25) from the speech made by the Mayor of Birmingham when the town was granted the status of a borough in 1839. Although women's help was solicited in political activities in the period 1780–1850, Hall stresses that the constitution of masculinity and femininity by the idea of *nature* produced characteristics that were in radical opposition to each other. Women's natures fitted them for caring; passivity and gentleness were the private qualities that maintained the domestic sphere. The exclusion of bourgeois women from the public realm meant that they were excluded from the very practices that produced the bourgeois *individual*. Because they were private, they were not *someone*, and had therefore no claim to the individuality which might give them a public place. Catherine Hall's chapter indicates one aspect of the practice by which the modern individual is claimed as universal – a gender- and class-neutral category – and yet one which contains within it a series of systematic exclusions.

Within the spaces provided by such exclusion, the mid-nineteenth century witnessed the dramatic eruption of women's voices against a set of public practices that systematically denied them a hearing. In her examination of nineteenth-century spiritualism, Alex Owen demonstrates the way in which those characteristics forbidden to women – active sexuality, political positions, the assertion of public rights – were voiced by women as mediums. Through their demonstration of an ultimate passivity, women as a vehicle for *another*, they were able to be all the things that were systematically denied, bringing forward to stand on the platform the shade of another self. At the same time, the medical professions consistently attempted to understand spiritualists as insane – and fraudulent – exposing in particular the fragility of the 'innocence' that supported the preference for very young, or child mediums, especially within domestic spiritualism.

For the middle-class woman of nineteenth-century Britain the private realm was inhabited by children. In Karen Clarke's chapter these children come into sharper focus. By examining the early infant school movement, 'Public and private children' shows how there was a systematic shift away from understanding a parent and teacher to be a man, to an understanding of both these positions being filled by a woman. But there was also a clear social class split in recommended practice towards children. Middle-class women were to educate their children at home, systematically mothering individuals with special gifts and unique personalities. Working-class women, on the other hand, had to engage in paid employment and their children were inculcated with habits of obedience in the public classroom, through a pedagogy that emphasised character rather than intellect.

Writing about the period immediately before and after the First World War, Jacqueline Rose takes issues of nineteenth-century pedagogy further. By this time the construction of the unitary and universal child, the 'common-sense' starting point of modern pedagogy, was almost complete. She shows this child to be a fiction by considering the case of one text, Barrie's *Peter Pan*, and how the idea of the child was created to be the recipient of specifically modified literature like this. School editions of *Peter Pan* from this period use a language pruned of literary allusion, a simplified 'plain English' for use by children in school. This socially produced language, from which all differences of rhetoric were extracted, later served as the data base for various linguistic theories in which universals of this 'natural' language were understood to have their origin in the brain. 'Plain English', and English designed for working-class children, was naturalised in this way, but 'there is no natural language, least of all for children. . . .' (page 100).

The legacy of this kind of practice that the re-writing of *Peter Pan* represents is a set of modern understandings in which a particular kind of language is taken to be both natural and normal. Its absence is seen as a kind of pathology, an object for intervention programmes. Aimed in the first instance at compensating for the inadequacies of a home environment that gave rise to abnormal language use, the language of intervention itself played an important role in creating the image of the good mother. Conflating natural language with domestic nurture the Bullock Report (which Jacqueline Rose considers in her chapter) told mothers: 'when you give your child a bath, bathe him in language' (page 93).

But the effect of this construction on the child cannot be understood only in terms of coercion, or the child's passivity. What the next chapters do is explore the relationship between the social practices that produced particular texts, and the experience of children using them. Gill Frith considers the boarding school fiction that is read by some adolescent girls and the systems of regulation that it embodies. Boarding school fiction is embarrassing because it celebrates the very institution of power and the transmission of privilege in a class society. But Gill Frith shows that modern working-class girls enjoy this fiction not because it is understood to portray boarding school life as it really is, nor because they do not realise that it embodies class contempt and xenophobia. Rather, she argues, it appeals because it allows them to engage with powerful fantasies of a world in which girls can be active, adventurous, resistant to the enforced passivity of adolescent femininity, and set free by the imagined institution from the confines of the family.

Private lives, private histories, marginalised and secret stories . . . Carolyn Steedman examines one example of modern pedagogic practice which turns difference (the difference of being an Asian child in mid-twentieth-century, white, racist England) into a kind of deficiency. By looking at the way in which a young Punjabi girl made a song out of her reading of books, Carolyn Steedman shows how the child moved between two representations of herself, the one she knew from her own experience and the one that fiction offered her. This 9-year-old girl's manipulation of meaning at the intersection of two cultures is one example of a child's move into historical time, bringing with her the hidden interpretive devices of an experience that is given no place in the educational theories that have been formulated to 'explain' children like her.

Fictions of the normal – of normal child development, of normal mothering – are inscribed in institutional practices concerned with the regulation of child care in the modern state, and also in modern child care manuals. In her analysis of such practices and manuals, Cathy Urwin shows the powerful effects that these normalisations have on the day-to-day lives of young mothers. In all of them, 'normal' development is heralded as at once natural, and yet also the responsibility of the mother, who might be doing something wrong, but can never be quite sure. The interviews she bases her chapter on show how the reassurance offered by professionals could feel empty, so that the mothers were caught between two impossible and limited alternatives, either to be the mother of a 'normal' or of a 'problem' family; neither of these addressed the material and emotional problems of being a young woman at home with children.[5]

In the final chapter of this book, Valerie Walkerdine considers other aspects of the modern pedagogic practices which define and produce the normal child. She looks specifically at the occurrence of 'normal' and 'natural' reasoning in children. By examining the regulation of speaking and silence in contemporary schooling she reveals the avoidance of conflict which underpins current practices in their assumption of a natural and active masculinity nurtured by a complementary and passive femininity. Existing practices, aiming to produce coherent and autonomous individuals, freed from overt regulation through its internalisation inside themselves, assure a family and more particularly a mother who provides a facilitating environment to prepare an active and talking learner. But such practices also provide traps and boundaries for those very children they aim to liberate. She explores the possibility of an approach to the production of subjectivity using the couplet power and desire to understand the painful silencing experienced by many children.

Most of the chapters that have just been summarised originated in History Workshop 14, 1980, 'Language and history'. HW13, 'People's history and socialist theory', the last History Workshop to be held in Oxford, was a dividing place for more than the Workshop itself. It brought a tradition of people's history and workers' writing into direct confrontation with new sources of socialism from Europe, and there was a dramatic enactment of this confrontation in the darkness of a deconsecrated church in Walton Street, where titanic figures of the left boomed the struggle in imperious male voices; and the only woman on the platform stood up to say that, excluded from the form and rhetoric of the debate, she could only stay silent.

In some ways, the idea of HW14 was thought of as a healing device, with 'language' as representative of a set of problems that all historians would recognise, that might unite the disparate forces that revealed themselves in November 1979. At the same time, certain aspects of this new topic hearkened back to much earlier Workshops (the debate of the early 1970s, for instance, on restricted and elaborated codes), and to a continuing concern with problems of representation.

The 'Language in history' collective met in a spirit of amicable conciliation throughout 1980. But the silent woman on the platform remained a problem, though we did not always realise that her shade was there. Straightforward attempts were made to redress the balance of the previous year when so often the proceedings had demonstrated the form and rhetoric of a man. Two convenors of subplenaries, for example, decided that they would make sure that half, or more than than half, of their contributors were women. Fewer than half those making up the collective were women though.

We recruited no sociolinguist to the collective; but rather brought back warnings from those we spoke to about the dangers of treating the discipline of linguistics as a kind of tool kit that would help us reconstruct our own. The sub-plenary 'Language and learning' necessarily recruited contributors from fields other than history, notably from those of psychology, education and literary theory. It is still talked of as an odd Workshop, because those who turned up in Brighton were not the traditional attenders. Some of them, perhaps a majority of the audience for this particular sub-plenary, were not historians. Often this mix was felt as deeply unsatisfactory. But such encounters stake out a new place.

We looked so consistently at women and children within the sub-plenary not simply so that the silent figure on the platform might be given space to speak, but so that women and children – those who dwell outside the conventional devices of historical inquiry – might make revelations about the political and social structures from which they appear to have been excluded. Looking at those other disciplines revealed that, far from being excluded, women and children were the central target of theories and practices aimed at the prescription and regulation of public and private life. More generally the investigation showed how the historical study of gender and childhood is integral to an understanding of the social and political forms which produce them. From this vantage point the experience of our history and the history of our experience can no longer be separated.

Notes

1 See, for example, Adrienne Rich, *On Lies, Secrets and Silence*; L. B. Tanner (ed.), *Voices From Women's Liberation*; Dale Spender, *Man Made Language*.
2 For example, S. Hall and T. Jefferson (eds), *Resistance Through Ritual*; Paul Willis, *Learning to Labour*, and Angela McRobbie, 'Settling accounts with subcultures'.
3 L. Segal, S. Rowbotham and H. Wainwright, *Beyond the Fragments*.
4 Section 3 of Henriques *et al.*, *Changing the Subject*.
5 The question of the use of the natural and then normal as prescriptions for child rearing is taken up by Cathy Urwin in her chapter on modern baby care.

2

Private persons versus public someones: class, gender and politics in England, 1780 – 1850

CATHERINE HALL

In 1810, Martha Syms, the daughter of an Evangelical clergyman, was writing to her father from India, where she was living with her husband who was in the Indian army. 'Syms desires me to present to you his best regards,' she wrote, continuing, 'and to add that he perfectly coincides with you in the political opinion contained in your last letter, I do not understand and therefore do not enter into these subjects myself. . . .'[1] Martha's assumption, that she did not understand political matters and would not risk expressing a political opinion, was one that was shared by many middle-class women in the early nineteenth century. But the process whereby that assumption came to be shared is one that is worth examining. Dorothy Thompson has explored the ways in which working-class women became marginalised in radical politics in the 1830s and 1840s and has demonstrated the extent to which that marginalisation was associated with the increasing formalisation of working-class politics.[2] Barbara Taylor has analysed the problems involved with developing a socialist feminist politics in the 1820s and 1830s and the decline of that politics as industrial capitalism established a more stable base and ideologies about masculinity and femininity became more rigidly defined.[3] But both these case studies deal with the experience of working-class women in relation to politics and as yet the experience of middle-class women has been relatively neglected. The entry of middle-class women into politics has tended to be constructed in terms of their entry into organised feminist movements in the mid-nineteenth century, with an assumption that between Mary Wollstonecraft and early Victorian forms of feminism little happened other than a few hiccups on the radical sidelines. It would be possible to construct this period rather differently and to see it as one in which a whole set of ideologies and social practices developed which saw middle-class women as essentially non-political beings, belonging to the private rather than the public sphere, having at most a supportive role to play in the rapidly expanding political world of their fathers, husbands and brothers. The ways in which such definitions were built into political institutions and related social practices ensured that the barriers against women thinking or acting politically were very extensive.

At one level the exclusion of middle-class women from the public world of politics is hardly surprising. After all, women never had been very involved in the political sphere. But neither had middle-class men. Their active involvement in the political process was a development largely associated with the late eighteenth and early nineteenth centuries. It was also an involvement of their own making, fought for and insisted upon in a society which had traditionally only legitimated the rights of the landed to be directly represented. After 1832 that legitimation was extended to all those men with sufficient property to ensure that their voices should be heard. It was in 1832 that for the first time the prefix 'male' was inserted into the act defining the right to a vote, thus making crystal clear something which had always been assumed previously, that in naming the propertied as those with the vote it was men of property who were being demarcated, not women. This process, of defining middle-class men as within the political arena and middle-class women as outside of it, did not simply happen by default. It is undoubtedly true that had a demand been made for the inclusion of women it would have been even more surprising, and certainly very much harder to achieve, than the demand on behalf of men. But many precedents were broken and assumptions challenged in the struggle by manufacturers, merchants, professional men and farmers to win the vote for themselves. The process whereby women were marginalised from that struggle needs explaining and documenting, rather than being assumed.

The late eighteenth and early nineteenth centuries marked a period of transition in English society when traditional values and beliefs were subjected to attack and criticism. Established social hierarchies were breaking down and common-sense notions being turned upside down. It was in this context that middle-class men articulated their new demand for representation. This was a demand which did not grow naturally by a process of evolution, but rather was forged out of the recognition that political influence was a necessary concomitant to their economic power. In the same way, there was nothing 'natural' about the process whereby women were not included in that demand. Certainly it coincided with custom. But middle-class men were busy challenging custom in other arenas. Customary patterns about gender divisions were re-worked in this period of transition. It was in that re-working that men were firmly placed in the newly defined public world of business, commerce and politics; women were placed in the private world of home and family.

Wherever public power has been separated from private power women have tended to be excluded from that public power.[4] As Rosaldo and Lamphere show in their anthropological work, those societies in which men and women inhabit the same domain tend to exhibit more egalitarian patterns of power and authority.[5] Historically the same patterns can be illustrated. In Roman society, for example, where there was a clear concept of public power, women were expressly excluded from it. In Carolingian times, however, there was scarcely any distinction between public and private power and consequently few restrictions on the power of women in any spheres of activity. It was landed families which were central to the exercise of power, rather than the state. Sons and daughters were able to share inheritance and some women were able to exercise considerable power. As the machinery of government was gradually developed and some control wrested from the aristocracy, so the influence of women declined.

It was difficult for them to become part of the new state bureaucracies in the way men did.[6] The early nineteenth century marked a point when the division between public and private became very highly demarcated. The notion of the division between public and private was an old established one but it always has to be understood as historically specific and socially constructed.[7] In classical Greece, for example, the public or *polis* was seen as purely political; it was separated from both production and reproduction. Both production and reproduction were centred on the household, but political life was carried on by a small number of adult male citizens who depended on women and slaves to provide for their social and economic needs. The Greek household, with its many functions, was seen as the private sphere. Such a narrow definition of the public would have been mysterious to Victorian men and women who understood the public as including the world of business and commerce, the market, and the world of politics. The private, on the other hand, was the haven from the anxieties of the market, and was constituted around the home and family. This notion of public and private was itself significantly re-worked from the late eighteenth century. Adam Smith, for example, conceptualised the market, governed as it was by freely made contracts, as part of the private, different from those public elements in life which were governed by the state.[8]

This re-formulation of the public and the private was to do with making sense of a world which was changing very rapidly and in which pre-existing definitions and boundaries no longer fitted very well. Central to this was the development of the market and of wage labour and the subsequent decline of paternalism in its eighteenth-century form. The social relations of industrial capitalism were not easily contained within a pre-industrial mode of thought. Not surprisingly, however, the traditions of classical liberal theory remained very important in the struggle to establish new values and beliefs. The work of Hobbes and Locke, resting squarely as it did on the notion of theoretical individualism, at least in the public sphere, had marked the initial course. They were both concerned to critique and undermine the case made by Filmer for the divine right of kings – which rested on a notion of patriarchal power as natural and given by God. The line of command for Filmer passed from God to the king and then to the father in the household. He insisted on an analogy between kingly civil authority and husbandly familial power. There was no split between the public and the private – the family was politicised and the state familiarised. Hobbes and Locke both rejected familial authority as the paradigm for political authority and rejected divine sanction in favour of rationality. Locke saw the development of rationality as going together with a split between public and private. Reason was for him separate from passion. Reason existed in the public world, where individuals were free and equal and made contracts. Passion or desire survived in the private world, a world in which contracts and rationality had no place. In arguing against Filmer's case for patriarchy Locke had presented women almost as men's equals for he claimed that both male and female parents had power over children. He claimed that the fifth commandment called for the child to honour his father and his mother and that the father should do nothing to discourage respect for the mother. But although he used parental equality to combat absolutism in the political realm he concluded elsewhere that there was a natural foundation to the customary and legal subjection of wives to their husbands. He assumed that fathers would represent the interests of their families in the wider society. For both Hobbes and Locke the fundamental subject matter of political philosophy was not the adult human individual but the male-headed family.

Locke's argument that women by consenting to marriage gave up their civil rights to their male protectors was mirrored by Rousseau's views on the distinctiveness of male and female characteristics.[10] And Rousseau was another powerful influence on late eighteenth- and early nineteenth-century thinking. Rousseau understood women as being defined by their natural procreative functions. He categorised man in terms of his limitless potential for rationality and for abstract thought. Women were seen as physical and sensual, deficient in rationality and incapable of rational thought. The nuclear family and patriarchy were both seen by Rousseau as natural. The sexes were complementary and man was free to become whatever he could or would whilst women were defined in terms of their capacity to bear children. Men were to do, whilst women were to be, as Charlotte Brontë put it.[11] Rousseau had no notion of citizenship for women; their influence should be exercised through their husbands.

The assumption that women should be represented politically by their husbands or fathers, whether it descended from the classical English philosophical tradition or through the French, continued to govern thinking about the political position of women in the late eighteenth and early nineteenth centuries. Fox, the great Radical, when asked why it was that women should not have the vote, replied that nature and convention had made women dependent on men and, therefore, 'their voices would be governed by the relations in which they stand to society'.[12] This view, enunciated in 1797, was little different from that of Hannah More, whose conservative thinking was central to the emergence of Evangelicalism in the 1780s and 1790s as a powerful social and political force.[13] It was reiterated in 1824 by John Stuart Mill in his *Essay on Government*:

> One thing is pretty clear, that all those individuals whose interests are indisputably included in those of other individuals, may be struck off without inconvenience. In this light may be viewed all children up to a certain age, whose interests are involved in those of their parents. In this light also, women may be regarded, the interest of almost all of whom is involved either in that of their fathers or in that of their husbands.[14]

Mill's formulation caused considerable offence at the time but the position he enunciated was widely accepted. As the *Edinburgh Review* was to put it, women should be represented politically *in* their families.[15] The common-sensical character of the view that women should be represented by men is even reflected in Harriet Martineau's novel *Deerbrook* where the two sisters Hester and Margaret accept unquestioningly the political wisdom and principles of Hester's husband Edward, who by voting against the interests of the landlord in a county election finds himself ostracised and his practice as a doctor almost destroyed. They are proud to see Edward representing their principles for them.[16] As Harriet Martineau herself commented, 'I want to be doing something with the pen, since no other means of action in politics are in a woman's power.'[17] Such a view co-existed comfortably with the definition of women as exercising power through a beneficial moral influence over men – a view which was again held by both conservative and feminist thinkers. Hannah More, Mary Wollstonecraft and Harriet Martineau could all have agreed on the central importance of women's influence.

The issue of the vote for women was not a central political issue in this period; indeed it hardly surfaced until mid-century when the suffrage societies began to be organised. One explanation for the lateness of the emergence of this issue lies in the existing assumptions which have been mapped out here. Another important explanation, however, focuses on the activities of middle-class men and the ways in which they moved towards the struggle for the vote. Merchants, professionals and the 'middling sort' had, in the late seventeenth and the eighteenth centuries, tended to rely on influence and pressure on their MPs to get their views represented in Parliament. The City of London had its own representatives, as did the established boroughs. But in the rapidly expanding industrial provincial towns such as Birmingham, Manchester and Sheffield the commercial interests had to rely on the county members to make their voice heard. As the 'middling sort' became increasingly important, and as the old established client economy gradually began to break down in the face of the broadening of the market and the growth of liquid forms of capital, so these commercial men began to seek more independence from the patronage and power of the aristocracy. 'Traders and merchants saw independence not as freedom conferred by landed property but as . . . freedom from the economic political control of the patricians', as John Brewer has put it.[18] Joseph Priestley, the Unitarian scientist and theologian, was one of the most influential voices articulating the new demands of the 'middling sort'. 'A sense of political and civil liberty', he wrote,

> though there should be no great occasion to exert it in course of a man's life, gives him a constant feeling of his own power and importance, and is the foundation of his indulging a free, bold and manly turn of thinking, unrestrained by the most distant idea of control.[19]

The connections made here between political rights, power, control and manliness were to become part of the rhetoric of middle-class men's politics in the early nineteenth century.

The 'middling sort', who probably constituted roughly

one-seventh of the English population, began during the eighteenth century to separate themselves both socially and politically from those above them and those below them. Crucial to this process of the establishment of an independent social and political identity were the clubs. There were clubs of every kind, from masonic lodges to clubs for drinking, for singing or for organising the raising of capital. The economic and social functions of such clubs were always closely intermixed, since in a period before the development of a commercial and financial infrastructure arrangements for credit and other forms of economic support relied on family first, but second on friends. The existence of such clubs and voluntary societies gave their members a sense of collective identity such as they had not previously enjoyed. The power of this collective sense was well illustrated by the support for Wilkes, which relied heavily for its orchestration on the clubs. In less troubled times many of the societies 'boasted of the way in which they united Anglicans and dissenters, men from different trades, merchants and gentlemen, whigs and tories, in a common association, promoting unanimity and harmony where only conflict had previously existed.'[20] The atmosphere of these clubs is well evoked by a painting of 'Freeth's Circle', a group of Birmingham men who met regularly in the pub run by Freeth for a pint, a pipe and a chat. The twelve men are represented as sitting around the table with their drinks and tobacco, ready for any discussion. Such convivial evenings were characterised by being exclusively male; these were not the kinds of occasions at which women were welcome. James Bisset, a Birmingham japanner and member of Freeth's circle, recalled in his memoirs his membership of a whole range of groups of this kind:

> [We] used often to meet at 'The Poet Freeth's, as also at Joe Warden's and at 'The Fountains', where I very frequently attended, but my general evenings were spent at 'The Union', 'Shakespeare', or 'Hen and Chickens Tavern', then kept by Mrs Lloyd. I was president for many years of a debating society, and president also of Saint Andrew's Club, and in the Masonic Order, I was Provincial Grand Master for the County of Warwick.[21]

Bisset loved convivial evenings of this kind and being of a cheerful disposition, and always good for a song, he was greatly in demand. It was only in retrospect that he was sorry for leaving his wife alone so many evenings, after she put the children to bed, whilst he enjoyed himself with his friends. In later life he decided to give up this social round and devote himself more to the pleasures of domestic life, and this decision reflected a growing interest in domesticity amongst men of his class.

The fact that the location of so many of these clubs was in the tavern clarifies one reason for women's exclusion from them. Pubs were increasingly being defined as inappropriate settings for women who wished to maintain their gentility in the late eighteenth and early nineteenth centuries. At one time they had provided an easy and informal social space for both men and women.[22] But the attack on drinking habits associated with the rise of temperance, together with the general attempt which was spearheaded by the Evangelicals in the late eighteenth century to improve the manners and morals of the nation in an attempt to raise the moral tone of English society and fend off a social upheaval such as that which had afflicted France, made the pub increasingly a place where respectable women should probably not be seen, except perhaps behind the bar. But the pub remained vital to middle-class men, a central meeting place, though sometimes it was transformed into the more genteel 'hotel'. Eliezer Edwards in his recollections of Birmingham in the early nineteenth century stressed the importance of tavern life: 'As in the West End of London, every man has his club, so in Birmingham, about the commencement of the present century, almost every man had his tavern, where he regularly spent a portion of each day.'[23] The tavern was 'the exchange and news-room of the period'. Often the taverns were divided into separate rooms, with facilities for different classes. 'Commercial rooms', 'smoking rooms' and 'snuggeries' abounded, with the landlady often making herself responsible for preventing any breach of decorum.

'The Union', another Birmingham hostelry, had two special rooms for their most favoured clubs.[24] One was for the Bucks Society, or 'The Order of Bucks', which was devoted to the promotion of 'good fellowship, freedom of conversation and innocent mirth';[25] the other was for the Staffordshire Ironmasters who had been meeting regularly since the late eighteenth century to defend their interests and promote their trade.[26] Initially the ironmasters at their quarterly meetings had dealt with questions about prices and conditions of sale but very soon became involved with political issues too. Samuel Garbett, a prominent Birmingham ironmaster, having failed to persuade Burke 'to take the lead in considering our commerce as a subject of politics', decided that he would have to lead the way himself and played a significant part in the opposition to Pitt's excise scheme in 1784.[27] The iron trade was not an arena in which women could easily engage and the ironmasters' meetings were certainly no place for women. Richard Reynolds, a Quaker ironmaster, thought of the quarterly meetings as 'times of peculiar trial' and warned his son about the temptations he would encounter there. 'I will not say', he wrote,

> that the consideration of the dangers to which I was about to be exposed, and the desire that sometimes accompanied it for preservation from them, was always attended with that degree of watchfulness and circumspection which would have ensured the plaudits of my own conscience after it was over. For though I may say, with humble thankfulness, I hope my conduct did not bring any reproach on my religious profession . . . yet, when I reflected upon the levity of the conversation (to speak of it in the mildest terms) and how far I had contributed to it, or at least, countenanced it by sitting longer among them than was absolutely necessary, it has brought sorrow and condemnation on my part.[28]

The ironmasters' meetings were clearly times of excess and intemperance and by the early nineteenth century these meetings were taking place weekly at 'The Union' with a grand dinner after the main part of the business was concluded. 'Money was easily made, and freely spent in those days,' recollected Edwards, and the share of the dinner bill 'was often a heavy sum, such as even such potentates as ironmasters would not care for their wives to know of.'[29]

Groups such as the Staffordshire Ironmasters, which started off with a commercial rationale but gradually became involved in more directly political matters as these impinged on their business, were responsible for much of the political education of men of the 'middling sort'. It was an education which women were excluded from. It was sufficient for family businesses to be represented by their male head at such gatherings, even when wives and daughters were actively involved in the running of the enterprise. When large public meetings were held the patterns of male conviviality tended to be maintained, with drinking and toasts. The General Chamber of Manufacturers, the first nationally organised expression of manufacturing opinion, was established in this sort of context. It relied on the activities of a group of men who were both friends and business associates. Its immediate trigger was the threatened lowering of the tariffs between Britain and Ireland but as its founding document pointed out it was high time that the manufacturers as a group should have their interests represented. 'It seems hitherto to have escaped the notice of the manufacturers', proclaimed their manifesto:

> That whilst the *landed* and the *funded interests*, the *East India* and other *commercial bodies*, have their respective advocates in the great council of the nation, *they* alone are destitute of that advantage; and it is probable from this source that many of their grievances have arisen – that they have repeatedly and perhaps inadvertently been oppressed by ministers unacquainted with their real interests, and misled by the designs of interested individuals.[30]

This Chamber of Manufacturers, which provided the basis for the Chamber of Commerce in Birmingham, played an important part in defining and articulating the interests of manufacturers and merchants. No women were ever listed in the press reports of those attending the meetings, nor were there any women subscribers. Yet it had been resolved at the founding meeting of the Chamber of Commerce, at Birmingham's Royal Hotel in 1813, that 'All persons interested in the manufactures and commerce of this town and neighbourhood, subscribing a sum of not less than one guinea, be considered members of the society'.[31] 'Persons', from the point of view of the Chamber of Commerce, were clearly men. Similarly when the voice of the town of Birmingham was to be heard, it was the principal male inhabitants who collectively spoke.

The formation of the Chamber had been immediately preceded by the struggle nationally amongst manufacturers and the commercial interest to get the Orders in Council revoked which were having such disastrous consequences on trade. Birmingham, led by Thomas Attwood the banker, had been very prominent in this agitation which was widely understood as a triumph for the middle classes. As Castlereagh wrote gloomily to Wilberforce, 'One does not like to own that we are forced to give way to our manufacturers.'[32] Those manufacturers were increasingly finding it necessary to instruct the governing classes on trading matters and to insist that their voices should be heard. It was this experience which fed directly into the demand for the reform of Parliament and for the vote for middle-class men. It was Attwood who led the Birmingham Political Union to their great victory in 1832, and it was he and his like who were extolled in the liberal poet Horton's poem about the town,

> The noblest men that dignify our age,
> The brightest names that live on history's pages.[33]

Middle-class men made their claim for direct representation on the grounds of the contribution which they were making to national wealth and prestige; it was their industriousness and their competence which meant that they had earned political recognition. It was clear that men and women were not in the same place and would not expect to be treated in the same way. Thomas Wright Hill and his sons, who were running their school for boys at Hazelwood in Birmingham, and whose venture had gained fame through the publication of *Public Education* and the recognition of Bentham, were so committed to the fight for reform that it was decided that Frederick, one of the sons, should devote himself fully to activity in the Birmingham Political Union. This was a decision for the men of the family and was made at one of the Family Councils, which it appears that neither Mrs Hill nor her daughter Sarah attended, even though they were both fully involved in the running of the school as a family enterprise.[34] Women attended the great political rallies organised by the Birmingham Political Union and were encouraged to wear blue garters inscribed with 'Attwood forever' but they played no part in the political discussions or decision making.[35] They were *spectators* and *supporters* rather than being active in their own right and on their own behalf.

The Political Union was revived in Birmingham in 1837. There was a serious economic depression and Attwood revived his plans for currency reform in response. He had always been very enthusiastic about the reforming potential of currency policies but it was the vote, not currency, which had made him popular. This time the Union had little middle-class support, since the middle classes had fundamentally got what they wanted in the Reform Act, and the platform soon became universal male suffrage. Faced with an urgent need for support and a less genteel membership, a Female Political Union was formed. Part of the strategy for reform was that all taxed or excisable articles should be abstained from until the demands were won. Since tea was one of these it was thought by Titus Salt, one of the leaders, that the support of women was essential. He called upon the women of Birmingham to break their normal patterns and 'meddle with politics'; the 'whole family of the people' must unite.[36] The Female Political Union was established and its meetings were regularly reported in the *Birmingham Journal*, the paper of the reformers. The purpose of the Union was seen as to provide support for the men. Women should not be indifferent to politics but should be active on behalf of their men. Needless to say this was in itself a progressive position and would certainly not have been supported by conservative thinkers. The radical/liberal position was that women should participate in politics through men, using their moral agency. As the Whig *Edinburgh Review* trumpeted:

> we assume that it is never contemplated that the right of voting should be claimed for married women during their husbands' lives; or for unmarried women living under the protection of their parents. The divisions

> which would thereby be created in the heart of families, and the extensive injury consequent therefrom to domestic peace, are objections too obvious to require discussion.[37]

The male leaders of the Birmingham Political Union had no illusions about the supportive functions of their female counterpart. At a large tea-party held at the Town Hall, at which Attwood was the main speaker, all of the public speaking was done by men. Even the address from the Female Political Union which was presented to Attwood was read by a Mr Collins. As Scholefield, one of the town's first MPs, declared, 'it was gratifying to him to meet so many excellent and intelligent women, who, by their presence, showed very plainly that they took a lively interest in all that concerned the welfare of their husbands, fathers, brothers and sons . . . ' and, he quickly added, 'which also deeply affected their own interests'.[38] He went on to argue for women's involvement in politics and cited their participation in the storming of the Bastille as an historic precedent of their engagement with the struggle for liberty. Mindful of the criticisms which had been made of the Union for encouraging women to desert their proper duties, he argued that he was 'far from wishing that politics should ever supersede the important duties of social and domestic life, which constituted the chief business of the female', but he still hoped that 'the women of Birmingham would never become indifferent to politics'.[39] Still it was clear that the leadership of the Political Union had a limited view of what the women could achieve. The women themselves sometimes had to insist on the part which they were playing. A meeting was reported in February, for example, at which Mr Collins spoke. In his address to the women he assured them that 'he could not but congratulate them on the glorious victory that had been that day achieved in the Town Hall by the men of Birmingham'. A 'female' present at this called out sharply, 'And by the women, Mr Collins; for we were there.' Mr Collins, chastened, 'was willing to admit the assistance the women had rendered.'[40]

This marginalisation of the contribution made by the women with its concurrent assumption that women were not really a part of the 'body politic' is nowhere better illustrated than in the ritual celebration of Birmingham's winning of borough status. This had been a long-drawn-out battle. Only the Liberals had been enthusiastic for incorporation in the wake of the Municipal Reform Act of 1835. The Whigs were neutral since their interests were well covered by the existing Street Commissioners, while the Tories were hostile. The charter was finally granted in October 1838 and in February of 1839 a dinner was held in the Town Hall to celebrate. This event was described in the *Birmingham Journal*, the wonderful decorations were enumerated, the atmosphere evoked . . .

> When to the effect of these very tasteful decorations, we add the attractions of the hall itself, with the blaze of light running along its extensive walls, the cheerful faces of not less than five hundred gentlemen at the tables below, and above all the blooming cheeks and bright eyes of nearly twice that number of elegantly dressed ladies in the galleries, the rich tones of the magnificent organ, and the pealing anthem swelling the note of praise. . . .[41]

The symbolic importance of this occasion was clear to all – the town was now both represented in Parliament and had its own local government. But the presence of the 'blooming cheeks' in the galleries was less straightforward than it might have seemed. Those 'bright eyes' were only in the side galleries in 'consequence of many pressing applications'. Initially it had been intended to put them in either the grand gallery, where they would have been able to hear nothing, or in the side gallery, where they would have been able to neither see or hear. As the editor of the *Journal* commented, however, their voices, usually gentle and low, became sharp when faced with this relegation and the seating arrangements had to be re-thought.[42] This did not mean that the ladies were able either to dine or to drink, but they were able to enjoy a toast being drunk to them. The mayor, in his toast, made the traditional invocation to women as being above politics, and in that way morally superior to men:

> 'Gentlemen', he cried, 'we live in times of great political strife and exasperation. We sometimes forget in the animosity of our contentions, that differ as we will, we are still of the same kind and of the same country, kith and kin one of another, united by one common bond of mutual dependence and of mutual interest. We often forget this. Woman's gentle nature never forgets it. She knows no hatred, nor will let us know any, if we but appeal to her. Let us then, gentlemen, whenever we feel our hearts hardening towards each other, or towards our political opponents, let us fly for counsel to those whose province and whose dearest task it is to soften, to bless, and to purify our imperfect nature. Then, believe me, we shall ever find a store of charity, large as our deficiencies, and learn how easy a thing it is to conciliate, without the sacrifice of independence, and to contend without the bitterness of animosity.'[43]

Those 'elegantly dressed ladies' could not have been told more clearly that they did not occupy the same political sphere as men. Those 'fit and proper persons' who had voted both nationally and locally and stood as candidates in Parliamentary and council elections relied on their women to soften, bless and purify their imperfect, and political, natures.

The marginalisation of women in the political world has to be understood as part of a larger process whereby women were being marginalised from, or indeed excluded from, the public world generally. The debate over what part women should play in philanthropy illustrates this very clearly. As long as they were concerned with private philanthropic work, visiting people in their homes in particular, there was no problem.[44] The difficulties arose when they attempted to step outside of that domestic arena and take on a more public role. We can find the same pattern repeated in the churches; women were, again, at least amongst 'serious Christians', encouraged to engage in visiting and tract distribution but anything more public, or indeed more official, was discouraged. The formalisation of philanthropic and religious societies invariably marginalised women from the process of decision making; their role was to support privately rather than engage publicly.

Nevertheless, 'serious Christians', with their belief in spiritual equality, did provide women with some basis for trust in their own individual and independent judgment and their own moral sense. It was possible, if difficult, to argue that women's special moral sense should be interpreted in political terms and indeed that argument underpinned many feminist interventions in the later nineteenth century. But the move from spirituality and morality to politics was a difficult one to make.

One arena in which women had asserted their right to a political engagement was on the issue of anti-slavery. Here the line between philanthropic work and politics was hard to draw and it was this blurring which had made it a possible area for women. The female anti-slavery societies were mainly established by Quaker women, who had benefited from their traditions of autonomous organisation. This in its turn stemmed from the Quaker belief in the spiritual equality of men and women. But the female anti-slavery societies never did the same kind of work as their male counterparts. Rather than lobbying Parliament or organising demonstrations they relied on appealing to women as wives and mothers, preferably in their own homes. The Birmingham Female Society for the Relief of British Negro Slaves was established in 1828 and initially concerned itself with producing workbags, albums and portfolios to raise money for the relief of neglected and deserted negro slaves. In a discussion in their report of 1828 as to why more women had not got involved with their activities, they concluded that few realised how useful they could be. Female 'weakness and feebleness', they argued, far from meaning that women had nothing to offer, guaranteed them a special kind of strength. For God had chosen 'the weak things of the world, and the things that are despised, and the things that are not, to bring to naught the things that are'. Women must use their special skills and gifts rather than pretending to be like men. The Birmingham Society appealed to women as consumers not to buy slave-grown sugar and to engage in house-to-house visiting in the town on this issue, saying:

> Is it for Christian females to be bribed by the greater *cheapness* of this, or the other articles of daily

> consumption, to lend themselves to the support of a flagrant system of blood-guiltiness and oppression, which cries to heaven for vengeance? – and can we think the cry will not be heard? The influence of females in the minor departments (as they are usually deemed) of household affairs is generally such, that it rests with them to determine whether the luxuries indulged in, and the conveniences enjoyed, shall come to them from *the employers of free men, or from the oppressors of British slaves.* When the preference is given to the latter, we see, therefore, with whom the responsibility must mainly rest; – we see at whose door the burden of the guilt must lie.[45]

Women should use their power as household managers to see that slave-grown sugar was not bought; this was the kind of political sphere in which they could have legitimate influence. Even this legitimacy was, however, contested. There were many men involved in the anti-slavery agitation, indeed Wilberforce himself, who were unhappy at this uncalled-for forwardness from ladies whom they preferred to think of as existing quietly in the domestic sphere.

The contestation over what were, and what were not, appropriate public arenas for women continued throughout the nineteenth century. It was not a contest which could be easily resolved since boundaries were open to change. Furthermore the debates over the nature of woman's influence and woman's mission embraced a wide number of issues. Politics, indeed, was rarely mentioned directly for it was assumed that it was not a sphere appropriate to women. What was 'political' was indeed partly defined by where the men were. Influential texts such as those by Mrs Ellis on the duties of the wives, mothers and daughters of England did not discuss the question of women's involvement in politics at all.[46] Mrs Ellis, like many others, believed that moral influence was the key. Nevertheless on occasions the support of 'the ladies' could be very useful politically though this could lead to acute disagreements.

There was of course a well-established tradition of aristocratic ladies using what influence they could in support of their candidates. In Emily Eden's novel *The Semi-attached Couple* Lady Teviot wanted to do what she could for her husband's candidate in an election. She acquired a poll book and went through it carefully to see whether any of her tradespeople were in it so that she might be able to exert some pressure. She and her mother:

> drove into the town constantly, and seemed suddenly to have discovered that they were without any of the necessaries or luxuries of life, for the extent of their dealings with well-thinking tradespeople was prodigious, and it might have been supposed that they were covertly sullying the purity of election; but, as they justly alleged, shopping was what every woman was born for, and could not, under any circumstances, be considered illegal. . . .[47]

Undoubtedly there were middle-class versions of this kind of pressuring. George Eliot observed in *Felix Holt* that at a time when controversies between the Church and Dissent were very sharp retailers who were Dissenters had to keep a strict hold on their tempers.[48] Tradespeople could not afford to be too sectarian. Similarly, Dr Hope's friends in *Deerbrook* assured him that no one would expect him to vote in a disputed election. 'You are quite absolved from interfering in politics', he was advised. 'Nobody expects it from a medical man. Everyone knows the disadvantage to a professional man, circumstanced like you, of taking any side in a party matter.'[49] No doubt well-to-do female customers and patients had ways of indicating their political preferences to those who provided them with services. But there was a marked difference between aristocratic and middle-class patterns when it came to the relation between women and politics. One aspect of the middle-class critique of aristocratic culture was that society hostesses neglected their families and their religious and moral responsibilities to their children in favour of more worldly pursuits.[50]

Sometimes this kind of 'behind the throne' influence was exercised more openly. The Anti-Corn Law League was quite prepared to utilise the support of middle-class women in their agitation for repeal. They were encouraged to run bazaars and fancy fairs as ways of raising money, capitalising on the experience gained from such activities in the philanthropic world. The League was of course a Radical organisation and as such took a more progressive position on the question of appropriate spheres for women than more conservative groups. They were happy to use lady collectors for the collecting of subscriptions and it was resolved by the Council of the League that 'in every town a committee must be formed, consisting of ladies and gentlemen, having a secretary and treasurer . . . '.[51] Not surprisingly, however, these committees represented the highest echelons that ladies could reach. J.W. Croker in the *Quarterly Review* denounced the use that the League made of women as providing a clear indication of the Jacobin influences at work. 'It has been a frequent device of revolutionary agitators', he asserted, 'to bring women forward as a screen and safeguard to their own operations.' He regarded the great bazaar held by the League with its stalls organised by women as 'a practice in our opinion equally offensive to good taste and good feeling, and destructive of the most amiable and valuable qualities of the female character'. Of a tea-party held with sixty lady stewardesses he commented:

> We exceedingly wonder and regret that the members of the Association and League [the *Councils* of these two bodies organised the bazaar], and still more that anybody else, should have chosen to exhibit their wives and daughters in the character of political agitators; and we most regret that so many ladies – modest, excellent and amiable persons we have no doubt in their domestic circles – should have been persuaded to allow their names to be *placarded* on such occasions – for be it remembered, this Bazaar and these Tea-parties did not even pretend to be for any *charitable* object, but entirely for the purposes of *political agitation*.[52]

J.W. Croker was right to be worried, for many of the daughters of Radicals who were involved in the agitation over the Corn Laws later became committed feminists. One thing could indeed lead to another! Many of the same objections had, however, been made to women's involvement in philanthropic bazaars, for, amongst other things, such occasions invited easy mixing between young men and women.[53] For many people amongst the respectable middle class there was a prohibition on genteel ladies appearing in public at all, except at church or chapel. The stress on the *private* definition of women made participation in the political world exceedingly difficult. For the political world was quintessentially a public world. The kinds of public recognition that were an essential part of political involvement were not accessible to women. Hobsbawm in his *The Age of Capital* tackles the question as to what defined the bourgeoisie as a class:

> the main characteristic of the bourgeoisie as a class was that it was a body of persons of power and influence, independent of the power and influence of traditional birth and status. To belong to it a man had to be 'someone'; a person who counted *as an individual* because of his wealth, his capacity to command other men, or otherwise to influence them.[54]

Such a definition is essentially male. There was no way in which women could be 'someone' in this sense. They did not have that kind of power or influence in either the world of business or in the sphere of voluntary associations of any kind. They were *private persons*, not *public someones*. As such they did not possess the necessary prerequisites for citizenship, nor indeed did they expect to occupy the world of political ideas. It was a source of acute amazement when a woman, Harriet Martineau, published a series on political economy, a subject not often associated with the 'fair sex'. When George Dawson, the influential preacher who inspired the 'civic gospel' which was taken up by Joseph Chamberlain and the Birmingham Liberals in the 1850s, fired his initial sally it was addressed to the 'Men of the Middle classes'.[55] He would have been breaking with custom to have appealed to women as well, despite the fact that his church, with its large female congregation, provided the base for the civic gospel. He would also have been breaking with new social practices in relation to gender and politics which had been established in his own lifetime. Middle-class men had successfully established their pitch; middle-class women were firmly outside of it.

Acknowledgment

This article is part of a larger study, sponsored by the Social Science Research Council, on the relation between domesticity and the development of industrial and agrarian capitalism in the late eighteenth and early nineteenth centuries. The study was jointly undertaken by Leonore Davidoff and myself at the University of Essex. All my ideas have been discussed with her.

Notes

1 Martha Syms, 'Letters and reminiscences'. This manuscript was kindly lent to me by the late Margaret Wilson.
2 Dorothy Thompson, 'Women and nineteenth century radical politics: a lost dimension', in J. Mitchell and A. Oakley (eds), *The Rights and Wrongs of Women*.
3 Barbara Taylor, *Eve and the New Jerusalem*.
4 M. Stacey and M. Price, *Women, Power and Politics*.
5 M.Z. Rosaldo and L. Lamphere, *Women, Culture and Society*.
6 J.A. McNamara and S. Wemple, 'The power of women through the family in medieval Europe: 500–1100', in M. Hartman and L.W. Banner (eds), *Clio's Consciousness Raised*.
7 J.B. Elshtain, *Public Man, Private Woman*.
8 Adam Smith, *The Theory of Moral Sentiments*.
9 S.M. Okin, *Women in Western Political Thought*; E. Fox-Genovese, 'Property and patriarchy in classical bourgeois political theory', in *Radical History Review*; R.W. Krouse, 'Patriarchal Liberalism and beyond: from John Stuart Mill to Harriet Taylor', in J.B. Elshtain (ed.), *The Family in Political Thought*; G. Schochet, *Patriarchalism in Political Thought*.
10 Okin, op.cit.
11 Elizabeth Cleghorn Gaskell, *The Life of Charlotte Brontë*, p. 123.
12 Quoted in R. Fulford, *Votes for Women*, p. 23.
13 C. Hall, 'The early formation of Victorian domestic ideology', in S. Burman (ed.), *Fit Work for Women*.
14 Quoted in Fulford, op.cit., pp. 26–7.
15 *Edinburgh Review*, vol.73, 1841.

16 H. Martineau, *Deerbrook*.
17 Quoted in E. Moers, *Literary Women*, p.20.
18 J. Brewer, 'Commercialization and politics', in N. McKendrick, J. Brewer and J.H. Plumb, *The Birth of a Consumer Society: The Commercialization of Eighteenth Century England*, p.199.
19 Quoted in R. Porter, *English Society in the Eighteenth Century*, p.274.
20 Brewer, op.cit., p.219.
21 J. Bisset, *Memoir of James Bisset*, p.76.
22 M. Girouard, *Victorian Pubs*.
23 E. Edwards, *The Old Taverns of Birmingham*, p.5.
24 Ibid.
25 J. Money, *Experience and Identity: Birmingham and the West Midlands, 1760–1800*, p. 138.
26 T.S. Ashton, *Iron and Steel in the Industrial Revolution*.
27 Ibid, p.164.
28 B. Trinder, *The Industrial Revolution in Shropshire*, p.202.
29 Edwards, op.cit., p.77.
30 Ashton, op.cit., p.169.
31 G.H. Wright, *Chronicles of the Birmingham Chamber of Commerce*, p.54.
32 C. Emsley, *British Society and the French Wars 1793–1815*, p. 160.
33 H.H. Horton, 'Birmingham', poem, Birmingham, 1851.
34 F. Hill, *An Autobiography of Fifty Years in Reform*.
35 C. Flick, *The Birmingham Political Union*.
36 T.C. Salt, 'To the women of Birmingham', 16 August 1838.
37 *Edinburgh Review*, vol.73, 1841, p.203.
38 *Birmingham Journal*, 12 January 1839.
39 *Birmingham Journal*, 12 January 1839.
40 *Birmingham Journal*, 2 February 1839.
41 *Birmingham Journal*, 16 February 1839.
42 *Birmingham Journal*, 16 February 1839.
43 *Birmingham Journal*, 23 February 1839.
44 A. Summers, 'A home from home – women's philanthropic work in the nineteenth century', in S. Burman (ed.), *Fit Work for Women*; F.K. Prochaska, *Women and Philanthropy in Nineteenth Century England*.
45 Female Society of Birmingham for the Relief of British Negro Slaves, Album, c.1828.
46 Mrs Ellis, *The Women of England, Mothers of England* and *The Daughters of England*.
47 Emily Eden, *The Semi-Attached Couple*, p.215.
48 George Eliot, *Felix Holt*, p.226.

49 Martineau, op.cit., p.183.
50 L. Davidoff, *The Best Circles*.
51 N. McCord, *The Anti-Corn Law League*, p.139.
52 *Quarterly Review*, vol.71, 1842–3, p.262.
53 J.A. James, *Female Piety*.
54 E. J. Hobsbawm, *The Age of Capital*, p.286.
55 G. Dawson, 'A letter to the middle classes on the present crisis', Birmingham, 1848.

3

The other voice: women, children and nineteenth-century spiritualism

ALEX OWEN

It was through the mediumship of two young girls that the spirits first made known their intention to establish regular communication with the modern world. In 1848 Kate and Margaret Fox were 12 and 13 years old, and lived in the family home in rural upper New York state. Their house was reputedly haunted and the 8-year-old daughter of the previous occupant had already experienced frightening occurrences there, but the inexplicable knockings and rappings which broke out shortly after the Fox family moved in did little to daunt the young sisters. On the contrary, they discovered that they could 'talk' to the unseen source of the disturbances by establishing a simple code involving a specific number of raps for Yes and No, and in this way ascertained that the cause of all the trouble was the spirit of a murdered pedlar who was supposedly buried in the cellar. From such humble beginnings the girls became a local and then national sensation, and precipitated the phenomenon known as modern spiritualism. As the spiritualist craze raged through the eastern states of America and swiftly found an enthusiastic reception in England and Europe, resolute non-believers and sceptics could only wonder that 'with the snap of a toe joint'[1] two young girls could wreak havoc in the theological world, and send parlour furniture in a million homes creaking and knocking in response to unseen spirit hands. During the next four decades spiritualism retained much of its popular appeal and throughout these years women continued to be considered central to the successful practice of mediumship.

From the beginning it was commonly accepted that women made the best mediums and that 'the power' often manifested itself in childhood or adolescence. The essential factor in the entire, and often bizarre, business of mediumship was the ability of these young practitioners to communicate with the spirits of the dead. At first the spirits made their presence felt via a series of knocks or raps which the medium then decoded, but later, when the trance state became the order of the day, she literally 'spoke spirit'; that is, the spirit entered her and spoke through her. Between these two extremes lay a range of interpretive devices – she might hear the spirit voice and then relay the message to the seance circle, see a spirit and describe it, feel an emotion and express it – but what was at issue at every stage of the procedure was the unopposed authority of the medium and of her claim to speech.

Spiritualism was brought to England by the American medium Mrs Hayden and by the following year, when Harriet Beecher Stowe arrived fresh from the triumphs of *Uncle Tom's Cabin*, abolition and spiritualism were the great topics of the day. In America, where spiritualism and radicalism were more readily linked, it was not unusual to find spiritualists who were also abolitionists. Robert Dale Owen, the son of the great reformer, anticipated his father's conversion after being introduced to spiritualism by the feminist and abolitionist, Frances Wright. Henry James used the convergence of feminism, spiritualism, and abolition for his own ends in *The Bostonians* where one of the major female characters was described as 'a female Jacobin' whose friends were all 'witches and wizards, mediums, and spirit-rappers, and roaring radicals'.[2] Harriet Beecher Stowe, although not a spiritualist at the time of her visit to England, later became concerned with it after the tragic death of her son. Her subsequent friendships and correspondence were evidence of the extent to which literary and reforming circles in England, Europe and America were shot through with spiritualist sympathies during this period – the Barrett Browning circle in Florence, the coteries of Ruskin and Rossetti in London, surviving Owenite and socialist communities in America. Like many others who took the spiritualist path Harriet Beecher Stowe's way was paved by an existing knowledge of mesmerism, whilst her husband had long since accepted the reality of the spirits which had visited him from boyhood. As George Eliot was later to observe on this very subject, 'the division between within and without in this sense seems to become every year a more subtle and bewildering problem'.[3]

In mid-nineteenth-century England all manner of persons enjoyed the latest rage of summoning the spirit bands. Throughout the land solemn Victorian furniture creaked, tipped and danced at the behest of small assembled companies sitting in the darkness in states varying from uncontrolled mirth to ghastly apprehension. But despite the fact that Queen Victoria and Gladstone were known to have dabbled, it was in the Midlands and the North, among the industrialised working class, that spiritualism initially took a firm hold.[4] David Richmond, a former member of a New York Shaker colony, gave a series of demonstration seances in Lancashire and the West Riding during 1853 and it was in these areas that spiritualism established itself most firmly, only later moving more solidly into London and the South. Working-class spiritualists, who tended to be more secularist and radical than their middle-class counterparts, explained their beliefs within a rationalist and materialist framework of quantifiable fluids and forces and it was here that the mesmeric tradition was important. Spiritualism enabled such believers to experience the joy of renewed contact with lost loved ones without having to accept any part of establishment theology, and proof of immortality had an enormous appeal when bereavement was still a constant feature of everyday life. The restoration of children to the bosom of their living family was an especially moving feature of spiritualist communication, and the death of a child was often a precipitory factor in conversions. This was true for all believers but middle-class spiritualists, who invariably retained their Christian worship, also derived religious consolation from their beliefs. They were often those who felt that the church had become a wasteland of dogma and ritual and discovered in the seance a direct experience of Divinity and the immortality of the soul.

Although there were divisions across class lines, particularly with respect to this vexed question of whether or not spiritualism constituted a religion, shared beliefs tended to have an homogenising effect. English spiritualists rallied behind a number of progressive causes including an improvement in women's rights, changes in the lunacy laws, and prison reform. Close attention to the health of body as well as soul also made 'clean living' an issue amongst spiritualists, and many favoured temperance, vegetarianism and natural healing. Class uneasiness did sometimes manifest itself in relations between a working-class medium and her middle-class sitters (the medium often adopted a refined name or blurred her class background; sitters were more prepared for fraudulence) but there was usually enough of a shared frame of reference for the class issue to remain secondary to the business in hand. On the whole, spiritualist mediums were accepted without reference to gender, class, education or training. The sole requirement was the possession of 'inspiration' or 'gifts', the ability to communicate with the other world. If a working-class girl could achieve successful seances without provocative fraudulence (and as we shall see, even this was forgiven) she was accepted, and often pursued, by society at large. For young girls of 15 or 16 the almost overnight change of status that resulted from high-quality mediumship presented temptations that were hard to resist, and the rate of fraudulence was high. Even where the rate of exchange was not money – and mediums seldom became wealthy – heightened prestige, new social opportunities, even brief moments of glory in a darkened room, were worth a few risks. Talented young actresses with quick wits and winning ways could do a lot worse. And then there were always those who were never caught in trickery, who appeared to be genuine. . . .

Women and the inheritance of spiritual power

Spiritualists were concerned with questions relating to the rights of women but it was as mediums that women assumed their positions of centrality. This was because they were thought to make particularly effective spiritual communicators, and this in turn was tied to culturally received notions of what was innate to the female personality. Passivity was one of the major normative constructs of nineteenth-century femininity and women were considered to lack the will-power and strength of character of men. Although passivity supposedly gave rise to the yielding feminine attributes so beloved of prescriptive ideology, it carried an essentially negative value and was used to reinforce the idea that women were unable to function successfully outside the domestic domain. Spiritualism, whilst itself maintaining an internal contradiction, viewed passivity in a different light. Here it was validated as the most important and powerful quality a medium could possess because it was the most necessary for effective spirit possession. Male believers strove to cultivate a passive attitude in order to counter-balance the domination of the masculine Will, thereby struggling to renounce what the medical profession held to be the very cornerstone of psychological health. So that whilst spiritualists reinforced the notion of immutable gender difference by their insistence on passivity as an innate feminine characteristic, they also privileged the construct and gave it a positive interpretation.[5] Thus the term remained but the meaning was altered, even subverted, and the resulting 'possessed' behaviour construed as evidence – not of hysteria or insanity, as medicine maintained – but as an indicator of great power and facility.

In order that the different energies should complement each other men and women were placed alternately in the seance circle, and would sit in dim light or total darkness waiting for a sign of spirit presence. The time was passed in light conversation or suitable singing until, usually within the hour, a cold breeze could be felt passing over the sitters' hands, or limbs and bodies would begin to twitch involuntarily. One person would then take charge of the seance and invite the spirit to make itself understood via raps on the table; one rap or tilt for No, three for Yes, and two to express doubt or uncertainty. The majority of seance circles began in this way and it would then gradually become clear which of the sitters had a 'gift'. It was at this point that women often came to the fore, developing more rapidly and confidently than the men. As the powers and experience of the medium increased so too did the seance phenomena, and this often progressed from raps to the playing of musical instruments by unseen hands, 'apports' of flowers and presents into the room, and finally to physical manifestations like the levitation of the medium's body. By the early 1870s good mediums were able to facilitate the appearance of materialised spirit forms in the semi-darkness, or parts of a form like disembodied hands or faces, whilst trance mediums took on the appearance and personality of a possessing spirit. Materialisation and trance mediums were greatly valued by sitters because it enabled them to take a more active part in the seance, and women were the most skilled in both these areas.

The ready acceptance of female spiritual power, however, was clearly related to the established 'separate sphere' philosophy which cast women in the role of superior moral beings possessing an innate religious sensibility. The Evangelical movement during the first half of the century had largely contributed to the notion of women as guardians of spiritual and domestic values, but the persistence of this ideology enabled women in the seance room to assume spiritual authority without it being seen as an assault on patriarchal esteem.[6] Male sitters, involved in a ritual within which women (by very dint of their femininity) were accepted as powerful voices, could accede to female directives without any loss of masculine prestige. The double-speak of the situation, and an aspect of its impasse, was epitomised by the use of the term 'control'; for whilst the medium controlled the events of the seance she herself was 'controlled' by the spirit. The question of responsibility and subjectivity then arises. Who or what was the acting and speaking 'I'? Was it an actress cleverly faking possession, a woman in a state of unconscious trance (in which case, again, who was speaking?), or a spirit? One thing was certain; whilst a medium was in the process of speaking spirit she was not held responsible for her actions or words, and this enabled her to say and do things that would have been unacceptable elsewhere.[7]

Many mediums took this to its logical conclusion and disclaimed any responsibility for their choice of career, maintaining that it had been thrust upon them by the demanding spirit world and that they were but reluctant vehicles for the promulgation of great truths. The ultimate irony of spirit mediumship was that the most powerful were in a sense the most powerless, the final coinage of exchange being the abdication of self for possession by another. In this sense mediumship inter-acted with, and to some extent dramatised, prescriptive notions of femininity and female sexuality. But where mediums managed, in part, to escape these contradictions was in the practical gain that could be extracted from spiritual prerogative. As recent work on the Owenite women has indicated, it was possible to transform a moral-mission ideology into the basis for a more overtly feminist endeavour, and there was already ample precedent for women entering the political and feminist fray through the vehicle of religion and the language of heresy.[8] Spiritualist women discovered that their mediumship could offer a way out of the limitations imposed by a separate spheres ideology, whilst those who otherwise would have been forced into the marketplace found in the seance room an acceptable alternative to less amenable forms of drudgery.

Women in the public sphere

The nineteenth century saw the development of a 'separate spheres' ideology which supposedly relegated women to the private domain of home and hearth. In practice this clearly delineated schema was constantly undermined by contradictions and tensions which blurred perimeters and indicated instead the distinction between prescription and reality.[9] However, within the spiritualist vocabulary the terms 'public' and 'private' mediumship were a matter of everyday parlance and so have relevance here. The meaning attributed to the terms had been roughly assumed from that accorded to the notion of separate spheres, but in the process some slippage had occurred which warrants closer attention because it illustrates the way in which class concerns cut across ideological categories. A public medium was one who had entered professional life, who gave seances to which there was general entry, and who was paid for her activity which could be re-classified here as work. A private medium invariably operated within the small domestic or private circle, her seances were closed to outsiders, and she was never paid. As might be expected, what usually happened was that girls from working- or lower-middle-class homes became public mediums, and those who had no need to earn a wage remained in the private category. What was important here was that for spiritualists the terms 'public' and 'private' had clear class connotations, and from this other assumptions about the veracity of the medium tended to follow. However, where the public/private distinctions broke down was when a medium (often of lower-class origin) was taken up by a wealthy benefactor who would support her financially in return for constant access to her seances. These providers were invariably spiritualist gentlemen, although in some cases a medium was able to survive financially through the generosity of several favourite sitters. The mediums who were maintained in this fashion were highly talented, had a good success rate, and consequently became the most sought-after and famous. The anomaly thus arose of the private medium, one who did not charge for her services, who, far from being cloistered in the bosom of her family, was kept by a man, gave famous seances to which the elite of society clamoured for entry, and whose activities were often more public than the most public of mediums. Furthermore, such private mediums were often not middle-class. What this means here, in terms of a 'spheres' analysis, is that there were quite clearly private mediums operating in the public arena, and I have therefore taken my criteria of 'public' to refer to those women who did not restrict their mediumistic activities to their domestic circle.

The onset of mediumistic powers usually occurred within the privacy of the home, but the growth of the spiritualist cause was associated with the development of public mediumship which steadily gained ground from the 1860s. Large public meetings and discussions attracted many people and during one quarter of 1878, in Lancashire alone, an estimated total of 9,000 individuals attended spiritualist gatherings.[10] This public aspect was one in which women shone in a variety of capacities, and they were extremely popular with their audiences. At first these women in public life tended to be middle-aged and, as one male observer later remarked, this was a period when lady mediums were apt 'to run to eighteen stone, or be old and frumpish'.[11] This was a reference to the talented Miss Nichol, later to become the second Mrs Guppy, whose great bulk defied gravity in a series of startling levitations. She was reportedly able to sail through the air with such speed that on one occasion she knocked two of her sitters to their knees, and on another was borne through the skies of London on a nocturnal flight. Her considerable abilities included being able to produce flowers covered in dew during a seance, gifts of fruit (and vegetables), and a live dove for a particularly valued friend.[12]

But Mrs Guppy's celebrated reign was overshadowed in the early 1870s by a new and altogether different breed of women mediums. These were the young, unmarried and attractive girls who began to make their appearance in London and the provinces, many of whom, had they not been mediums, would have been forced to earn their living in some other way. A flourishing spiritualist press and consequent publicity, the establishment of local societies which encouraged young developing mediums, and the prospect of a certain degree of limelight, all contributed to the propagation of new spiritualist stars. Suddenly the emphasis was on youth and beauty and spiritualists and non-believers alike flocked to the performances of pretty inspirational speakers, mediums and healers. Their male admirers were not slow to register the change:

> . . . of the many fluctuations to which Spiritualistic society has been exposed of late is a very prominent irruption of young lady mediums. The time seems to have gone by for portly matrons to be wafted aerially from the northern suburbs to the W.C. district, or, elderly spinsters to exhibit spirit drawings . . . and we anxious investigators can scarcely complain of the change which brings us face to face with fair young maidens in their teens to the exclusion of the matrons and spinsters aforesaid.[13]

In the opinion of the same observer the undisputed princesses of the 'two worlds' were Florence Cook and her friend Mary Rosina Showers. Both girls were accomplished materialisation mediums, and were examples of the private medium who operated within the public sphere.

Florence Cook was born in 1856 to respectable working parents, and as a young medium lived with her family in Hackney. She was the eldest of three daughters, all of whom claimed to be mediums, and began giving seances at the age of 15. At first she was only able to produce vague spirit faces which appeared in the gloom of gas or candle light, but after

'Katie King' became her regular spirit control the manifestations swiftly increased and improved. By 1873 Florence, in complete trance but hidden from view behind a heavy curtain, was able to produce the full-form materialisation of 'Katie'; that is, a young female figure would emerge from behind the curtain, completely covered from head to foot in white robes, and would pass amongst the sitters. To selected friends she would give little gifts, fragments of her clothing or a lock of her hair, and some of these sitters also heard her speak. At the end of the seance she would glide back behind the curtain, and after a decent interval Florence would indicate that she had come out of trance and the lights could be turned up. These performances were greeted with wild excitement on the part of believers and outraged wrath in the case of hostile critics. The general furore that they precipitated made them ever more in demand, and the medium became one of the most famous in the history of spiritualism. Meanwhile Florence was 'freed from all the troubles and anxieties of professional mediumship, chiefly through the kindness of Mr Blackburn of Manchester'. Charles Blackburn, a wealthy and devoted spiritualist, undertook to make a regular annual payment to Florence so that she could remain 'private'.[14]

During the early part of 1874 Blackburn passed the management of Florence's seances to the scientist William Crookes who was engaged in a laboratory investigation of the young girl's powers. Crookes was clearly enamoured of 'Katie', if not Florence, and his ardent espousal of the spirit's authenticity, together with his interest in other young mediums like Miss Showers, began to earn for him the dangerous reputation of a philanderer. There was undoubtedly an implicit (if not explicit) sexual element to many of the materialisation seances, and the libidinal context is an important one which I have considered elsewhere. There were certainly also strong rumours of a spiritualist sexual underworld, and Mrs Guppy's name was mentioned in connection with these, but the involvement of Crookes in any explicit misbehaviour has never been proven.[15] However, Crookes was sufficiently interested in both Florence and Mary Rosina to invite them to give joint seances for scientific purposes, and he claimed to have seen 'Katie' and 'Florence Maple' (Miss Showers's control) walking about his laboratory arm in arm. Mary Rosina, so like Florence Cook in most respects, differed in one fundamental way; she was the daughter of a colonel in the Indian army and came from a middle-class Devonshire home. She was one of the few girls to escape from a sedate provincial existence to the exciting world of London high-class seances through the exploitation of her mediumship.

The two girls, despite their different class backgrounds, were friends, and it seemed that they were happy to give their joint seances to other interested observers besides William Crookes. Edward Cox, a lawyer who made a keen study of spiritualism, stated that he had also seen 'Katie' and 'Florence' together:

> I have seen the forms of Katie and Florence together in the full light, coming out from the room in which Miss Cook and Miss Showers were placed, walking about, talking, playing girlish tricks, patting us and pushing us. They were solid flesh and blood and bone. They breathed, they perspired, and ate, and wore a white head-dress and a white robe from neck to foot, made of cotton and woven by a loom.[16]

Cox was by no means convinced that these girlish spirits were genuine and emphasised their similarity to their young mediums, but other sitters were able to counter his claims with instances of the differences between spirit and medium. However, he thought that he had proved his point when Miss Showers was discovered perpetrating what appeared to be a blatant fraud during a seance at his own country home at Hendon. Whether by design or accident, at the point in the seance when 'Florence' had poked her head out of the curtain, Cox's daughter reached forward and widened the gap so that the sitters could see behind the scenes. What met their fascinated gaze was the sight of the medium standing just behind the curtain dressed in her own black gown, wearing a 'ghost head-dress', and imitating the fixed glassy stare of 'Florence'. In the ensuing mayhem there was a violent struggle, 'the spirit head-dress fell off', and Miss Showers went into a state of wild hysterics. In his attempt to 'soothe and mesmerise' the young girl Cox enraged his own wife who stood crying, 'He has no mesmeric power, none whatever. Make him get up. Do make him get up.' During all this confusion there could still be heard the voice of 'Florence', presumably uttering from the lips of the distraught Miss Showers, 'You have killed my medium!'[17]

What was proof of fraud for one, however, was merely evidence of a brutish mishandling of a seance for another. Spiritualists rallied to Miss Showers, just as they did in most of these cases, and the entire episode was put down to 'unconscious somnambulism'. In other words, the figure of 'Florence' was really Miss Showers dressed as a spirit, but the medium was in a trance state and did not know what she was doing. Another favourite spiritualist explanation that removed all blame from the medium's shoulders was that she had been possessed by wicked spirits who forced her to perform the masquerade. Cox, presumably thinking of the future of his investigations, tactfully acceded to the somnambulist explanation and agreed that this might well have been the case. William Crookes later became convinced that Miss Showers was fraudulent but he never recanted his defence of Miss Cook. The difficulty of his position, given his espousal of the girls' joint sessions, has been admirably treated elsewhere,[18] whilst the authenticity or otherwise of materialised spirits remains a hotly debated subject amongst interested parties. Beguiling though these discussions are, however, they occlude the important wider issue of what mediumship offered young women during the second half of the nineteenth century, and why public mediumship might have seemed an attractive option for a working-class girl.

The public careers of private mediums like Florence Cook and Mary Rosina Showers were echoed by those of other young women during this period. Miss Showers was exceptional in that her middle-class background did not prevent her from moving out of the domestic sphere, but the majority of mediums in public life were of more humble origin. Materialisation mediums were in great demand and girls like Miss Wood, the daughter of a Derbyshire mechanic, and her friend Miss Fairlamb were visited, reviewed, and persuaded to go to London in order to give exhibitions of their powers. These young women were paid for their services and were often hired for a series of seances by spiritualist societies, and later by the newly formed Society for Psychical Research. Weekend house parties in the country and invitations to comfortable London homes were exchanged for the privilege of the undivided attention of the medium, and social advancement was the order of the day. Doors were opened to young women who could not have dreamed of such social mobility under any other circumstances. Less happy, of course, were the mediums who were eclipsed, and in the early 1870s a bitter quarrel broke out between Florence Cook and Mrs Guppy. The older woman was thwarted in her attempt to throw vitriol into 'Katie's' face during a seance, but the jealousy and back-biting were real enough.

If the materialisation mediums represented one aspect of novel spiritualist spectacle, they were equally matched by women inspirational speakers. This form of mediumship broke all the taboos relating to respectable women; it established the platform as the medium's rightful domain, and public speech as her *raison d'être*. The inspirational discourse was a female speciality and involved the medium speaking at length without any prior preparation, and solely at the behest of the spirits. These addresses were very popular with spiritualist audiences, but speakers could travel throughout the country on a circuit which included not only Spiritualist Associations but also other acceptable venues like Mechanics' Institutes and Temperance Societies. The theme was invariably uplifting, often religious (although by no means narrowly Christian), and usually had a didactic flavour. In 1874, when Florence and Mary Rosina reigned supreme in the materialisation world, the undisputed queen of the public platform was the beautiful American medium, Cora L. V. Tappan. She had been addressing audiences since she was 13, had come to England in 1873, and now in her early thirties presented a visual delight which gladdened the heart of many an enthusiast:

> Mrs Tappan was dressed neatly in black, with a profusion of golden hair – very golden indeed, falling in studied negligence over her shoulders. She had a tasteful bunch of flowers on her head, and another on her

> bosom. She is a fine woman, above the middle height, and decidedly good-looking.[19]

When Cora Tappan mounted a public platform a great hush fell over the audience, and after delivering a prayer she would begin to speak. As she discoursed on the value of Christian observance at Easter, the relationship of that rite to those of Pagan antiquity, or the need for greater spiritual harmony in the world, her listeners underwent an emotional experience that far outweighed the actual content of her words. The spectacle that she presented, the actual theatrical quality of the woman, the spiritual presence that she managed to bring to the proceedings, combined with the belief that she was actually communing with the other world, all contributed to a sense of occasion that far outstripped her use of language. In fact, what mediums actually said was rarely innovative, and was often rambling, obscure and repetitive, but the best of them could hold an audience for hours at a time. For Cora Tappan and other good inspirational speakers it was not merely a question of 'The Word' – the dead letter of the text was indeed a dead letter! – but also one of context. Respectable Victorian audiences were familiar with the religious diatribe, and with male propounders of The Word; they were not familiar with beautiful young women who dared to make the public platform the place from which to 'speak spirit', who created a specular display that was at once pleasurable and modest, and who were linked by an invisible thread to all that was best in the next world. So that not only the Cora Tappans but the lesser-knowns, Miss Brown of Howden-le-Wear, Miss Keeves and Miss Record of London, could hold audiences 'spellbound', fill rooms 'to overflowing'.[20]

But if the use of language was not the sole key to their success, the mediums' spiritual authority nevertheless gave them an unusual degree of access to speech. Spiritual gifts were the gateway to public discourse but, like mediumship in general, they also provided a rationale for avoidance of personal responsibility in the matter of what was actually spoken. Emma Hardinge Britten, a woman of great sense and intelligence who became a leading figure amongst British spiritualists, reported that on the occasion of her first speaking engagement:

> . . . my last clear remembrance was of listening to a lovely quartette beautifully sung by the 'Troy Harmonists', and then I had a dim perception that I was standing outside of myself, by the side of my dear father – dead – when I was only a little child – but whose noble form I could plainly see close by me, gesticulating to, and addressing somehow, my second self, which was imitating him, and repeating all the thrilling words he was uttering.[21]

Emma, famous for her public support of abolition and feminism, felt the need to resurrect her father (what better patriarchal precedent?) as the source of her words. She merely imitated and repeated, and even as her confidence and renown grew she still adhered to a paradigm of a second self. Emma maintained that when she began to speak she seemed 'to be two individuals', one whose lips were 'uttering a succession of sentences, sometimes familiar to me, still oftener new and strange', and the other 'an onlooker and occasional listener'.[22] This type of double-consciousness effect was familiar from other varieties of mediumship, but here it permitted one part of the personality to speak and the other to represent the disclaimer. Modern psychoanalytic theory in its various guises has contributed to an understanding of the psychical process known as splitting – *Spaltung* – which can result in the co-existence within the psyche of different and distinct personalities. Freud maintained that such splitting was the result of conflict, and noted that the ego comprises a part that observes and a part that is the observed. Jacques Lacan then postulated the importance of what he called the 'mirror phase' in the early development of the ego whereby the first faltering steps towards a unified sense of self are taken with the help of an identification with a separate and coherent counterpart (for example, the infant's reflection in a mirror). These psychoanalytic concepts are complex and by no means uncontested but in representing the fractured nature of the 'I' they throw light on the experiences of mediums who consistently reported having a sense of themselves as two people, either entirely different entities or carbon copies. The image of the counterpart, the medium's two 'Is', personified the myth underlying the constructed sense of a unified self. The medium was manifesting what we might now think of as split subjectivity.[23]

Emma's fractured identity, a concept which helps provide one of many explanations of mediumship, lays bare the paucity of any analysis based on the notion of a unified subject. Mediumship, particularly speaking mediumship, reveals the inconsistency, heterogeneity and precariousness of human identity. The experiences of these women would indicate that mediumship was not simply a question of play-acting and conscious fraud. Two selves, one speaking, one silent, took the floor for an inspirational address; two selves, one the spirit, the other the sleeping medium behind her curtain, manifested themselves at materialisation seances. Meanwhile, the spiritualist explanation for the phenomena provided something else yet again; spiritualism offered both context and permission, quite literally, for new 'forms' of signification. Materialised spirits were not mediums dressed up (in whatever state of mind), and inspirational speakers were not deranged exhibitionists. This was a new reality in which it was quite normal to be two individuals at once, and each with only the vaguest cognisance of the other. Not only a complete subversion of common-sense notions of the world, but also carte blanche to be another – even the Other. If the inspirational discourse still poses the question, 'Who was speaking?', it also provides another example of the way in which mediumship precipitated women into a different frame of reference.

The religious imperative got women the floor but, as we have seen, once there they were not responsible for the dictates of the spirits. Mediums might mount the platform in the name of spiritualism but discourse at length on anything from the structure of the spirit realm to politics. Cora Tappan could move smoothly from the spiritual world to the social, linking an attack on the materialism of the age to an outright condemnation of the London slums.[24] Emma Hardinge Britten braved bitter cold, hardship and abuse during her early speaking tours in America where her addresses invariably centred around abolition and women's rights. She could fill a hall with anything from 1,500 to 3,000 people and her personal charisma was sufficient to keep her audience enthralled. In 1859 she was telling her American audiences that the time had come for women to claim full social, religious and political equality. Woman:

> requires equality with man in the right to govern her person, her property, her children. She requires equality with man in the right to enter into schools, and the associations of commerce and trade, and to hold positions in the government.[25]

Emma believed that women had specific qualities which made them more readily spiritual than men, but denied that they should be exercised solely in the home. Women, she argued, must go out into the world of men, and each must learn to become more like the other. Like other spiritualists who had inherited some of the earlier Owenite heterodoxy, she dwelt on the androgyny theme speaking of women as 'the half which must complete the angel', and of the 'heart of mother and father God'.[26] These opinions, with their echoes of heresy ancient and modern, enabled speakers like Emma to field an impressive array of arguments in favour of women's emancipation. They were also examples of the way in which a spiritual or religious theme could support a more overtly political imperative. Careers like Emma's were a testimony to the feminist possibilities of a strategy based on women's spiritual equality, even superiority, and the way in which this could be conflated with the demand for rights in the temporal world.

Whilst some exceptional women made public platform appearances in their own right and not as inspirational speakers, it was usual for women to claim spirit guidance and mediumistic ability as the credentials for a public speaking career. This undoubtedly eased the difficulties involved in a woman appearing on the public platform[27] and enabled gifted orators to make a reasonable living by travelling the spiritualist circuit. In general the public world of mediumship opened fresh channels of advancement for women, and despite the fact that spiritualists sometimes complained that the more rarefied aspects were being lost to 'the business interests and abnormal practices of professional mediums'[28] the fact remained that it offered a means of decent livelihood. By the early 1870s young girls were entering public life prior to marriage and at a time when they were often least socially secure, and they were able to do this within the auspices of a movement that looked with favour on its gifted female practitioners. However, for every medium who went public there were at least three more at home, and it is to the private sphere that I should now like to turn.

The spiritualist family in the private sphere

Despite the increase in public activity dating from the 1860s spiritualism remained an essentially private affair practised by families within their home circle. Private mediumship was greatly revered on several counts. It was regarded as the mainstay of a happy and united family, the love and trust generated by the family circle encouraged refined and powerful manifestations, and a closed and intimate circle was thought to eliminate the problem of fraud. There were also, however, implicit class assumptions. Although family spiritualism was obviously practised by all classes, private mediumship was largely associated with middle-class women, 'ladies'. There was an assumption, especially amongst middle-class believers and researchers, that these women would be morally beyond reproach and would never stoop to fraud. Indeed, as no money ever changed hands (the financial motive being the most suspect) there seemed to be no reason for trickery. Spiritualists preferred to emphasise family unity rather than any class aspect when they praised private mediumship, but class was an important underlying issue. In a rare explicit statement of class feeling Mrs Showers, in the aftermath of her daughter's experiences at the home of Edward Cox, exclaimed that it was unthinkable 'to attribute imposture to people in our position of life: people who . . . had but one object, viz., the advancement of truth'. Her fury at being treated like 'conjurors' wives' knew no bounds, but she placed her faith in 'gentlemen and ladies in the world' who would 'ask by what right Serjeant Cox rates his word higher than mine? Our social position is the same. . . . '[29] The fact that it was difficult for believers to associate fraud with lady mediums, and hard to credit imposture within the family circle, is relevant for what follows and for any consideration of private mediumship.

Amongst middle-class believers the home circle provided the focus for domestic and spiritual harmony, and the family was considered to be the most perfect focus for uplifting manifestations:

> Spiritualism is essentially a domestic institution. . . . Spiritual manifestations have been most successfully evolved in select companies, more particularly in the family circle, or where there is a kinship of spiritual development similar to true family affinity. Mediums have the greatest degree of power, the phenomena are of the most unmistakable description, and communications are purest, when presented in select and harmonious gatherings of which a well-ordered family is a type.[30]

When the Theobald family began experimenting with spiritualism in the early 1860s it was Mrs Theobald, mother of a growing family, and her unmarried sister-in-law, Florence, who provided the initial stimulus. Morell Theobald, a widely read, cultivated man who was an active partner in the family business in the city, was less enthusiastic but did nothing to prevent the women of the household from pursuing their interest. Florence, known affectionately as Aunt Fanny, introduced the family to spiritualism after having discovered in herself the talent for passive writing. This was a well-known technique and did not require a seance circle or medium in order to be effective. The writer simply held her pen over a blank sheet of paper, emptied her mind, and allowed the spirits to move her hand across the page. The essential factor was that the writing should not be achieved by conscious volition, and experimenters usually discovered that it took a while before actual writing emerged from the jumble of haphazard strokes.

There were dangers associated with passive writing. It was very popular with women because they could practise it in their own home whenever they chose, and it was often adopted by newcomers to spiritualism who were unaware of its addictive qualities. It was not unusual for the writing to become a focal point for lonely lives and for a particular spirit, often named and with a complete history of its own, to begin to dominate the relationship. Unfortunately the spirits were often not satisfied to remain on a religious level and, just when the writer had become most trusting, the unseen communicator would begin to reveal fragments of salacious gossip about friends, relations, husbands and even children. Not content with the havoc that this could wreak in quiet lives, the spirit then advanced to unambiguously sexual, cruel and grotesque revelations which sometimes drove writers to the point of suicide. Spiritualists put these 'unsuitable' communications, the exact nature of which were rarely articulated, down to possession by an evil spirit. Experienced practitioners knew all the signs, the wildly shaking hand and uncontrolled script, and would stop immediately any unsavoury presence threatened. It did not seem to be a problem for these writers to exercise a degree of control or judgment over content whilst maintaining the required passivity of mind for the process to continue. Putting aside a spirit-based explanation it is not difficult to see that an activity which encouraged the relaxation of conscious censorship was likely to permit an upsurge of 'language'.

At all events, after a variety of false starts and difficulties, it was by this means that the Theobald women began to communicate with spirits. During the 1860s the family lived in a large comfortable house in Highgate which was run by a staff of servants including a cook. The children, Ernest, Franky, Teddy and Nellie, were educated at home by a governess until the boys were old enough to go away to school, then Nellie remained on her own. Florence was a frequent visitor to the house, although many of the winter months were spent nursing her health in the more bracing climate of Hastings. The family was a happy one but, like many others during this period, it had its share of grief. Although there were four living children there was finally to be a total of five in the spirit-land. What Florence and Mrs Theobald discovered when they took up passive writing was that it was these little spirits who were most eager to 'come through'. The eldest of the spirit children was Louisa, who had been a stillborn baby, and it was she who communicated most freely and vividly with Florence and later with the rest of the family. Louisa received each new child under her wing as it passed from this world to the next, and was quick to report the safe arrival of two-month-old Horace in 1868, and baby Perceval two years later. She sought to reassure her parents that the children continued to live and grow in the spirit world, that their education was not neglected, and that they were unmarred by the experience of death. Her message was constant over the years: no germ of life is ever lost. After the arrival of a new baby the tiny spirits reported:

> We are all connected together by a bright cord of light, and we are told it is God's love. We saw the dear little germ-spirit come to us at the end of light. God has given him to us, your little children in the spirit-home. . . . We are all joined in one magnetic circle, which little Horace saw as a chain of flowers. By this chain we can all communicate at any time when the conditions are favourable. . . . All of you are more or less mediums, because you are all in such strong sympathy with the unseen and the spiritual. We all mesmerise you to draw you to us.[31]

The spirit children continued to give endless encouragement to the development of their parent's powers, noting that 'Mama might write if she tried . . . and we could more easily influence her than you, dear old Pa'.[32]

Morell remained the most sceptical and for some time was inclined to put the entire proceedings down to the workings of a vivid imagination. But as the months passed and the spirit dialogue continued, his wife now achieving identical types of communication, his disbelief slowly eroded and he finally became a convinced spiritualist. The belief that their children had survived death was a source of inestimable consolation to the Theobalds, and it was this communication which became the centre of their domestic and spiritual life. The entire family settled down to a pattern of regular seances led by the two women, and attended weekly by the servants who would stand respectfully at one side of the room. This was the equivalent of family worship (although for many years the Theobalds also attended the local Non-conformist chapel), and included prayers and hymn singing. Morell accepted without question the women's dominance of the seance and the primacy of Louisa's communications, whilst the spirit children continually emphasised the need for passivity and the fact that they found this quality most readily in their mother and aunt. As the power of the family circle grew and developed, the spirits found it increasingly easy to communicate and began to indicate their presence with louds raps. Meanwhile, the living children were growing older and were taking an increasingly active part in the seances where their position was accepted as perfectly natural and normal. The spirits were particularly attracted to the eldest living boy, Ernest, but they began to warn the family that great care should be taken of him. Florence was also receiving messages full of foreboding, and at this point Ernest was taken seriously ill with scarlet fever. In this extremely dramatic and touching episode of the family's history Ernest, with spirit help, recovered from his illness and emerged with the power of trance mediumship.

By the early 1870s, the height of this phase of the Theobalds' spiritual development, there were two writing mediums and one who could go into trance and 'speak spirit'. The family circle was now also joined by a gifted neighbour, Mrs Everitt, and life became increasingly centred around the seance table. Lengthy discussions of family matters, theology, healing and cosmology, as well as simple messages of love and greeting, became regular elements of the sittings. Ernest's mediumship meant that the communications were now much faster and the family could speak directly to the possessing spirit. Increasingly the Theobalds came to rely on spirit wisdom and family decisions were debated and settled within the context of the seance. This meant, of course, that the women and children were playing a vital part in matters from which they might normally have been excluded. Although this was accepted with perfect assurance and matter-of-factness by the entire family it nevertheless constituted an extraordinary reversal of contemporary familial power relations, in which status and autonomy were granted to both women and children. The answers to questions that emanated from the lips of 12-year-old Ernest and the pens of Florence and Mrs Theobald were taken to be sacred. The family was completely committed to its spiritualism and none of them ever appeared to entertain the notion that a member of the seance could be guilty of fraud. The fact that there was no apparent motive for trickery seemed to satisfy even Morell. In his own account[33] Morell outlined the many original doubts that he had concerning the authenticity of spirit communication but once he was convinced of their genuineness there was no going back. When the seances brought so much joy, and the participators were all loved and trusted, how could anyone believe that a hoax was being perpetrated? Individual credibility was everything, and the question of 'unconscious somnambulism' never seemed to come up.

Their credulity, however, was to be tried to the limit ten years later. The boys were now no longer at home, and the family circle, and its manifestations, was severely reduced. This was a fallow period for the remaining members but Morell was consistently advised by the spirits that a new medium was developing in their midst. Nevertheless it came as a great shock when their cook of some years' standing suddenly announced that she could see spirits. Mediumistic sight was a highly prized gift, and they considered Mary to be a cut above the usual 'servant class', but the family were still confused and at a loss as to how to proceed. After much seance consultation it was decided that she should begin to sit in the family circle on an *ad hoc* basis whilst maintaining her status as a servant. In this situation Mary made swift progress and the circle was completely rejuvenated. Under her auspices a new burst of spirit activity began. Household tasks were completed by unseen spirit hands, tables were laid, kettles boiled, shaving water floated up and down stairs, messages were written and secreted in hidden places. The family were overawed, mystified, thrilled and finally convinced. Despite all their precautions and a wave of class-based suspicion and prejudice, they could not detect Mary in fraud. Reluctant as they were to accept her socially, and concerned as they were with her motives, Mary was finally accepted as an equal member of the circle and, in the end, of the household. Morell, recounting this bizarre episode, asked his reader:

> look upon Mary as we did – no longer as a mere servant, but as a friend, tried and trusted; my daughter's inseparable companion, with conditions in the house for investigation almost perfect; all being sensitives and all interested. This social difficulty has, I know, distressed some of our friends; not more so, I think, than it has ourselves. . . . Doubtless Spiritualism comes somewhat as a leveller of social distinctions, and although we are slow to learn such a lesson, I am not sure it is not one very needful for an age which is so much fettered by the 'sickly forms' and 'social wrongs' by which classes and castes are hedged in.[34]

It was a remarkable coup. The respectable middle-class Theobalds overcame the class difficulties to accept Mary as an intimate family friend. She moved up from the basement to share Nellie's room and assumed a status on a par with that of the daughter of the house. Fraud or not, Mary was there to stay. Even the disquieting probings of the Society for Psychical Research failed to dislodge her.

The issue of the servant, that intruder from another class nestled in the bosom of the family, is an important one that extends way beyond the considerations of spiritualism. But here it can be seen that Mary's prominence within the closed family unit was truly remarkable because of the subversion of accepted class relations that it represented. This servant was indeed 'the hole in the social cell'.[35] Within the privacy of the home she succeeded in undermining a rigid class structure, just as the women of the family had effectively challenged gender norms when they asserted their complete spiritual superiority. This in turn had implications of a more material nature. Mary acquired status, the women gained respect and greater autonomy. None of this was achieved through any conscious feminist or oppositional framework. The women were allowed, or permitted themselves, to fulfil the expectation that they would make better mediums than men, and from that other gains followed. Mediumship offered a very great deal to women in the private sphere; a way out of loneliness, bereavement and silence. They now had a voice . . . well, if not of their own, at least another voice. The lengths that some no doubt went to in order to gain the authority to speak is yet another issue. And what of the children? They too had found a voice, both in the seance and in the spirit-land.

Mediumship and childhood

One of the most consistent reasons put forward by believers for their initial interest in spiritualism was the death of a loved one, and the most moving and compelling the loss of a child. As we have seen, communication with their dead children became the lynchpin of the Theobalds' family life and lay at the heart of their spiritualist convictions. Each spirit child was highly individualistic with a style and personality of its own. When the little sprites were still communicating solely through passive writing, the handwriting of the medium would change radically as a new voice came through and the family could tell at a glance which of them was now 'speaking'. Louisa and her younger sister, 'N', were calm, loving and authoritative, Horace and Perceval were cute and full of fun, and baby 'Dewdrop' (a final stillborn child born in 1876) was a mischievous imp who claimed a large part in the wonders worked by Mary. The two girls took it upon themselves to ease the anxieties of their parents, 'N' assuring them that she had not 'caught her death' the day they allowed her to go out on her pony and that they were in no way responsible for her sudden demise. Furthermore, she emphasised that her passage to the beautiful gardens of the spirit-land, where she was able to ride her very own spirit pony, was in no sense harrowing:

> My room became, to my earthly vision, invested in a cloud as of the purest downy appearance, which gradually gave place to ineffable brightness. All earthly

> things had receded. I found myself alone with one resplendently beautiful figure. It was in human form, and yet it was formed of dazzling whiteness – whiteness and brightness such as can proceed only from Divinity. He was gazing at me; his hair was flowing, showered over with brilliant gems of star-like form and wonderful radiance. . . . He looked at me, and thereby was my spirit drawn to him; it gave me spirit-birth. I was gathered to his arms and slept in Jesus.[36]

These sentimental descriptions of a gorgeous Jesus, and a spirit-land that matched item for item any large Victorian garden, might seem hackneyed when read in cold blood but the effect they had on grieving parents was riveting. To be told by the lost children themselves that all was well 'in God's home for his little ones', and that the babies had been taken early to save them greater suffering later on, all helped initiate an acceptance of the earthly loss.[37] At the same time the living children were having great fun discovering whether baby Horace had wings, if the spirit children had to learn Latin, and whether or not there were dahlias in heaven. Teddy wondered if they had seen Jesus or the moon, and a young cousin once asked plaintively if his pet canary had safely reached the other side. The children's continued curiosity about angels and God's throne seemed to be accepted in good part by the participating adults who allowed them a free rein during these question and answer sessions.

The popularity of child spirits was also reflected in the public seances, and certain materialisation mediums specialised in their production. Miss Wood, who began her public career at the age of 18, was renowned for her little black sprite, 'Pocha', whose favourite tricks were stealing money from sitters and sitting on the laps of the gentlemen. Her friend, Annie Fairlamb, countered with the 4-year-old 'Cissie' who ran about the seance room sucking proffered sweets, and showing her little feet to prove that she was not her medium. 'Cissie' also indulged in baby talk: 'me will do all me can for Mr Burns, he was so kind to my medium whenever she was in London', and would sing and dance for her delighted sitters. When the two mediums gave joint seances the sprites would come out of the cabinet together and embrace each other in great shows of friendship.[38] The fact that both young women had at various times been detected in fraud, and 'Pocha' and 'Cissie' discovered to be none other than Miss Wood and Miss Fairlamb on their knees, did not deter ardent believers. They remained in demand. Miss Wood was later to enchant the Theobalds with a materialisation of Louisa, and Mrs Mellon (*née* Fairlamb) was still going strong in 1931!

The popularity of child spirits was paralleled by the importance attached to youthful mediumship during this period. It had always been emphasised that the instigators of modern spiritualism, the young Fox sisters, had scarcely reached their teens when they first heard the spirit rappings, and British mediums followed their example. The Cook girls were 15 when they began their careers, Mary Rosina Showers was about the same age, Miss Wood and Annie Fairlamb were in their later teens. As it was, mediumship itself began early enough but these girls were also keen to accentuate childhood intimations of their spiritual gifts. Florence Cook spoke of childhood visions, exposure to a grandmother who saw visions and fell into trance, and experienced trance herself at the age of 14. Annie Fairlamb had her first supernatural experience at 9, 'seeing' her brother at sea and in danger of drowning, and was then encouraged within a family circle. As a little girl the materialisation medium Elizabeth d'Esperance saw 'shadow people' and adopted them as her friends and playmates. Emma Hardinge Britten, a highly gifted child with a fine voice and love of music, had childhood clairaudient (she could 'hear') as well as clairvoyant experiences.

Many of their memories played upon the same theme. These were lonely children, somehow different from the rest, who sought in their imagination compensations for losses in the real world. Emma Hardinge Britten recalled:

> Looking back upon my earliest recollections I fancy that I was never young, joyous or happy like other children; my delight was to steal away alone and seek the solitude of woods and fields, but above all to wander in churchyards, cathedrals and cloisters, and old monastic ruins. Here strange sounds would ring in my ears,

> sometimes in the form of exquisite music, suggesting new compositions and pathetic songs, sometimes in voices uttering dim prophecies of future events, especially in coming misfortunes. At times forms of rare beauty or appalling ugliness flitted across my path, wearing the human form and conveying impressions of identity with those who had once lived on earth.[39]

This morbid sensibility, even if embroidered to heighten the spiritual nature of their later calling, was invariably cited by mediums as an important aspect of their young years. Emma also lost her father at an early age, and spent a solitary childhood amidst her daydreams and music. Later, a promising musical career was nipped in the bud by persistent somnambulism, a state of mind characterised by loss of normal consciousness and sleepwalking. Elizabeth d'Esperance (her professional name) also recalled a lonely and unhappy childhood marred by the absence of her beloved father who, like Emma's, was a sea-captain – no doubt a suitably romantic figure. Elizabeth grew up in a large gloomy house in London's East End, ignored by a sickly mother and for many years an only surviving child. She was a daydreamer and spent much of her time in her own world, disliking to be shaken out of it and resenting attempts to force her into pretty feminine ways. As a result she gained the reputation for being 'a little vixen' and 'decidedly queer',[40] and when her mother later produced several living children in quick succession Elizabeth was pushed even further into the background. She began to experience terrible problems with her school lessons and found it increasingly difficult to separate the real from the imaginary. Finally, upon hearing that those who saw 'shadow people' could be confined as lunatics, she began to fear for her sanity and her former spirit playmates became hated and feared. On the verge of a complete nervous collapse at the tender age of 14, she was saved by her father who carried her off on a three-month sea voyage in the Mediterranean and then established her in a boarding school where she spent two happy years. By the age of 18 she was married.

These were lonely and difficult childhoods, then, where young girls inhabited rich worlds of their own creation, fleeing from the present into the comfort of daydreams and imaginings: 'Muffled throughout their history, they have lived in dreams. . . .'[41] If the daydreaming was compensatory, making up for neglect and isolation, substituting a world in which they were central characters for a life in which they were peripheral, glossing the pain of being unloved (Emma's dead father, Elizabeth's harsh mother), then it was only a step away from mediumship which was also an enterprise that placed these young women at centre stage. Medicine seized on daydreaming as a feminine and infantile activity and related it to serious personality breakdown in adult life. The French psychologist Pierre Janet used spiritualist mediumship as a good example of the abnormally developed daydream. It was an extension of the old equation of femininity with unwholesome pathology, a question of innate characteristics. But if, as seems likely, there was a connection between childhood daydreams and adult mediumship, or even daydreams and mental breakdown, this had little to do with an essentialist psychology of woman.[42] Instead, it indicates the extent to which the needs of the individual psyche, and the way in which it deals with pain and conflict, can only be understood within the context of contemporary power relations. Daydreams, like mediumship, offered a way out.

Daydreams were one means of flight and illness was another. Within spiritualism illness held a privileged position because it was seen as a kind of cleansing of the body in preparation for the reception of higher gifts. But there was also, of course, considerable value to be gained from illness, particularly for women and children whose positions of powerlessness made escape routes one of the few practical (if problematic) means of rebellion. Emma Hardinge Britten, never a robust woman, was under no illusions as to her childhood relationship with sickness:

> The happiest period of these immature years was, strange to say, when I was, as frequently happened, laid on a bed of sickness. To pass away in dreams, as I then believed, into lovely green fields amidst strange and beautiful people, was such rapture to me, that I was wilful enough to try and take cold, so that I might be

> laid up and go off to my unknown and fascinating fairy land.[43]

Florence Cook experienced poor health as a young girl and was the despair of her family. She 'was so drowsy and heavy she scarcely ever seemed to be fully awake' – one of Miss Showers's characteristics was also this 'heaviness', and there was Emma's somnambulism – and she would sleep on a sofa all night, going into violent hysterical fits if roused.[44] Mrs Cook was in despair about her daughter until, upon the advice of a friend, she took her to a seance circle. Immediately Florence's health improved, she experienced a feeling of enormous relief, and felt like a new person (an interesting reflection!). As her mediumship developed all her old drowsiness and hysterical symptoms disappeared and she became the vivacious and playful Florence Cook of later reports.

The notion of motivational illness, the idea of falling ill with 'the intention of securing some gain',[45] is relevant to these girlhoods. In this connection it is interesting to note Freud's comments:

> The motives for being ill often begin to be active even in childhood. A little girl in her greed for love does not enjoy having to share the affection of her parents with her brothers and sisters; and she notices that the whole of their affection is lavished on her once more whenever she arouses their anxiety by falling ill. She has now discovered a means of enticing out her parents' love. . . . When such a child has grown up to be a woman she may find all the demands she used to make in her childhood countered owing to her marriage with an inconsiderate husband, who may subjugate her will, mercilessly exploit her capacity for work, and lavish neither his affection or his money upon her. In that case ill-health will be her one weapon for maintaining her position. It will procure her the care she longs for. . . .[46]

It is necessary to leave aside the many contentious issues involved here, pausing only to note that it was written when Freud's eldest child, Mathilde, was 14 (the age of the drowsy

Florence) and had five younger siblings. For our purposes we can see that ill-health was the means of regaining her father's love and attention for Elizabeth d'Esperance, and it got her out of the home and away from her mother. In the same way, Florence escaped from a home environment dominated by Mrs Cook and three younger siblings, and entered a world where she was to become a star. So that illness, an important aspect of the mythology of mediumship and one of its childhood credentials, had many uses.

Again, in this context it is interesting to note what happened when these young mediums married, and many of them were teenage brides. Florence Cook, whose husband refused to allow her to continue with her mediumship once she became Mrs Corner ('an inconsiderate husband, who may subjugate her will. . . '), very quickly succumbed once more to lethargy and symptoms of hysteria. He was finally forced to agree to the continuation of her private mediumship, whereupon her health and happiness once again revived ('it will force her husband to . . . show her consideration . . . for otherwise a relapse will threaten').[47] Elizabeth d'Esperance, who had remained well since her schooldays, became badly depressed within days of her marriage at the age of 18. Once more she was haunted by visions of 'shadow people' and an encroaching sense of unreality. Her health began to suffer in a direct repetition of the earlier events but this time she was saved, not by her father, but by the seance. Friends introduced her to a seance circle and there she quickly regained her equilibrium and emerged an accomplished and powerful medium. Far from being a step into freedom, or the promised enhancement of status, marriage had relegated Florence to the rank of a child who must beg permission for her activities, and Elizabeth to the loneliness and isolation of her previous years. Great expectations were not fulfilled, conflicts were resurrected, and illness resulted. Successful mediumship mediated these problems and difficulties, and presented a kind of safety valve for their contained expression.

Contingent to the emphasis on youthful mediumship was the implicit assumption of childhood innocence. Although this was rarely articulated it undoubtedly lay behind much of the pleasure and enthusiasm with which child spirits were received, and the ready acceptance of young girl mediums. William Crookes, in paying tribute to the frank straightforwardness of Florence Cook, related his claim for the authenticity of the spirit to the youth of the medium:

> to imagine that an innocent school-girl of fifteen should be able to conceive and then successfully carry out for three years so gigantic an imposture as this, and in that time should submit to any test which might be imposed upon her, should bear the strictest scrutiny, should be willing to be searched at any time, either before or after a seance . . . to imagine, I say, the Katie King of the last three years to be the result of imposture does more violence to one's reason and common sense than to believe her to be what she herself affirms.[48]

Babies in the spirit-land and English schoolgirls could not possibly be capable of fraud. It was unthinkable that they could possess the perverse morality necessary to instigate such monstrous proceedings. But elsewhere in the spiritualist literature it is clear that youthful mediums were as likely to attract disreputable spirits as any other, and this was certainly a feature of Florence Cook's career. During the early phases of her mediumship Florence apparently complained of the presence of malignant spirits. Noises, disturbances and small thefts, all the type of Poltergeist phenomena usually associated with children, became common in the Cook household. 'Katie' explained through her medium that this was a period of some danger for Florence, that there were indeed disreputable influences present, but that it was a phase through which all mediums must pass. Other reports claimed that Florence had been appalled at the wickedness of some spirit communications, and as early as 1872 there had been talk of an evil presence (which presumably spoke and acted through her) purporting to be the Devil.[49] It was also well-known that materialised child spirits enjoyed taking money and trinkets from sitters, whilst one report of an American seance featuring a 12-year-old girl noted that items were stolen and 'the bosoms of ladies' were 'partially unbuttoned' by spirit hands.[50] Stealing, sexual impropriety and devilish communications were hardly consistent with a concept of innocent childhood, but as usual spiritualists did not ascribe the behaviour to the medium. The gentle girl who, only minutes before, had been possessed by the archetypal drunken sailor with his swaggering coarseness and demands for strong drink, emerged from the ordeal quite unscathed. She was once more simply 'a little country girl, pure and innocent of harm as mortal is but rarely found'.[51] The fact that such purity of mind could attract the 'disgusting' and 'loathesome' was put down to lack of experience, and this a good developing circle could provide. The reputation of the fair-faced daughters of Albion remained intact.

It was from a different direction that danger threatened. Physicians were not slow to see that many of the manifestations of mediumship were similar to those of hysteria, and were used to dealing with uncontrolled outbursts of behaviour and language even in young girls. The medical literature abounded in references to the moral and sexual perversity of the female hysteric, of her ability to deceive, to act a part, to manipulate, to express (in short) every conceivable attribute that was the very antithesis of 'normal' femininity. The fact that this discourse subverted the prescriptive norms that medicine was keen to espouse as scientific truths was a contradiction that the profession was not anxious to address. Consequently medicine could continue to harp on the subject of innate female virtue whilst at the same time standing by the old adage, 'hysteria is most frequently seen in lascivious girls'.[52] This was the explicit recognition that hysteria and rampant sexuality were linked, and were to be found in female children. So that when Freud openly attacked the concept of childhood 'innocence of mind', claiming that it was perfectly possible for a child of 10 to possess 'forbidden knowledge', he was simply stating what many doctors already knew but were reluctant to express as a generic fact.[53] This had severe implications for a spiritualist rationale based on the assumption of childhood innocence which was thought, in itself, to be a protection against deception. To make matters worse, the physicians who showed most interest in spiritualism were just those who often followed up other cases of youthful female fraud, albeit in a different line. These were the infamous fasting cases of the 1860s and 1870s, epitomised by that of Sarah Jacobs. This 10-year-old Welsh girl with pretensions to sainthood claimed that she was miraculously continuing to live without any intake of nourishment beyond that of constant Bible reading. She and several other angelic little girls became the local wonders of their small rural communities, and eventually attracted the attention of the physicians. After detailed investigation medicine had no hesitation in denouncing these would-be miracle workers as hysterial impostors. Linking the eating disorders, and claiming them as feminine prerogative, the investigators went on to enumerate the variety of ruses that young women would resort to in order to appear to be eating. Pretending to fast whilst obtaining secret sources of food, masquerading as a healthy eater but in fact digesting nothing, these were merely different forms of moral debasement and youthful female perversion. Claims to authentic mediumship based on the concept of innocence cut no ice with these medical critics, and others who were happy to adopt the medical paradigm of the association between hysteria and mediumship continued to reinforce the connection:

> The acts of the hysteric, again, are like those of the medium and the Poltergeist child . . . the study of hysteria paints for us in rather coarser colours just such a weakening of the moral sense, such an inextricable mingling of imposture and reality and such examples of unnatural cunning posing under the mask of innocence, as we find in mediumship.[54]

It was a harsh condemnation for those accustomed to welcoming loving child spirits during a family seance, or for parents who believed passionately in the mediumship of their own child. But that innocence of youth which was proof for the believer became, for the sceptic, a grotesque mask. Behind the blasts and counter-blasts that signified every engagement between the embattled positions of believer and non-believer, lay the precarious, painful and infinitely delicate terrain of the psyche of a child.

It has not been my intention here to present a theoretical

analysis of altered states of consciousness, or of the relationship between subjectivity and language. Instead, I have tried to indicate some of the issues involved in the attainment of speaking mediumship by women and children, and the wider implications for their lives. Despite its many inconsistencies and complexities nineteenth-century spiritualism did offer an opportunity for greater effectivity and improved status, and through it the prescriptive virtue of silence could be confounded. The ambiguity lies in the fact that, having claimed the right to be heard, the medium then went to great pains to disassociate herself from her words. Leaving aside the question of fraud (and the important issue of choosing to 'act the part'), the means for this deflection of personal responsibility was the renunciation of a unified sense of self. As far as the medium was concerned a second 'I', often a mirror image, emerged to take control of the proceedings: 'I might have been regarding my own reflexion in a mirror. . . . '[55] And it was another voice which spoke. So that an activity which emphasised the centrality of the medium and the importance of utterance rested on the assumption that it was not she who was the speaking and acting subject. Mediumship operated as both resistance and acquiescence to the patriarchal order; transgression and conformity. Like hysteria, this marks not the feminine tendency to insanity of medical discourse but a severely contained oppositional politics. However, the hysteric's revolt was closed off by familial and medical intervention, and in order to maintain her outbursts she was forced to submit to the definition of 'patient'. The medium, on the other hand, operated within the same frame of reference as her sitters, and was encouraged in an activity which had wider social implications. Her world was opened up rather than shut down. Involved in an intricate interplay of projection and desire, both medium and sitters gained from the exchange. For the medium, another voice. Another who is, and is not, me. For the believer, 'the touch of a vanished hand, and the sound of a voice that was still'.[56]

Acknowledgment

I should like to thank Alison White for her help in clarifying some of the points I have made here.

Notes

1 'The professor at the breakfast table', *Atlantic Monthly* 3 (January 1859), p. 90. Cited by R. Laurence Moore, *In Search of White Crows: Spiritualism, Parapsychology, and American Culture*, New York, Oxford University Press, 1977, p. 44.
2 Henry James, *The Bostonians* (1886), London, Sidgwick & Jackson, 1948, p. 3.
3 George Eliot in a letter to Harriet Beecher Stowe, 24 June 1872. She was most intrigued by the fact that Harriet had used her husband as the model for 'the visionary boy' in *Oldtown Folks* (1869), and for a discussion of the subject see Charles Edward Stowe, *The Life of Harriet Beecher Stowe*, London, Sampson Low, Marston, Searle & Rivington, 1889, pp. 419–44. Mesmerism claimed to have established the presence of a magnetic force or fluid which emanated from the human body, and which could be manipulated and transmitted by an experienced operator. This had significance for spiritualists who believed that the spirits communicated via this force, and that spirit existence was proof of the materiality of a hitherto unknown element in the universe.
4 For a discussion of nineteenth-century working-class spiritualism see Logie Barrow, 'Socialism in eternity: the ideology of plebeian spiritualists, 1853–1913', *History Workshop Journal* 9, (Spring 1980), pp. 37–69.
5 For an interesting discussion of the so-called feminine qualities in relation to American mediumship during this period see, Moore, op. cit., p. 106.
6 For a discussion of the separate spheres see Catherine Hall, 'The early formation of Victorian domestic ideology', *Fit Work for Women*, London, Croom Helm, 1979, pp. 15–32. The notion of feminine religious influence as a cohesive force has interesting cross-cultural parallels. See, for example, I.M. Lewis, *Ecstatic Religion – An Anthropological Study of Spirit Possession and Shamanism*, London, Penguin, 1978, p. 86.
7 Elsewhere I have dealt more directly with these issues, and with the subversion of normative femininity that they entailed. See

Alex Owen, 'Women and nineteenth century spiritualism: strategies in the subversion of femininity', in J. Obelkevitch, L. Roper and R. Samuel (eds), *Religion and Society*, London, Routledge & Kegan Paul, forthcoming.

8 See Barbara Taylor, *Eve and the New Jerusalem: Socialism and Feminism in the Nineteenth Century*, London, Virago, 1983. For an elaboration of these points in relation to Joanna Southcott, a prophetess who attained a wide following during the early nineteenth century and whose heretical ideas were to prove formative for the socialist feminists of the Owenite movement, see Barbara Taylor, 'The woman-power: religious heresy and feminism in early English socialism', in Susan Lipshitz (ed.), *Tearing the Veil: Essays on Femininity*, London, Routledge & Kegan Paul, 1978, pp. 119–44. J.F.C. Harrison, *The Second Coming: Popular Millennarianism 1780–1850*, London, Routledge & Kegan Paul, 1979, pp. 31 ff., has a discussion of the role of women within millennarian movements.

9 For a useful and cautionary discussion of the use of the public/private distinction in feminist analyses, see Sarah Fildes, 'The inevitability of theory', *Feminist Review* 14 (Summer 1983), pp. 66–8.

10 Geoffrey K. Nelson, *Spiritualism and Society*, London, Routledge & Kegan Paul, 1969, p. 112.

11 Reverend Charles Maurice Davies, *Mystic London: or, Phases of Occult Life in the Metropolis*, London, Tinsley Bros, 1875, p. 262.

12 See Georgiana Houghton, *Evenings at Home in Spiritualist Seance*, London, Trübner & Co., 1881, pp. 126, 128, 180.

13 Davies, op. cit., pp. 313–14.

14 *Spiritualist*, 12 December 1873, p. 451. Relations between Florence Cook and Blackburn had deteriorated by the mid-1870s and he then turned his attention to the second daughter, Kate Cook, and her spirit form 'Lily Gordon'. He finally left the bulk of his estate to Kate and her mother.

15 For a consideration of mediumship and the expression of sexuality, see Owen, op. cit. Trevor H. Hall was the first to make out a case against Crookes citing the 1922 statement of Francis Anderson who claimed to have had an affair with Florence Cook in the early 1890s, during the course of which she admitted to the earlier affair with Crookes. See Trevor H. Hall, *The Spiritualists. The Story of Florence Cook and William Crookes*, New York, Helix Press, Garrett Publications, 1962. An excellent antidote is the scrupulous case presented by Mr R.G. Medhurst and Mrs K.M. Goldney, 'William Crookes and the physical phenomena of mediumship', *Proceedings of the Society*

for Psychical Research vol. 54 (March 1964), pp. 25–157. Despite this meticulous contribution, the Hall thesis continues to be trotted out by those seeking quick and easy explanations. Interesting from other points of view, but still leaning heavily on Hall, is Vieda Skultans, 'Mediums, controls and eminent men', in Pat Holden (ed.), *Women's Religious Experience*, London, Croom Helm, 1983, pp. 15–26.

16 *Spiritualist*, 15 May 1874, p. 230. Crookes's similar account appeared in ibid., 10 April 1874, p. 176.

17 Ibid., 15 May 1874, pp. 230, 232. My account is drawn from the versions offered by both Edward Cox and Mrs Showers.

18 Medhurst and Goldney, op. cit., pp. 122–3.

19 Reverend Charles Maurice Davies, *Heterodox London, or, Phases of Freethought in the Metropolis*, vol. 2, London, Tinsley Bros, 1874, p. 44.

20 See *Medium and Daybreak*, 7 September 1877, p. 572; ibid., 28 June 1878, p. 411; and ibid., 15 August 1879, p. 508.

21 *Autobiography of Emma Hardinge Britten*, Mrs Margaret Wilkinson (ed.), London, John Heywood, 1900, p. 50.

22 Ibid.

23 Sigmund Freud, 'Splitting of the ego in the process of defence' (1938), *The Standard Edition of the Complete Psychological Works of Sigmund Freud*, London, Hogarth Press, 1953–74, vol. 23, 1951, pp. 273–8; Jacques Lacan, 'Le stade du miroir comme formateur de la fonction du Je' (1936), *Ecrits*, Paris, Seuil, 1966, pp. 93–100, and *Ecrits: A Selection*, tr. Alan Sheridan, London, Tavistock, 1977, pp. 1–7. I have found psychoanalytic theory, particularly in the connection it makes between sexuality and the unconscious, invaluable in interpreting many of the more bizarre spiritualist incidents. However, I have tried to avoid here a full-scale engagement with theory, preferring to allow the concepts to emerge in the context of the material. A useful translation of the central Lacanian texts relating to feminine sexuality, together with lucid introductions, is Juliet Mitchell and Jacqueline Rose (eds), *Feminine Sexuality: Jacques Lacan and the école freudienne*, tr. Jacqueline Rose, London, Macmillan, 1982.

24 An inspirational address delivered at Cleveland Hall, London, and reported in the *Spiritualist*, 10 April 1874, p. 174.

25 Emma Hardinge, *The Place and Mission of Woman – An Inspirational Discourse*, Boston, Hubbard W. Swett, 1859, p. 6.

26 Ibid., p. 3.

27 R. Laurence Moore, 'The spiritualist medium: a study of female professionalism in America' in Esther Katz and Anita Rapone

(eds), *Women's Experience in America: An Historical Anthology*, New Brunswick, Transaction Books, 1980, pp. 145–68, makes a similar point in relation to American female mediumship. One of the major British exceptions was Chandos Leigh Hunt, a remarkable spiritualist healer who travelled the country during the 1870s to speak out against compulsory vaccination.

28 James Burns speaking at the Second Jubilee Convention of Spiritualists, 1 and 2 November 1879. Reported in the *Medium and Daybreak*, 12 December 1879, p. 773.

29 Mrs Showers's account, *Spiritualist*, 15 May 1874, pp. 231–2.

30 Editorial, *Medium and Daybreak*, 12 October 1877, p. 649.

31 F.J.T., *Heaven Opened; or Messages for the Bereaved from Our Little Ones in Glory*, London, J. Burns, 1870, p. 42.

32 Morell Theobald, *Spirit Workers in the Home Circle*, London, T. Fisher Unwin, 1887, p. 43.

33 Ibid.

34 Ibid., p. 135.

35 Catherine Clément/Hélène Cixous, *La jeune née*, Union Général d'Editions, Collection '10/18', 1975, p. 184. Cited by Jane Gallop, *Feminism and Psychoanalysis: The Daughter's Seduction*, London, Macmillan, 1982, p. 144, in considering the seduction role played in Freud's case histories by the maid/governess, nurse.

36 F.J.T., op. cit., p. 13.

37 Ibid., p. 38

38 See *Medium and Daybreak*, 27 July 1877, p. 475; ibid., 21 September 1877, pp. 596–7. The 'cabinet' was the term used for the alcove or box covered by a heavy curtain, behind which the materialisation medium sat in order to produce the phenomena.

39 Wilkinson (ed.), op. cit., p. 3.

40 Elizabeth d'Esperance, *Shadow Land, or Light from the Other Side*, London, George Redway, 1897, p. 3.

41 Hélène Cixous, 'The laugh of the Medusa', *Signs*, Summer 1976, vol. 1, no. 4, p. 886.

42 Frank Podmore, *Modern Spiritualism: A History and a Criticism*, vol. 2, London, Methuen & Co., 1902, pp. 309–12, discusses the significance of daydreaming and mediumship. He cites statistics on daydreaming as an activity predominantly related to women and children from the *American Journal of Psychology* 7, (1895), p. 86. For a quite different personal account of the importance of daydreams in his own boyhood, see Laurens van der Post, *Jung and the Story of Our Time*, London, Hogarth Press, 1976, pp. 7–15. Van der Post was another child whose early years were peppered with remarks like, 'Would you be

good enough, sir, to step out of your trance?' (p. 9). He, too, became a leading exponent of the importance of spiritual life, although not of spiritualism.

43 Wilkinson (ed.), op. cit., p. 3.

44 Mrs Everett was a passive writing medium who knew Florence Cook, and she recorded this observation in her diary. The Everett Diaries are held by the Society for Psychical Research, London. Cited by Medhurst and Goldney, op. cit., pp. 72–3.

45 Sigmund Freud, 'Fragment of an analysis of a case of hysteria ("Dora")', (1905 [1901]), *The Pelican Freud Library*, vol.8, London, Penguin, 1980, p. 75. Footnote added in 1923.

46 Ibid., p. 77.

47 Ibid.

48 William Crookes, 'The last of Katie King', *Spiritualist*, 5 June 1874. Reprinted in full in M.R. Barrington (ed.), *Crookes and the Spirit World*, London, Souvenir Press, 1972, pp. 137–41.

49 *Spiritualist*, 12 December 1873, p. 452. References to the Devil were made in 1872 by a Dr Purdon who had invited Florence Cook to his home on the Isle of Wight in order to carry out a series of private seances. His letters on the subject are cited by Medhurst and Goldney, op. cit., pp. 53–4.

50 Letter to Frank J. Garrison, 18 January 1867, held in the Boston Public Library. Cited by Moore (1977), op. cit., p. 17.

51 *Spiritualist*, 2 November 1877, p. 689.

52 Thomas Laycock, *A Treatise on the Nervous Diseases of Women*, London, Longman, Orme, Brown, Green & Longmans, 1840, p. 163.

53 Freud, op. cit., p. 83.

54 Podmore, op. cit., pp. 323–4. For two examples of hostile physicians who were keen to debunk spiritualism and expose female eating disorders, see William A. Hammond, *Fasting Girls: Their Physiology and Pathology*, New York, G.P. Putnam's Sons, 1879; L.S. Forbes Winslow, *Fasting and Feeding Psychologically Considered*, London, Baillière, Tindall & Cox, 1881.

55 D'Esperance, op. cit., pp. 289–91.

56 Theobald, op. cit., pp. 80–1.

4

Public and private children: infant education in the 1820s and 1830s

KAREN CLARKE

In 1819 a group of Whigs and Radicals, led by Henry Brougham, set up an infant school for working-class children at Brewers Green, Westminster, under the supervision of James Buchanan, who had come from Robert Owen's pioneering infant school at New Lanark. The Westminster school was the first infant school in England and its establishment was quickly followed by the opening of a number of others in London and elsewhere. By 1825, thirty-eight towns outside London had one or more infant schools and there was an Infant School Society, set up the previous year, to provide general support and publicity for the establishment of schools throughout the country.[1] Interest in the infant school movement was manifest not only in the setting up of schools, funded locally by public subscription, throughout England, but also in the appearance of numerous books and articles in the religious and educational press. But by the late 1830s this interest had all but died away, despite the availability of government grants for infant schools from 1833 onwards and support for the schools from at least some of the government inspectors.[2]

This paper will look at the political and ideological context for the sudden rise of the infant school movement and examine the aims and methods of the schools before going on to look at some of the possible reasons for the movement's equally rapid decline.

The interest in infant education has to be seen in the context of a more general interest in working-class education among liberal Whigs and Radicals who saw it as a necessary condition for social harmony. Education was seen as the solution to the social and political threat to the ruling class posed by the concentration of large numbers of working-class people in the rapidly expanding cities of the early nineteenth century and their political autonomy.[3] The Sunday School movement and the establishment of monitorial schools in the late eighteenth and early nineteenth centuries may both be seen as attempts to control and contain the political energies of the working class.[4] However, the specific interest in infant education was a new phenomenon in the early 1820s and has to be seen in the light of the changes taking place within the middle-class family, in particular, the separation of spheres into male-public and female-private (discussed in this volume by Catherine Hall), which led to a self-conscious examination of the maternal role and the focusing of attention on early childhood. The middle-class mother came to have an increased responsibility for the provision of a suitable moral and physical environment for her children, particularly in the early years. The spectacle of large numbers of working-class children on the streets, in the public eye, became an irritation and an anomaly in the light of the developing ideology of the family, which gave an important place to the protection of the mother and child within the private sphere, safe from the dangers of the public domain. Ideally, the child's place was in the home, under the parental eye, but where the exigencies of working-class life made this impossible, it was preferable that children should be gathered together in properly conducted schools than that they should be left to roam the streets.

David Goyder, master of the first Bristol infant school, bemoaned the degraded state of the poor and the frequent sight of children of the working classes:

> wandering about the streets, lanes and avenues of our populous cities and towns, disgusting the beholder with their pallid, filthy appearance, imitating successfully the example of their more mature but vicious associates, their countenances the just index of the vacuity of their minds, and their general appearance exhibiting their progressive advancement in vice, misery and ruin. Such beyond all doubt is their state, if allowed their liberty unrestrained by paternal authority.[5]

Sir James Mackintosh, at the meeting to inaugurate the Infant School Society, spoke of how families were 'schools appointed by Providence to implant virtue in the hearts of the young and to inculcate affection and every kind of feeling'; only when this was lacking could it be justifiable to establish infant schools.[6] The failure of the working-class family to provide the right kind of care for their children gave educators the opportunity to 'go back and find the very germ of the child's intellect before its roots were shot forth into an unhealthy soil and ere it was engrafted upon from the very fulsome plants by which it was surrounded'.[7]

This horticultural metaphor runs through much of the writing on infant schools (and continues to be the metaphor in some writing on early education today).[8] The infant school, placed in the working-class district it was to serve, was to provide a contrast with the houses and streets from which it drew its pupils.[9] Samuel Wilderspin, master of the second London infant school in Spitalfields and effective leader of the infant school movement, specified that the schoolroom should be a 'light, airy, cheerful place, which the mind can use to give to itself agreeable sensations'.[10] The provision of a playground with swings, trees and flowers was seen as very important, with the breath of the countryside which that introduced: 'these schools are intended to supersede everything that is confined and limited, so does the health of the children demand a free access to fresh air as often as may be convenient.'[11]

Wilderspin, on a more practical note, pointed out that the flowers in the playground would 'tend to counteract any disagreeable smell that may proceed from the children, and thereby be conducive to their health as well as to that of those who have charge of them'.[12]

More importantly, the playground had a central pedagogical role, as the place where the master could assess his success in inculcating particular habits. Wilderspin wrote:

> The playground may be compared to the world, where the little children are left to themselves, there it may be seen what effects their education has produced, for if any of the children be fond of fighting and quarelling, it is here that they will do it, and this gives the master an opportunity of giving them seasonable advice, as to the

> impropriety of such conduct; whereas if kept in school . . . these evil inclinations, with many others, will never manifest themselves, until they go into the street, and consequently the master would have no opportunity of attempting a cure.[13]

Aims and methods of the infant schools

The young child was seen by those promoting infant schools as a bundle of faculties whose development was largely determined by the environment in which s/he was placed. The faculties were seen as a set of mutually independent qualities, each of which had its own particular stimuli in the environment, exposure to which exercised that faculty and thereby strengthened it. In addition to the five senses, the faculties included moral propensities, such as affection, conscience and kindness, and also undesirable ones such as envy, hate, etc.[14] The master's example constituted the stimulus which would strengthen the desirable moral faculties by exercise; simultaneously the undesirable ones were weakened by lack of exercise: 'The better feelings of the child must gradually become most prominent since they are constantly excited, while the bad passions are put and kept in subjection by this more and more predominating influence.'[15]

This belief, deriving from phrenology, in the exercise of pre-existing faculties as the basis for the development of character and intellect, clearly made infancy a period of crucial importance.[16] It was the failure of working-class parents to recognise this, as well as the practical constraints which their circumstances imposed, which, in the eyes of their advocates, made infant schools so necessary as a means of bringing about social reform.[17] By the time children reached the age where they were accepted by monitorial schools the damage was already done.

The infant school literature had a view of education broader than that of established educational institutions; it argued against a concept of education that concentrated on the intellect, and within the intellect on the faculty of memory in particular, at the expense of all other faculties.[18] The movement's aim was rather to mould the whole character of the child, by encouraging a set of habits of behaviour, which would remain with the child throughout its life:

> to implant good *habits* of body, heart and mind which . . . shall grow with their growth and strengthen with their strength, is the largest part of the work undertaken by the best infant schools for those portions of our juvenile population who more particularly need such asylums.[19]

Wilderspin's characterisation of habits as 'living rules' illustrates an important contrast between teaching a set of precepts, i.e. externally given rules which have to be remembered and then obeyed, and rules of behaviour which are totally internalised and which become inseparable from the character of the child.[20] There are very obvious parallels in these contrasting beliefs about the nature of education with changes in the dominant ideology of power. The dominant view in the eighteenth century was that power was something visible and imposed from outside, and could therefore be resisted; that becoming dominant in the nineteenth century, through utilitarian philosophy, was that government should be based on consent, on a common set of values, and in the interests of all, with every individual governing himself.[21]

The methods to be followed in the schools similarly reflect this political philosophy. The master of the school was to rule the children by *love* not fear; his first task was to win their *hearts*, and this would provide the key to his future success in teaching them. Rev. William Wilson, in his book *The System of Infant Schools*, pointed out the dangers of ruling by fear, saying that fear would lead to a dislike of the master, and by association, to a dislike of what was being taught, and would also produce a feeling of resistance to *all* control. David Goyder described his own method of gaining the children's affections by 'humbling himself to the character of a little child . . . until at length I so won their affections that I could turn and regulate them at my pleasure.'[22]

Most of the writers on infant schools were opposed to any form of corporal punishment and used methods of public shaming such as the method known as the 'jury system' to correct behaviour. The child who had misbehaved was to be questioned on his behaviour by the master before the whole school, who were to decide his punishment. Here again, the emphasis is on consent and shared values. In the examples of jury trials given, the children's kindness, mercy and sense of justice unmotivated by revenge is stressed, and the process is always portrayed as a beneficial experience for all present.[23]

The particular habits in which the children were to be trained were those of obedience, cheerful subordination, cleanliness and order – characteristics which were clearly desirable in the future working class.[24] An equation was constantly made between moral and physical qualities, so that the physical environment created by the school was of great importance to the success of the whole undertaking.[25] Order as a physical and a moral virtue was taught by more or less elaborate drilling procedures, which were perhaps developed in their most extreme form by David Goyder, master of the Bristol infants' school in the early 1820s. He described how he had so trained the children that at a word of command or through signals from a whistle or the foot or hand of the master, the children would march around the room in complex zig-zag formations, clapping their hands in time to the stamp of their feet.[26] Thomas Pole, a Quaker doctor who wrote about the school, was much impressed by this drill which he described as 'the means of introducing them (the children) to habits of subordination; in these marches they are also obliged to attend to signals or the word of command and to obey them; there is in fact no part of the school employments so calculated to produce attention and obedience.'[27]

In the same way singing was seen as 'an essential part of the effort and means to awaken and excite human sympathy'. In Goyder's words, 'singing for the most part has the effect of tranquillizing the turbulent, and of subduing the unruly passions and produces in the infant a frame of feeling so humble and teachable that I always think it expedient to open the school with this exercise.' Similarly for the Mayos it was both physical exercise and a 'moral engine' used to excite religious and moral sentiments.[28]

Despite the constant emphasis on the education of the child

as a whole, development of the intellect was given less emphasis than the development of character in the early literature on infant schools. From the later 1830s the central technique, the object lesson, was written about very fully, and dominated the training literature for infant teachers produced by the central training institute, the Home and Colonial Infant School Society, established in 1836.[29] This relative lack of emphasis on the intellect is at least in part attributable to the fact that the faculties were seen as being hierarchically arranged, with an order of development reflecting the position of each faculty in the hierarchy. The physical and moral powers had to be developed before those of the intellect, but the infant school could lay the foundations for later learning through the development of the senses.[30]

The object lesson was a pure application of empirical philosophy deriving from Locke, that is, the belief that all ideas derive from impressions received by the senses. The formation of clear and correct ideas and the cultivation of the faculties of observation, thought and expression were to be encouraged by the exercise of the senses on different objects. Once clear ideas were established, words could be attached to the ideas. The method by which this was to be achieved was to present the whole school with an object and elicit from the children, by questioning, what ideas they already had, extending their understanding by drawing attention to further qualities.[31] The objects used and the qualities emphasised were 'natural' ones, on the implicit assumption that the natural was simpler than the artifactual, and therefore more suitable for young children. In addition to leaves, twigs and flowers, and *pictures* of animals whose characteristics included moral virtues, e.g. the busy bee, the faithful dog, the hard-working ox or horse, common objects such as coal, glass and milk were used. The natural qualities of the last three objects systematically overlooked the place of *labour* in bringing the objects before the children, with the consequence that the labour involved in their production appears as a natural quality of the object itself.

This view of the natural order extended to the social position of the children themselves. Charles Mayo pointed out to teachers:

> It is very important also to accustom them [the children] to consider what is their right position in society. Teach them that the different grades of rank are established by the Lord, and that each has its appointed work, as each member of our body has its appointed office.[32]

Men as teachers

Almost all the authors of the books on infant schools were men who were themselves masters of infant schools. They assumed or explicitly advocated that the schools should be headed by a man with his wife or sister acting as an assistant, in order to reproduce the structure of the family in the public domain of the school:

> After the family order of father and mother, there ought to be a man at the head of every juvenile and infant training school, and when practicable, his wife or sister ought to be an assistant. This proposal to carry the family system into school is not to supersede parental training at home, but to assist and strengthen it.[33]

Stow also used this to argue for the education of girls and boys together so that men could take the chief burden of girls' education and women would be free to carry out their family responsibilities (on the assumption apparently that it would be improper for a girls' only school to be headed by a man).[34]

In Wilderspin's view, men made the best teachers because a man's position as head of the family gave him greater authority over the children; women had neither the physical strength, nor 'at present' the intellectual powers to manage a school.[35] Charles Mayo, discussing the importance of the character of the master (sic) made it clear that he felt that only men had the necessary spiritual and intellectual qualities required for 'the high object of inculcating Christian sentiments'. He informed his audience at the Royal Institution that if they merely wished to relieve parents of the burden of their children, 'any cheerful, good-tempered, and, if I may be allowed the term, motherly female, may be appointed', but in that case the school would be no more than a refuge for infants.[36]

The infant school movement saw itself as providing an education for children which was informed by a proper understanding of the nature of the young, not only as a substitute for the uncontrolled and dangerous education which the children of the poor received on the streets, but also as an alternative to the provision which already existed in the form of Dame schools. These were informal, locally based, casual, small-scale schools, which as their name suggests were mainly run by women.[37] There are interesting parallels in the rivalry between infant schools and Dame schools with the attempts of medical men to wrest the management of childbirth from midwives.[38] Thomas Pole, who was associated with the Bristol infant school, wrote of Dame school mistresses:

> How few of the ordinary class of school-keepers know how to correct the early tempers which ruffle the children's minds and which if not brought into subjection will grow up with them and in process of time destroy their own happiness as well as that of others with whom they may hereafter associate? Are these mistresses of schools likely to teach them by example and precept, to curb those tempers, to forgive injuries and to love those who have offended them? Are they likely to harmonise discordant minds, and strengthen the bonds of affection?[39]

Similar objections to the competence of Dame school mistresses for the task of educating young children were given by Wilderspin: 'since it has been proved that infants demand and are capable of extensive mental development, it cannot be supposed that ignorant and inactive old women are competent to undertake such a charge.'[40]

As with midwifery, little is known of Dame schools except through the eyes of their opponents. The Manchester Statistical Society, which clearly supported the establishment of infant schools, described Manchester's Dame schools as follows:

> This is the most numerous class of schools and they are generally in the most deplorable condition. The greater part of them are kept by females, but some by old men, whose only qualification for this employment seems to be their unfitness for every other. Many of these teachers are engaged at the same time in some other employment such as shopkeeping, sewing, washing etc. which renders any regular instruction among their scholars absolutely impossible. Indeed, neither parents nor teachers seem to consider this as the principal object in sending the children to these schools, but generally say that they go there in order to be taken care of and to be out of the way at home.[41]

It is the tension and contradiction between the attempt to assert men's role as the guardians and educators of the very young in the public sphere, and their eclipse from this role in the private sphere by the mother, which I believe explains the infant school movement's loss of impetus in the 1840s and 1850s. There seems to have been a subtle shift in the literature from men being both the theoretical experts and the practitioners in the field of infant education, to the role of advising *women* how to educate young children. Simultaneously there was a shift of focus away from the application of these ideas to the children of the poor, to their application in the home to the children of middle-class parents. This is reflected in the title of the Mayos' book on infant education, addressed to schools and *private families*. The preface states that it is hoped that the book will be useful to parents and governesses engaged in early education.[42]

The *Christian Mothers Magazine*, a monthly periodical addressed to middle-class mothers which started publication in 1844, contained several extensive reviews of books by Wilderspin and the Mayos, and a number of articles on infant education, which were clearly intended to instruct its readers in relation to their own children rather than urge them to set up schools for the poor.[43] Responsibility for the moral and spiritual welfare of young children was increasingly seen as resting with the mother rather than with the father or jointly, as the appearance of the *Christian Mothers Magazine* and innumerable advice books on infant education addressed to mothers indicates. Whereas twenty years earlier the *Christian Observer* had contained anxious correspondence from anonymous parents, clearly identifiable as fathers, on problems of child rearing, by the 1840s these problems were the mother's province. The word 'parent' by the 1840s implied 'mother' rather than being ambiguous or meaning 'father'.[44]

Other factors also contributed to the infant school movement's loss of impetus and to infant schools becoming the non-prestigious domain of women. In the 1830s religious divisions arose between those who wanted the schools to remain non-denominational in their approach to religious teaching and organisations like the Home and Colonial Infants School Society, set up in 1836, which represented the established church.[45] There were good financial reasons for rejecting the notion that infant schools needed a man with a female assistant at its head, rather than a single woman. David Goyder, who ran the Bristol Infant School in the early 1820s, had a salary of £90 a year; Wilderspin advocated a salary of £70–80 a year for a master and mistress, but a mistress on her own could be employed for as little as £35.[46] It was the cheapness of infant schools 'as they are usually taught by mistresses' which was one of the factors which the Newcastle Commission singled out in their favour in its report in 1861.[47]

However neither religious divisions nor purely financial considerations can explain the change in the gender of the ideal teacher of infants from male to female with the concomitant decline in interest in the infant school as an educational enterprise. The explanation for this has to be sought in the development of the definition of the public sphere as male and the private as female, with the responsibility of women for early education which this came to imply during the 1820s and 1830s. The infant school occupied an ambiguous position in relation to these two spheres, being a public substitute for an area of private responsibility. The resolution of the ambiguity was that the practice of infant education became a relatively obscure part of the public sphere occupied by women, while men retained their interest in it at the level of theory and training.

Notes

1 W.P. McCann, 'Samuel Wilderspin and the early infant schools', *British Journal of Educational Studies*, vol.14, 1966, pp.188–204; Samuel Wilderspin, *Infant Education*, London, Simpkin & Marshall, 1825 (3rd ed), ch.2; W.A.C. Stewart and W.P. McCann, *the Educational Innovators, volume 1: 1750–1880*, London, Macmillan, 1967, pp.241–72.
2 E.g. articles in the *Christian Observer*, 1824 and 1825.
3 For general background, see, e.g., Brian Simon, *The Two Nations and the Educational Structure 1780–1870*, London, Lawrence & Wishart, 1974, ch. 3.
4 Harold Silver, *The Concept of Popular Education*, MacGibbon & Kee, London, 1965, pp. 15–48.
5 D.G. Goyder, *A Treatise on the Management of Infant Schools*, London, Simpkin & Marshall, 1826, p. 5.
6 Wilderspin, op. cit., p. 26.
7 Wilderspin, op. cit., p. 32.
8 William Taylor, *Society and the Education of Teachers*, London, Faber & Faber, 1969.
9 Thomas Pole, *Observations Relative to Infant Schools*, Bristol, 1823, pp. 23–8.
10 Wilderspin, op. cit., p. 276. For a detailed discussion of Wilderspin's life and work see Philip McCann and Francis Young, *Samuel Wilderspin and the Infant School Movement*, London, Croom Helm, 1982.
11 D.G. Goyder, *A Manual Detailing the System of Instruction Pursued at the Infant School, Bristol*, London, Thomas Goyder, 1824 (3rd ed), p. 43.
12 Wilderspin, op. cit., p. 204.
13 Wilderspin, op. cit., pp. 201–2.
14 PP 1835 VII, *Select Committee on Education in England and Wales*, evidence of Samuel Wilderspin, qn. 236; Charles and Elizabeth Mayo, *Practical Remarks on Infant Education*, London, Seeley & Burnside, 1837, pp. 48, 54–5; David Stow, *Supplement to Moral Training and the Training System*, Glasgow, 1839, p. 26.
15 Wilderspin, op. cit., pp. 276–7.
16 For an extensive discussion of the place of phrenology in nineteenth-century thought, see Roger Cooter, *The Cultural Meanings of Popular Sciences*, Cambridge, Cambridge University Press, 1984.
17 William Wilson, *The System of Infants' Schools*, London, George Wilson, 1825, p. 5.

18 Wilderspin, op. cit., pp. 273–4.
19 PP 1846 XXXII, pp. 353–4, report on infant schools by J. Fletcher.
20 Wilderspin, op. cit., p. 281.
21 See M. Foucault, *Discipline and Punish*, London, Allen Lane, 1977.
22 Wilson, op. cit., pp. 14–15; Goyder, 1826, op. cit., p. 20; Wilderspin, op. cit., p. 274.
23 Pole, op. cit., pp. 40–54; Wilson, op. cit., pp. 26–7.
24 Wilderspin to Select Committee on Education, op. cit., qns 195–6; Goyder, 1826, op. cit., p. 20; Charles Mayo, *Observations on the Establishment and Direction of Infant Schools*, London, Seeley & Sons, 1827, p.27.
25 Wilson, op. cit., pp. 19–20.
26 Goyder, 1824, op. cit., pp. 14–17.
27 Pole, op. cit., pp. 57–8.
28 Wilderspin, op. cit., p. 279; Goyder, 1826, op. cit., p. 23; Charles and Elizabeth Mayo, op. cit., p. 98.
29 Charles and Elizabeth Mayo, op. cit.; Elizabeth Mayo, *Model Lessons for Infant School Teachers*, London, Seeley & Burnside, 1838.
30 Wilderspin, op. cit., p. 278.
31 Elizabeth Mayo, op. cit., preface; Charles and Elizabeth Mayo, op. cit., pp. 67–70.
32 Charles and Elizabeth Mayo, op. cit., p. 49.
33 Stow, op. cit., p. 19.
34 Stow, op. cit., pp. 19–20.
35 McCann and Young, op. cit., p. 175.
36 Charles Mayo, op. cit., p. 16.
37 D.P. Leinster-MacKay, 'Dame schools: a need for review', *British Journal of Educational Studies*, vol. 24, 1976, pp. 33–48; A.F.B. Roberts, 'A new view of the infant school movement', *British Journal of Educational Studies*, vol. 20, 1972, pp. 154–64.
38 Jean Donnison, *Midwives and Medical Men*, London, Heinemann Educational, 1977.
39 Pole, op. cit., p. 30.
40 Wilderspin, op. cit., p. 277.
41 Manchester Statistical Society, *Report of a Committee on the State of Education in the Borough of Manchester in 1834* (2nd ed), London, James Ridgway & Son, 1837, p. 5.
42 Charles and Elizabeth Mayo, op. cit.
43 For example, a series of articles on Wilderspin's methods appeared in the *Christian Mothers Magazine*, September to De-

cember 1844. The issue of February 1845 reviewed a series of books on infant education, etc.

44 Contrast, for example, 'Parents and children', *Christian Mothers Magazine*, October 1845 with letters to the *Christian Observer*, e.g. 1812, p.425; 1814, pp. 703–5; 1815, p. 20.

45 McCann and Young, op. cit., chs 10 and 11.

46 D.A. Turner, '1870: the state and the infant school system', *British Journal of Educational Studies*, vol. 18, 1970, pp. 151–65, at p. 162.

47 PP 1861 XXI, vol. 1, part I, p. 32.

5
State and language: Peter Pan *as written for the child*

JACQUELINE ROSE

> The question we need to ask now is which Ideological State Apparatus is the site of production of literary fictions. (Balibar, 1974, p. 126)

> The conflicts inherent to the instigation and development of the linguistic-educational politics of our bourgeois democracy are the only ones excluded from the literary representation of social conflict. (Balibar, 1974, p. 58)

As a myth of our culture, *Peter Pan* shares with other myths a place which seems to transcend the local and historical conditions out of which it first emerged. As a myth of childhood, it adds to that transcendence the particular force of innocence. Myth and childhood belong together, in that myth is so often identified with what is primitive, even *infantile*, or is seen as a form of expression which goes back to the origins of culture and speech.[1]

But *Peter Pan* is also a story that was told and which, in the process of its telling, reveals something of the problem – specifically in terms of childhood and its institutions – of this very conception of myth, which can only operate if we abstract from it the history of the language in which it is spoken. In the case of *Peter Pan*, that history is particularly complex, touching on questions of literacy and schooling, and on different forms of language use between classes of child – differences which finally undermine the wholly general category of childhood on which *Peter Pan* rests its appeal.

Peter Pan has been one of the most overwritten texts of our century, existing in numerous versions by different authors,[2] each version seemingly expanding the universal nature of its value, each version in fact suggesting a serious problem of linguistic address. To which child does each version speak? At what class of child are they aimed? These are questions which exceed the fact of the different ages of childhood (May Byron's three versions of *Peter Pan* for boys and girls, for little people, for the nursery),[3] and the problem of language which they raise cannot be fully understood without reference to divisions inside the institution of schooling, the institution out of which modern childhood has more or less been produced (Ariès, 1960). Language for children – how it is spoken both by and to the child – is subject to strictures, and characterised by differences, which need first to be located inside the institution where language is systematically taught. This is an issue which bears on our relationship, not only to children's writing, but to literature as a whole – the fact that language has an institutional history which determines how it is written, spoken, and understood.

In her book on French literary language (from which the opening quotations of this chapter are taken), Renée Balibar shows how the specifically literary effect of a French classic (Flaubert's 'Un coeur simple') relies on a condensation of the new (post-1789) national elementary French grammar and the Franco-Latin Syntax and tropes of the Ancien Régime which were still being reproduced in the secondary schools. In England, the history is different and the lines of linguistic-educational privilege are differently drawn, but there is the same distinction between a language of elementary experience and one of cultural style. At the beginning of this century, when *Peter Pan* was written, state policy on language was directed towards a rigorous separation of these forms of language between the different sectors of the education system. A whole new concept of 'synthetic' language was developed in the public elementary schools, a language to be based on the impressions of the visible world, as distinct from the classical and literary language which was simultaneously being taught in the secondary schools. It was because Barrie's own narrative version of *Peter Pan, Peter and Wendy* (Barrie, 1911) persistently confounded this distinction, and revealed these differences as contradictions within its own language, that it had to be completely re-written in order for it to be accepted for use in the state schools.

The distinction is one which still affects the way we use language today, but it is rarely discussed in commentaries on children's writing, where attention to class difference has tended to concentrate on the values, or content, of children's books.[4] The re-writing of *Peter Pan* shows class difference operating at a more fundamental level – that of the base components of the language which the child is actually allowed to speak. In this chapter I want to examine this issue of language and institution (the institutional determinants of language) by focusing on that moment when the most enduring and universal of children's fictions came into direct confrontation with the educational policy of the state.

In 1925, Barrie wrote a short story called 'Jas Hook at Eton: or The Solitary' for inclusion in an anthology of short stories for children, *The Flying Carpet* (Barrie, 1926). Instead of being published in that anthology, the story was delivered as a speech to the First Hundred at Eton on 7 July 1927, and published in *The Times*. It was replaced in the anthology by 'Neil and Tintinnabulum', a story which describes how a male narrator loses his godson when he is absorbed into the life of a public school – the title reflects the loss as the little boy's name is changed at school from Neil to Tintinnabulum, from English to Latin. Latin is the element which connects the two stories. The autograph manuscript version of Barrie's 1927 story is accompanied by a leaf of manuscript in an unidentified hand which gives the following Latin inscription for James Hook:

> Gratissimus Almae Matris filius magistro inform. et alumnis omnibus avete hoc into Iunii die MDCCC? ex Moluccis Iacobus Hook Floreat Etona. (Barrie, 1927b)
> (A most grateful son of our Dear Mother to the headmaster and to all her pupils. Greeting! this 4th day of June 18 – from the Moluccas, James Hook, Eton for ever)

The story 'Jas Hook at Eton' is presented by Barrie as evidence for the Latinate and public school credentials which are given in Hook's dying words – 'Floreat Etona' – which he utters as he jumps off the edge of the ship in the last sequence of

Barrie's famous play. In the 1911 narrative *Peter and Wendy*, Barrie spells the association out in the form of a revelation or scandal – as the ultimate and the most carefully guarded secret of his story:

> Hook was not his true name. To reveal who he really was would even at this date set the country in a blaze; but as those who read between the lines must have guessed, he had been at a famous public school. (Barrie, 1911, p. 203)

Four years later, when *Peter and Wendy* was accepted by the London County Council Books and Apparatus Sub-Committee as a reader for use in the public elementary schools, every vestige of this reference was systematically cut.[5] In 1915, the public elementary school child, object of compulsory education since 1880 and recently re-differentiated from the middle-class child by the second education act of 1902,[6] did not speak Latin but English, and an English which was carefully distinguished from literary language by its reference to experience, to the 'sights and sounds, the thoughts and feelings of everyday life' (Government Circular, 1912 (BOE, 1912, p.27)). Against this language was set not only Latin, but literary language in general or, more specifically, the language of the literary trope. Matthew Arnold, one of the chief spokesmen on cultural values and education at this time (Arnold, 1864, 1869), was also HM Inspector of Schools from 1852–86. He offered the following two extracts in 1867 to illustrate the gulf which then separated the privately educated middle-class child from children in the elementary schools:

> My dear parents, – The anticipation of our Christmas vacation abounds in peculiar delights. Not only that its 'festivities', its social gatherings, and its lively amusements crown the old year with happiness and mirth, but that I come a guest commended to your hospitable love by the performance of all you bade me remember when I left you in the glad season of sun and flowers. (Arnold, 1889, pp.131–2).

> Dear Fanny, – I am afraid I shall not pass in my examination. Miss C says she thinks I shall. I shall be glad when the Serpentine is frozen over, for we shall have such fun; I wish you did not live so far away, then you could come and share in the game. (ibid.)

The pseudo-classicism which Arnold is commenting on in the language of the privately educated middle-class child is picked up by Barrie in his 1927 story about Captain Hook: 'But even so, what ardour to excel, how indomitable is the particle man' (Barrie, 1927b, p. 3). It also appears at various points in *Peter and Wendy*: 'O man unfathomable' (Barrie, 1911, p. 202); 'the elegance of his diction, even when he was swearing, no less than the distinction of his demeanour, showed him one of a different caste from his crew' (Barrie, 1911, pp. 80–1). Along with all mention of Hook's educational history, this language is edited out of *Peter and Wendy* when it is accepted by the schools. Thus the censorship does not only apply to the explicit references to the institutions of schooling. Equally, and more crucially, it takes out any signs of their associated forms of linguistic style.

For *Peter Pan* to become a *reader*, the overconscious signs of its status as *literature* must be erased. The distinction is one which was written into state educational policy on language in the first decades of the century, when the state faced a potential contradiction between an increasingly generalised policy of state aid to schools (the 1902 Education Act provided state aid for the first time to the previously private domain of secondary education),[7] and the continuing differentiation between classes of child.

The language of the child – the language which it speaks, the language it reads, and the relationship between the two – was one of the central arenas within which this contradiction was played out. Here, the question of language becomes the question of *literacy*, and the question of literature hands over to that of *literary language* (how and what to speak, what to read and to what end). By this almost imperceptible shift, both language and literature are released as objects of *policy* – policy by means of which the child's relationship to its culture can be defined. Language is not simply there to be spoken, any more than literature waits to be read, like matter almost to be imbibed by the child ('When you give your child a bath, bathe him in language' – the exhortation of the 1974 Bullock report on literacy, *A Language for Life* (Bullock, 1974, p.58)). Both the language and the literature available to the child fall inside institutions which constitute them differentially and with different values and meanings at different times. The point of examining *Peter Pan*'s encounter with the schools is not, therefore, so much to demonstrate an outrage – how the repressive educational machinery clamps down on the book for the child – as to show how both language and literature are constituted by just such 'machinery' in the first place. In this context, natural language or the idea of language as naturally expressive appears not as something outside the range of these determinations but as one pole of a fully structural opposition between natural and cultured language in the schools.

This is how the Board of Education Circular of 1912 on the teaching of English in the public elementary school concludes its final section on English teaching for its senior classes:

> in teaching children, failure to use a direct, simple, unaffected style is doubly harmful: it makes the teaching more difficult for the child to understand and remember, and it corrupts his natural taste. . . . To preserve and develop naturally the unsophisticated virtues of children's language is worthy of an effort and will indeed require an effort on the part of a grown-up teacher. He need not revert to 'childish' language, but if he can recover some of the directness and simplicity of thought and expression which education too often impairs, he will find that his effort has been of as great advantage to himself as to the children. (BOE, 1912, pp.31–2)

This from the opening section of the 1910 Board of Education Circular on English teaching in the secondary schools:

> It would only be wasting words to refute the view that knowledge of English in any real sense of the term will be 'picked up' naturally, or that though systematic

> instruction is necessary in such subjects as mathematics or foreign languages, the mother-tongue may safely be left to the occasional direction and influence of home, or to the rare chance of spontaneous liking for its study. The instruction in English in a Secondary School aims at training the mind to appreciate English literature, and at cultivating the power of using the English language in speech and writing. These objects are equally important, and each implies the other. Without training in the use of language, literature cannot be fully understood or properly appreciated. Without the study of literature there can be no mastery over language. (BOE, 1910, p.3)

The relationship between these two types of school was not one of a sequence – a journey through the educational system of an individual child (elementary *then* secondary). The age groups of the two schools partly overlapped (10 to 14 for the senior classes of the elementary school and 12 to 16 for the secondary school). The elementary school stopped at 14 because this was considered the appropriate educational span for the working-class child; and the secondary school made it clear that its methods should also be used for the elementary training of its pupils ('the whole spirit of the Circular must be regarded as applying equally to pupils of this more elementary stage' (BOE, 1910, p.3)). The differences between these recommendations on language – an unsophisticated language on the verge of 'childishness' versus literature as the precondition for mastery over language itself – cannot therefore be resolved into the stages of a continuous development or growth, but remain, precisely, a difference.

The language of the elementary school child was to be natural – which meant a vocabulary based on concrete objects, and written composition constructed on the basis of speech ('No attempt should be made to impose a difference in style in written and oral composition'; 'Written composition should be subordinate to oral' (BOE, 1912, p.16, p.14)). It meant literature based on physical actions, and on facts which could be added to the child's stock of information. The child should read literature for its story, poetry for its matter rather than its form. If literary taste was to be developed, it too should 'grow naturally by feeding on the best' (BOE, 1912, p.25) – although the child will not be fully cognisant of the process ('they will rarely be able to show reasons for their preference' (BOE, 1912, p.25)). In the secondary school, the priorities are almost exactly reversed. Since literary language predominates, so the child's speech is encouraged towards cadence and quality, its composition towards structure and style. Books of fiction are the one form of writing to be excluded from its reading. In the final stages, the study of literature leads to the analysis, appreciation and mastery of the classicism of Milton's style. Literature is to be selected for its 'specially fine passages' (BOE, 1910, p.6) which the child commits to memory by learning them by heart ('not so much a method as the presupposition of all methods' (BOE, 1910, p.6)). Literary language therefore becomes the fully internalised model of the child's own mental processes which reflect, not everyday concrete experience, but 'remembrances', 'unconscious associations' and a 'widening experience of life' (BOE, 1910, p.6). The image is that of a subjecthood which 'ripens' (BOE, 1910, p.6) in accordance with the truly organic nature of a literate culture ('nature' appearing with opposite connotations on either side of the educational divide).

Thus the secondary school remained, even after it had been taken partly under state control, the repository of a notion of literacy, whose objective was the classicism which Arnold's quotation (p.91 above) shows us was so slavishly imitated by the middle-class child. Meanwhile, the public schoolboy was himself learning English for the first time, a 'new subject' in 1906 according to the Assistant Master of Harrow School, but English as 'pure literature' (*The Public Schools from Within*, 1906, p.49, p.48), with composition taught on the earlier models of Latin prose.[8] In this context, therefore, Barrie's Latin reference places *Peter and Wendy* in the midst of a struggle about the appropriate ownership, patronage and reproduction of linguistic and cultural privilege in the schools. Even for Matthew Arnold, who pleaded for a 'humanising' (Arnold, 1889, p.87) influence to be exerted on the raw, uncultivated information of elementary education, Latin literature represented the one cut-off point of his cultural *largesse*: 'we do not want to carry our elementary schools into Virgil or Cicero' (Arnold, 1889, p. 166).

Elementary language is, however, no more natural than this classical prose. At the time when *Peter Pan* was written, elementary language, with its emphasis on natural expression, can clearly be seen as something in the process of being *constructed*. This can be seen most clearly in a new synthetic method for teaching English which was devised in 1914 in direct response to the 1912 Government Circular. Its objective – which it defined against the previous analytic method of teaching English by grammar, spelling and dictation – was to teach the child language by means of the visual image, in such a way that language should be seen to arise directly, and without interference, out of the objects of the visible world:

> 1 To name in turn various objects represented by the artist, e.g.: I see a horse.
> 2 To close book and name objects from memory, e.g. I saw a horse, or, I have just seen a horse.
> 3 To say what he will see when he opens the book, or, what his companions will see, e.g. I shall see a horse, etc. He will see a horse, etc.
> 4 To name 'actions' or 'states' represented by the artist, e.g. Grazes in the field. . . .

The method corresponded to the new utilitarianism (language as functional rather than style). It would also be seen later as arresting the working-class child at a concrete (i.e. non-abstract) level of development or growth. It was also perhaps appropriate for a child whose future was most likely to involve the physical manipulation of objects in manual work. (This has in turn produced a new crisis of literacy since this form of language is now considered unsuitable for a workforce no longer employed predominantly in manufacture, agriculture and mines (Bullock, 1974, p.4).)

The Government Circular of 1912 takes *Robinson Crusoe* as its image for the most proper, that is, physical and concrete, relationship between literature and the elementary school child:

> a child should not be expected to write a single composition upon a whole book or story, e.g. on *Robinson Crusoe*; it will be found far more profitable to call for a description of some particular scene or incident which is specifically interesting or even to frame two or three pointed questions on some portion of the book; e.g., what were the difficulties which Crusoe found in building his boat, and by what means did he overcome them. (BOE, 1912, p.26)

We can compare this with the use of literature in the secondary school, where the child's consciousness is directed at the language of the author (whose words 'express the meaning better than any other words can do' (BOE, 1910, p.8)); the aim being to produce an attention to language itself rather than to bypass it in the name of the event which it records.

In the elementary school the stress on the visible and manipulable aspects of physical experience, on concrete impression and on language as the direct extension of the visual sign, can also be seen as linked to a late nineteenth-century imperialism (*Robinson Crusoe* is often seen as the original colonialist fiction) which was simultaneously bringing subjects like geography, religion and comparative ethnography for the first time into the elementary schools.

The other face of this imperialism was the public school itself which was the recognised repository of Graeco-Latin culture. Threatened by the growth of a secondary education which partly reproduced its educational values and was sponsored by the state, the public school re-defined its status as the preserve of a fully classical heritage. It actually (statistically) produced a public service elite which serviced the Empire and nation.[9] The question of a classical (and superior) inheritance and that of cultural and political domination belonged together, and the Graeco-Latin privilege of the public school was inseparable from the nationalism/imperialism of the period leading up to and including the post-Boer war reaction to Tory imperialist politics. But the emphasis on this classical privilege in the public schools also acted as a bulwark against the equally nationalist emphasis on the mother tongue celebrated elsewhere in the education system.[10]

After the Clarendon commission of 1864, there were a number of moves to introduce new subjects into the public school curriculum but for the most part they were resisted or counteracted by the hostility to educational utilitarianism.[11] It was this which led to the paradox that the public school remained the repository of the ideology of imperialism, but the subjects relevant to the Empire (geography, religion, comparative ethnography) with their corresponding emphasis on empirical access to the real world, were only introduced into the state schools. The teaching of language in the secondary and elementary schools – literate expressivity on the one hand, language and literature subordinated to practical aims on the other – merely picked up the opposite linguistic poles of these divisions.

This moment of education history is, therefore, particularly helpful in allowing us to bring into sharper focus what it is we mean when we talk about language for the child. Children's language is not a concept which comes as readily and easily to mind as that of children's literature. The encounter between *Peter and Wendy* and the schools shows, however, that they are inseparable, insofar as what is allowable to the child as fiction – its literature – is in part an effect of what it is permissible at any one moment for the child to speak. 'Children's language' tends to be a differential term, meaning 'not adult' and associated with babbling, rhythm, puzzle or play. For the elementary schools in 1912, there is no doubt that any trouble which children's literature might pose at this level of impossibility and/or nonsense was to be subsumed under the correctness of the child's mother tongue:

> *Lesson XXIV 'Who'*
> Write down two sentences.
> 'Alice was a little girl.' 'She had many adventures in Wonderland.'
> Now join them by substituting *who* for she. Note that *who* comes near to the noun for which it stands.
> Now offer the following for similar treatment.
>
> 'Red Riding Hood was a little girl.' 'She met a wolf in the wood.'

> 'Tom was a boy sweep.' 'He was turned into a water baby.'
> 'Peter Pan was a little boy.' 'He did not wish to grow up.'
> (Wilson, 1914), Teacher's Lesson Book 3, p.43).

There is an obvious repressiveness involved in turning all these unlikely or miraculous characters (metamorphosised – Tom; in danger – Red Riding Hood; or desiring the impossible – Peter Pan) into familiar people 'who . . .'. But this deflation of the content conceals the more important transformation, which is the fundamental *ordering* of the language through which it takes place.

It would, therefore, be misleading to describe the relationship between elementary and cultured language as an ideal sequence from linguistic underdevelopment into literate civilisation – a sequence which, at the turn of the century, was only available to one class of child. Firstly, because the same child did not attend the elementary and secondary schools, and secondly because to conceive of the differences between them as a sequence can give the impression that the more simple language is uncorrupted and true, or else simply deprived – with the idea of the elementary as something lacking, or left out, as far as these educational determinants are concerned. The 1912 Circular ends, indeed, by recommending the teacher to put back the clock on her language and to start speaking almost like a child. But the fact that this statement comes at the end of a document designed to lay down the principles of natural language, plus the fact that it has to sidestep so carefully the more incoherent of children's speech, suggests that the idea that there could ever be a natural language is a myth. Rather there are two ideologies *of* language – one based on the visible, knowable and controllable of the physical world, the other based on the more numinous reaches of our higher cultural life. The most rudimentary laws of how to organise narrative fall under the rubric of each: for the elementary child, actions and their immediate consequences ('What happened and what happened next' (Wilson, 1914, Teacher's Lesson Book 6, p.3)); for the secondary school, the circular motion of a fully integrated teleology of prose ('the end would be in view from the beginning . . . the whole piece of composition shall be an organic whole in which each portion is related to all the rest' (BOE, 1910, p.12)).

What is striking about Barrie's *Peter and Wendy* is the way that it belongs on both sides of this cultural division, oscillating between these extremes of language, between elementary English and the periodic cadences of a more Latinate prose:

> Wendy came first, then John, then Michael.
>
> It was just at this moment that Mr and Mrs Darling hurried with Nana out of 27.
>
> He was a little boy and she was grown up.
>
> Fell from their eyes then the film through which they had looked at victory.
>
> the elegance of his diction, even when he was swearing, no less than the distinction of his demeanour, showed him one of a different caste from his crew
>
> That passionate breast no longer asked for life.
>
> (Barrie, 1911, p.3, p.556, p.262, p.174, pp.80–1, p.228)

The Latin style is conspicuous; the elementary English fades into the invisibility of an apparently natural, and universally comprehensible, linguistic form. But, as educational policy at the turn of the century makes clear, the most natural of languages only has a meaning in relation to that other stylistic quality against which it is set. There is no natural language (least of all *for* children); there is elementary English and cultured prose, evoking each other, confronting each other, or else coming together as here, only to be carefully orchestrated apart.

When *Peter and Wendy* comes up against the schools, it therefore reveals, almost accidentally, that it is speaking to two different children at once, and that its language is not cohered but divided down the middle. But, at a time when the state was particularly concerned to secure a differentiation in the language of its subjects-to-be, such a conflation was impossible to accept and every sign of it, therefore, had to be edited out.

The effect of that editing is to remove not only the signs of this linguistic disturbance but also all other elements which might be seen as incompatible with writing for the child. The authorised school version removes:

– all syntax (periodisation, inversion) or tropes (metonymy, synechdoche) which are resonant of a classical literary style;

– all specific cultural and material references (not just to Hook's educational history, but also the more middle-class associations of the nursery: Mr Darling's stocks and shares, and Mrs Fulsome's kindergarten for the children);

– all signs of play or parody of its own language, especially those which comment on language as institution or practice (' "I, George Darling, did it. *Mea culpa. Mea culpa.*" He had had a classical education' (Barrie, 1911, p.19); 'Feeling that Peter was on his way back, the Never Land woke into life. We ought to use the pluperfect and say wakened, but woke is better and was always used by Peter' (Barrie, 1911, p.75)); the implication here seems to be that language must not be seen to comment on itself;

– all those moments when the sexuality of the text becomes explicit (in one sequence, when Hook is being taunted by an invisible Peter, he feels 'his ego slipping from him. . . . In the dark nature there was a touch of the feminine, as in all the great pirates' (Barrie, 1911, p.149) and resorts to a guessing game to discover the identity of his taunter. The text drops the 'ego' and the 'feminine' but keeps the game, which was the one 'judicious form of play' recommended by the 1912 Circular (BOE, 1912, p.6));

– all episodes which disturb the logical narrative sequence of the story (*Peter and Wendy* describes the children's escape retrospectively, that is, it gives the outcome and then leads up to it; the school version picks out the story of what happened but drops the frame which gave it the status of a memory).

Above all, the school version cuts out virtually all signs of the presence of an identifiable narrator, that is, a narrator who forces on the reader's attention the question of who is telling the story. The school version is told almost entirely by an anonymous third person narrator who never appears explicitly in the text to trouble its linguistic norms or its utterly sustained cohesion of address. Thus, after dropping the first ten pages of Barrie's text completely, it opens, 'The children were in bed' (Barrie, 1915, p.5), a sentence which it lifts clean out of this one from the original: 'On the night we speak of all *the children were* once more *in bed*' (Barrie, 1915, p.14) (italics added).

Barrie's text is not the only version of *Peter Pan* accepted after alterations for use in the schools. Three years before *Peter and Wendy* was approved, D.S. O'Connor's *Keepsake* had been admitted as a reader (O'Connor, 1912). The complexity of the operation carried out on this text is less because its challenge is less. (It was, after all, a summary version of the play which went into circulation largely because Barrie had refused to write a narrative version of his story.) The *Keepsake* is not so much dramatically cut as corrected and its vocabulary simplified where this is too ponderous or literary: 'voracious saurian' to 'greedy crocodile', 'weird apparition' to 'strange figure', 'become inaudible' to 'died away'. Above all its syntax is simplified, which means that for a sentence like 'he was the best father who never forgot to be a little boy' (O'Connor, 1907, p.19), which grammatically can be read in at least three different ways ('of those fathers who never forgot to be a little boy, he was the best'; 'he was the best father because he never forgot'; 'he was the best father and never forgot'), the easiest and most banal is the meaning which is retained: 'He was the best of fathers; and he never forgot to be a little boy' (O'Connor, 1912, p.49) (the separation of the two clauses breaks the otherwise total and perhaps uncomfortable identity between fathers and little boys).

Barrie's text is never *re-written* in this way. It is *abridged*, which means that the form of language desired by the schools can be extracted out of the most recalcitrant of Barrie's prose. Unlike O'Connor, whose faulty grammar is corrected on a number of occasions, Barrie never makes a mistake. It is his precision in relation to both forms of language, which he so skilfully meshes together, that is the scandal.

In educational terms, Barrie's personal history can suggest

why he might have been particularly well placed to produce something which appears in *Peter and Wendy* as a type of condensation of these forms of speech, which for the schools were rapidly becoming seen, and were increasingly being defined, as incompatible. In relation to linguistic policy at the turn of the century, Barrie's text was full of interference or noise. In relation to Barrie, however, this can be seen as the logical outcome of a fairly remarkable educational history which stretched from the learning situation of a small domestic economy in Scotland, through the Dumfries Academy (Barrie's elder brother was, like Arnold, an HM Inspector of Schools, and the Independent Scottish Academies were renowned for their cultural standards), to Edinburgh University and then London.[12] The public school education which Barrie provided for the Llewellyn Davies boys, whom he finally adopted, is well known (Eton of course).[13] But it only makes sense when seen as the termination point, or fantasy, of a linguistic trajectory which runs right across the spectrum of educational institutions and practices at that time. Barrie spoke almost all their forms of language – and desired perhaps above all the one that he did not speak. The biographical reference is important here only because it shows up the complex institutional determinants – at the level of language and education as they bear most directly on the child (Barrie included) – of a work which has given to childhood the transcendent and ahistorical status of a myth.

The alterations carried out on *Peter and Wendy* suggest that it is not just the stylistic features of literary language which clash with the linguistic demands of the elementary school. The cutting out of the narrator's comment on Mr Darling ('He had had a classical education'), and of the more infantile voice which rebels against correct grammar in the name of Peter Pan ('we ought to use the pluperfect and say wakened, but woke is better and was always used by Peter'), removes from the text any linguistic self-consciousness, any drawing attention to language as something whose origins are never safely anonymous (a third person narrator who just *speaks*), nor single, but stem from what might be a multiple and contradictory source. One of the main achievements of many works which are successfully classified as literary might, therefore, be the extent to which they smooth over these differences, and integrate our own divisions in language into a coherent form.

In this sense, literary cohesion could be seen to involve a suppression of those aspects of our linguistic-educational history which are culturally divisive, or rather reveal the divisions of culture itself. The problem – like so many others – is shown up by Barrie's *Peter and Wendy*, but it is by no means restricted to that book. A more recent children's classic, Richard Adams's *Watership Down* (Adams, 1972), for example, can serve to show a different way of resolving those same linguistic tensions.

Watership Down follows the classical adventure format of a pursuit and a struggle for survival, carried out by rabbits who are given by the narrator something of the status of a lost tribe battling against the horrors of advancing civilisation. At the climax of the story, a final chapter suddenly brings to the reader's attention the issue of language and literacy, when a young girl, Lucy, is introduced into the book as a 'Dea ex machina' (the title of the chapter) to save the rabbit, Hazel, from destruction by the farmyard cat.

The moment stands out conspicuously from the rest of the book – because, up to this point, the humans have been villains of the story (it is their development of the land which precipitates the rabbits on their journey); because of the Latin which announces it; and because it is the first time, in a book in which rabbits speak the most finely tuned and cultured English prose (verging on the biblical in the mythical stories they tell), that dialect comes into the story: ' "Tab!" called Lucy sharply. "Tab! Wha' you got?" . . . "Git out, Tab!" said Lucy. "Crool thing! Let'n alone!" ' (Adams, 1972, pp.396–7). Lucy's dialect is, however, in transition. She is marked out as self-educated – the only person in the book with knowledge of rabbit life, that knowledge which the narrator provides for the reader and whose source in the work of Mr Lockley's *The Private Life of the Rabbit* is acknowledged before the book starts and at several points in the narration. And she is on her way to the grammar school: 'her father was proud of the way Lucy got on with Doctor. She was proper bright kid – very likely goin' to grammar school an' all, so they told him' (Adams, 1972, p.398).

The moment is almost an aside, but it fleetingly allows to be spoken the whole question of the child's relationship to knowledge, culture, language and the schools. Simply brought into focus here, it is a relationship which forms the pre-history of the book (the sources of the language in which the author writes) and the precondition of its reception (the child reader). But it figures, as it did in *Peter and Wendy*, throughout *Watership Down* – in the *range* of its language, which moves from Mr Lockley's nature study, to the mythical stories of 'El-ahrairah', through a whole history of literature, which is celebrated in the opening quotations to every chapter of the book (from Aeschylus and Xenephon to Malory, Shakespeare, Dr Johnson, Tennyson and Hardy with the occasional reference to popular literature and one children's book (*Alice*)). In *Watership Down*, practical down-to-earth knowledge is what matters (Lucy saves the rabbits), but literate culture is the framework and final objective of the story (Lucy goes to grammar school). Writing over fifty years after Barrie, Adams manages to balance out and co-ordinate these disparate voices in such a way that his version of *Watership Down* (as opposed to the film, book-of-the-film, calendar, long-playing record, and ceramic rabbits) remains the version which is still most widely acclaimed.

What appears so sharply thrown into relief by Barrie's *Peter and Wendy* reappears here in another form. *Peter and Wendy*'s encounter with the schools merely reveals a history which lies, necessarily, behind any children's book (behind any book), occasionally commented on, but mostly suppressed, or else ordered into the coherence of what we recognise as successful literary writing. Children's writers may well have a special relationship to that history – it may, quite simply, be one of the things to which they are endlessly returning, something they are writing *about*. Adams, for example, shares with other children's writers (Alan Garner, J.R. Tolkien) a working over of the origins of culture (more than once in *Watership Down* the rabbits are described as 'primitives'), which in his case brings with it a re-probing of the institutional beginnings of speech (Alan Garner has commented on the importance for him as a children's writer of an abrupt transition from dialect to the Latin of the grammar school).[14] Like the pleasure which

Lucy's father takes in the fact that she is going to grammar school, Barrie's revelation of the hidden educational history of Captain Hook, is therefore the wholly appropriate finale for *Peter Pan*.

The issue of literacy in relation to childhood continues to be an area of public policy and concern. In 1972, the year when *Watership Down* was published, the government commissioned a new report on literacy. We can see it as the official response to a set of dilemmas which were given one possible solution at the time of *Peter Pan* (a response also to some of the effects of that earlier solution). Looking forwards from *Peter Pan*, therefore, I want to end by taking the Bullock report as the most recent officially sanctioned statement of how language and literature are in the process of being reconceptualised for the child.

The report was published in 1974 under the title *A Language for Life* – a title whose generality (*a* language for *life*) already signals the broadness of the concept of literacy and culture which it is to offer. Like *Watership Down*, the report opens a number of its chapters with quotations from, or about, literature – Dickens, Hardy, I.A. Richards, J.D. Salinger – plus this one from Georges Gusdorf which begins the section on language and learning: 'Man interposes a network of words between the world and himself and thereby becomes master of the world' (Bullock, 1974, p.47). The purpose of the report – and the effect of *Watership Down* – could therefore be defined as the integration of that more general proposition about mastery of language (and of the world through language) with literature itself.

Unlike the 1910 and 1912 government circulars, the Bullock report does not wish to differentiate between classes of child. Rather its desire is to redress a balance, to halt a felt decline in standards of literacy (a decline which it traces to the children of the unskilled and semi-skilled workers), and to give back to children as a whole a culture whose carefully constituted divisions of half a century previously are now felt as an obstruction to the possibility of general social advance. The report explains that as a society becomes more complex, so it requires greater 'awareness' and 'understanding' on the part of its members, and its criterion of literacy will rise (Bullock,

1974, p. 11) (the implication is that standards have not necessarily declined but are now felt to be deficient in relation to social needs). For a society whose workforce is now predominantly employed, not in manual labour, but in the service sectors of industry, literacy is the *general* prerequisite for full participation in working life. Accordingly the stress is on a general language policy – language *across* the curriculum, *continuity* between schools (primary and secondary), *cross-age* tutoring and *mixed-ability* teaching (these are just some of the terms used). The idea that the problem can be resolved by these forms of continuity, and improved teaching methods inside the schools, blinds the report almost completely to what might be some of the divisive institutional origins of the problem it addresses (such as language policy just sixty years before), and the institutional conditions of their perpetuation (the different types of schools in England today). Instead language is seen as something which can cut across and harmoniously reconcile social differences in and of itself, as if language could magically wipe out divisions of which it necessarily forms a part. The report does not address this notion of origins as institution, but sees the source of the difficulty in more privatised terms: 'There is an indisputable gap between the language experience that some families provide and the linguistic demands of school education' (Bullock, 1974, p. 54) (hence the already noted exhortation to mothers: 'When you give your child a bath, bathe him in language' (Bullock, 1974, p. 58)).

It is, I think, precisely this way of conceiving of language (fount of all things) which allows the report to give to literature a similarly universal status: 'It would have been impossible for me to have told anyone what I derived from these novels, for it was nothing less than a sense of life itself' (Richard Wright, *Black Boy*, quoted in Bullock, 1974, p. 124). Quoting F.R. Leavis on the value of literary studies, on the vital *range* of their implication ('literary studies lead constantly outside themselves' (Bullock, 1974, p. 5)), it argues that literature should be allowed to *flow* where the child's interests take it. Thus the earlier distinction between natural and literary language in the schools, described in the first half of this chapter, is replaced with a conception of literature as something fully integral to the child's mind.

It follows from this that language belongs in the 'general context of childcare' (Bullock, 1974, p.58) and 'child growth' (courses on parenthood which 'direct the emphasis away from mothercraft to child growth as an aspect of human development' (Bullock, 1974, p.55)), an emphasis which links directly back to the time which saw the emergence of *Peter Pan*. For the word 'mothercraft' which is being moved out here in favour of 'child growth' was in itself only introduced into the English language in 1907. Dr John Sykes, medical officer of health for St Pancras, London, and founder of the St Pancras school for mothers, coined the word at a time when concern about infant mortality, precipitated by low recruitment figures for the Boer war, and anxiety about the effects of this on imperialism, produced a renewed concentration on the role of the mother as 'bearer of the Imperial race' ('a matter of Imperial importance', A. Newsholme, 'Infant mortality', *The Practitioner*, October 1905, p. 494, quoted in Davin, 1978). This moment, taken by historians (Davin, 1978) to show the historical determinations of the seemingly natural values which attach to the status of motherhood, is only one of a number of occasions when social anxiety about one form of policy (in this case imperialism) gravitates for its solution down to the felt source of all subjectivity and social life – that is, the primary relationship between the mother and child. That which is most 'natural' – mother, child, human development and growth (the unitary condition and eternal sameness invested in the image of each) – thus serves to syphon off the more urgently needed recognition of the social divisions and conflicts through which their ever-changing meanings are constituted at any one time.

There is, therefore, no question of denying here that some of the individual recommendations of the Bullock report may, indeed, represent an advance – better literature for all, one could say, than literature for some (that is, some literature for some children). Rather the point is to draw attention to what I would call the fundamental desire, or even fantasy, which underlines that call. A language for life and a literature for ever – it is the very innocence of the appeal which, like that of *Peter Pan*, requires scrutiny. This chapter has described just one small area in the cultural divisions and contestations which lie behind that generality and which continue to determine the history of childhood.

Acknowledgment

This chapter, originally presented with the other papers in this book at the 'Language and History' *History Workshop* Conference of 1980, forms part of a larger examination of writing for children with reference to *Peter Pan*, published as *The Case of Peter Pan or the Impossibility of Children's Fiction* (Macmillan, 1984).

Notes

1 For a much fuller discussion of this, see George Boas, *The Cult of the Child*, London, Warburg, 1966.

2 The first story about Peter Pan appeared in a novel for adults – J.M. Barrie's *The Little White Bird* (Barrie, 1902) – the chapters containing his story were published as *Peter Pan in Kensington Gardens*, with illustrations by Arthur Rackham, in 1906 (Barrie, 1906), two years after the play *Peter Pan* was first produced in December 1904 at the Duke of York's Theatre in London. Barrie did not publish his play until 1928, but narrative versions of the story (not the same as that of 1902 and 1906) were produced by other writers (O'Connor, 1907; Drennan, 1909, Byron, 1925). After some hesitation, Barrie did produce his own narrative version for children in 1911 – *Peter and Wendy* – but it never acquired the definitive status expected of it (see Mackail, 1941, p. 400, and Green, 1954, p. 115), and *Peter Pan* continued (and continues) to be re-written. The extent and value (material) of this output is perhaps best indicated by the fact that each contract issued by the Great Ormond Street Hospital for Sick Children, to whom Barrie left the rights in 1937, allows for a version of up to 7,500 words; the percentage demanded on merchandise is double that on producer's profits.

3 May Byron re-told the story for little people (Byron, 1925a), for boys and girls (Byron, 1925b), and for 'the littlest ones' (the nursery) (Byron, 1930).

4 See, for example, Dixon, 1977.

5 'Report of the Books and Apparatus Sub-Committee, July 19, 1915', *Greater London Record Office and Library, London County*

Council Education Minutes, 1915, 2, 28 July 1915, p. 164. Originally set up in 1872 under the School Boards to give instructions to local school managers (and then teachers from 1899) on the selection of books for use in schools, the policies of this Committee were adopted by the County Council in 1904.

6 The 1870 Education Act legislated for the state provision of elementary education by locally elected agencies, the School Boards, to supplement, where necessary, schooling provided by religious denominations; the Act is related by historians to shifts in the workforce in the second half of the nineteenth century which released the working-class child as an object of education (the development of a casual labour force) (see Simon, 1960, pp. 337–67 and Middleton, 1970). The 1902 Education Act was directed primarily at secondary education; it was introduced partly as a check to the increasing infiltration by the School Boards, via High Grade Technical and Evening Classes, into the domain of a predominantly private secondary education. The Act provided for state aid to the voluntary schools (a victory for the Anglican High Church Party in collaboration with the Liberal-Unionists). It was resisted by the non-conformists and by the School Boards which were effectively liquidated when the whole of educational policy became assimilated to the County Councils (see Halévy, 1926 and Rogers, 1959).

7 The Taunton Commission of 1864–8, investigating 'middle' (that is non-public) schools, had recommended a class-based tripartite division of the educational system (upper and professional, mercantile and higher commercial, upper working class). Despite the inclusion of secondary education in state policy after 1902, it is clear that the three types of school – public, secondary and elementary – correspond to and reinforce such a division. Sir Francis Sandford makes the distinction between elementary and secondary education the basis of his introduction to Matthew Arnold's *Reports on the Elementary Schools 1852–82* (Arnold, 1889): 'Education should be based upon three principles – the mean, the possible, the becoming, these three. The term "mean", used here in the ordinary Aristotelian sense, seems, as applied to elementary education, to be equivalent to what Mr. Forster called "*a reasonable* amount of instruction"; not confined to the three R's on the one hand, not trenching on the domain of secondary education on the other' (Sandford, Introduction to Arnold, 1889, p. viii).

8 In 1864 the Clarendon Commission, investigating the nine leading public schools, recommended the retention of classical

languages and literature as the central part of the curriculum, together with the introduction of arithmetic or mathematics, one modern language, one branch of science, either drawing or music, ancient or modern history, and a command of 'pure grammatical English' (quoted in Darwin, 1929, p. 110); for the public school response to the commission and their resistance to the introduction of new subjects, see the *Public Schools from Within*, 1906, esp. Introduction, p. xii, and T.E. Page (Assistant Master of Charterhouse School), 'Classics' (pp. 3–11); also Darwin, 1929, Chapter 8, 'The curriculum and the upheaval of the Royal Commission' (pp. 100–11) and Mack, 1941, Chapter 1, 'The Public School Commission' (pp. 3–49).

9 Classics were still the basis of the civil service entry examinations; on the close links between the public schools and the civil service, see Mack, 1941, esp. Chapter 7, 'Imperialism' (pp. 209–64); Guttsman, 1954; Woodruff, 1954; and Wilkinson, 1964; also Pitcairn (ed.), *Unwritten Laws and Ideals of Active Careers* (Pitcairn, 1899), esp. Rev. J.E.C. Welldon (late schoolmaster of Harrow), 'Schoolmasters' (pp. 269–85); and *The Public Schools from Within* (1906), esp. Rev. T.L. Papillon, 'The public schools and citizenship': 'Thus equipped he goes out into the world, and bears a man's part in subduing the earth, ruling its wild folk, and building up the Empire' (p. 283).

10 See Henry Wyld, 'The place of the mother tongue in the national education' (Wyld, 1906) and Brian Hollingsworth, 'The mother tongue and public schools in the 1860s' (Hollingsworth, 1974); also Richard Wilson, *Macmillan's Sentence Building*: 'Remember also that your mother tongue is a precious gift to you from many generations of patriotic Englishmen' (Wilson, 1914, Pupil's Companion, 7, p. 3).

11 Gladstone had written to the Clarendon Commission criticising the 'low utilitarian argument in matter of education' (quoted in Darwin, 1929, p. 110); Rev. T.L. Papillon specifically criticises the public school for the low level of teaching relevant to the Empire (geography, English history and literature, ethnology and religions) as part of his general exhortation 'learn to think Imperially' (*The Public Schools from Within*, 1906, p. 284).

12 Barrie's educational history was even more complex than this. It includes a free church school, a number of private schools, a seminary, the Glasgow and Forfar Academies as well as the Dumfries Academy which he attended before going on to Edinburgh University in 1878. Many of these changes were determined by his elder brother's career (he was classics master

at Glasgow Academy from 1867 to 1871) (see Mackail, 1941, pp. 18–73).

13 See Mackail, 1941, pp. 431–2.

14 'I realised that I had been taught (if only by default) to suppress, and even deride, my primary native North-West Mercian tongue.' 'All my writing has been fuelled by the instinctive drive to speak with a true and Northern voice integrated with the language of literary fluency.' (Alan Garner, 'The fine anger', in Fox and Hammond (eds), *Responses to Children's Literature*, London, K.G. Saw, 1978, pp. 1–12 (p. 5, p. 10)).

6

'The time of your life': the meaning of the school story

GILL FRITH

> It was at this point, when I was twelve years old, that I took to reading junk books the way some people take to eating junk food. I read long-forgotten authors of books about girls' schools in Switzerland or Paris, as well as Angela Brazil, Noel Streatfield, Pamela Brown and, above all, Enid Blyton. How I envied the schoolgirls of St Clare's or Malory Towers: they belonged to a safe, structured world where rules were rules, good was good, and bad was bad. And in spite of, or perhaps because of, this framework, they all seemed to have such fun, such carefree, girlish fun. My rebellion was only half-consciously directed at my father's choice of reading matter for me, although his disapproving and often angry comments made it clear that he took my behaviour as a personal affront. I wanted to choose for myself, yes, but I also wanted to escape into a world of certainties, which I knew to be unreal while desperately wanting to believe that it might have some reality. I wanted to escape from being at home, from being at school, and, quite consciously and openly, from being myself. (Sheila MacLeod, *The Art of Starvation*)[1]

The question I want to address in this essay is, quite simply, why it is that the boarding-school story is now (and has been for the past century) such a popular form of reading for girls. My purpose is to explore the meaning of the school story as a genre, the changes in that meaning since its inception, and its relationship to ideologies of female subjectivity. I shall argue that the pleasure which these stories offer has positive aspects which directly contravene the concept of femininity found in other forms of popular reading available to girls, but that this pleasure contains its own limits and contradictions. But first

I want to look at the ways in which schoolgirl fiction has more generally been perceived.

I

Discussion of the girls' school story has been characterised by two forms of unease. The first is an unease about the status of the genre as *literature*, and while this applies to the school story in general, it is particularly true of school stories for girls. They are not discussed, for example, in John Rowe Townsend's *Written for Children*, although it contains a chapter on 'The world of school', and Isabel Quigly's recent history of and apologia for the school story, *The Heirs of Tom Brown*, contains only a brief and dismissive chapter on stories for girls. Mary Cadogan and Patricia Craig's useful history of girls' fiction, *You're A Brick, Angela!*, attempts to distinguish between those examples of the genre which are relatively 'good' (Angela Brazil, Dorita Fairlie Bruce) and those which are not (L.T. Meade). The criteria at work here draw on a broad notion of the 'credible' reinforced by the 'natural': L.T. Meade's 'mawkish', 'irritatingly sentimentalised' schoolgirls with their 'unhealthily intense' friendships are seen to give way to the more plausible, though still ideologically suspect, representations of Brazil and Fairlie Bruce.[2] Cadogan and Craig suggest that these later writers, in giving a more energetic and realistic and less sentimentalised account of schoolgirl life as seen 'from the inside', lent an artificially extended lease of life to a form with inbuilt obsolescence. As the arch title of their work indicates, Cadogan and Craig perceive the school story as a quaint, if intriguing, relic of a former age; they argue that such stories are no longer read by working-class girls in comprehensive schools.[3]

In fact, this is simply not the case. While the boys' boarding-school story is now an anachronism, school stories for girls are both widely read and freely available. The most popular examples are still Enid Blyton's *St Clare's* and *Malory Towers* books, written in the 1940s, constantly in print ever since, and currently in Dragon paperback. Stories by Angela Brazil, Elinor Brent-Dyer and Antonia Forest are also available in paperback, but it is particularly significant that in the late 1970s an entirely new series in the traditional mould made its appearance: the *Trebizon* books by Anne Digby, now in Granada paperback. Nor is the readership confined to the white middle classes; as a teacher in comprehensive schools, I found that many working-class girls, some of them Asian, read these stories. Recently, with the help of three teachers who distributed questionnaires in their schools, I was able to confirm that this is still true.[4] The readership for these stories falls approximately between the ages of 8 and 12, with some overspill at each end; during this period, a significant number of girls go through a lengthy period of addiction, in which they not only read nothing *but* school stories, but return to the same books over and over again. It is important that this is a matter of choice, sometimes in conscious opposition to the wishes of teachers and parents (although the books may also be 'handed on' from mother to daughter). The books are borrowed from libraries, bought by the girls themselves, passed on from friend to friend. Few teachers will encourage girls to read boarding-school stories; many actively *discourage* them, and at best they are likely to take the liberal view that the addiction should be indulged, in the interests of developing a 'reading habit' until the addict can be weaned off them and directed towards more sophisticated and *realistic* literature, possibly via 'quality' school stories such as Penelope Farmer's *Charlotte Sometimes* and the novels of Mary K. Harris.

The second form of unease, which often coexists with the first, is a question of politics. Quite simply, school stories are embarrassing. Set in that institution which is so clearly a product and reflection of bourgeois capitalism, and a most effective instrument in its perpetuation – the private boarding school – school stories are complacent about class privilege, inherited wealth and xenophobia. Exclusive, expensive and enclosed, they represent a sealed, rigidly hierarchical world in which 'normality' is white and middle-class.

This embarrassment was strikingly evident in the reviews of Denise Deegan's play *Daisy Pulls It Off*, which drew on and crystallised the conventions of the boarding-school story: the scholarship girl, daughter of a 'widowed mother'; her loyal friend, the Madcap of the Fourth; her enemies, the rich girl and her toady; the adorable but endangered Head Girl; the stolen essay; the vital match; the clifftop rescue; the suspected Russian spy; the secret passage; the hidden treasure; the return of the 'lost' father. . . . Reviews in the radical press which praised the play when it opened in 1983 fell over themselves in their efforts to disclaim nostalgia, to emphasise that this was a spoof, a parody, *not* a celebration ('A dodgy message had this play been for real. But it's not – it is a send-up, and a very funny one at times' – *Spare Rib*) and drew on the recognised language of the genre to emphasise their own ironic distance ('a ripping night out' – *City Limits*). Yet *Daisy Pulls It Off* was precisely *not* a parody, for it contained nothing incongruous or exaggerated. Every character, every element in the plot, virtually every *line* in the play has its counterpart in the novels of Brazil and her imitators, in the school stories in *Girl* and *Girl's Crystal* in the 1950s. Deegan's carefully crafted play drew on *self-mockery* rather than mockery, and for the women in the audience at least, the response which the play successfully elicited was a complex mixture of recognition, embarrassment and nostalgia. Like the original title of Posy Simmonds's strip in the *Guardian*, 'The Silent Three' – a code-reference instantly accessible to any woman who had ever read *School Friend*, in which a long-running serial with the same name appeared – Deegan's play depended on the audience's ability to recognise the conventions of the genre, and on their astonishment at seeing this hidden, embarrassing, repressed aspect of women's culture represented publicly, barefacedly, *on stage*. Hardly any of the women with whom I saw the play had been to private schools, yet all 'recognised' it equally. Deegan herself went to secondary modern school; Angela Brazil's stories were based, not on her own unsatisfactory school experience, but on her fantasy of the schools she *wished* she had attended; L.T. Meade, the popular nineteenth-century pioneer of the 'college story' for girls, never went to university. The school story has always been a dream, a fantasy, has never had more than a tenuous connection with 'real life'; the nostalgia which *Daisy* elicited was not a nostalgia for a lived event or an irrecoverable 'golden age', but a nostalgia for a half-forgotten *reading experience*. It is the nature of this experience that I want to explore in this essay.

II

> 'I like them because they showed the tricks and scandals children get up to. It wasn't very realistic but I still enjoyed it because I like fantasy stories.' – Manjit, aged 12

The first point I want to emphasise is that the girls who read school stories are aware from the start that they are *fictions*. Almost without exception, the girls in my survey said that they did not believe real boarding schools would be like the schools in the stories, and that they had no desire to go to such a school themselves. Most thought that the teachers and girls in the stories were not at all like the ones they knew. They were drawn to the stories because they were *fun*, because the girls in them were having the time of their lives: they particularly enjoyed the tricks played on teachers (a central feature in Blyton's stories), the jokes, the breaking of bounds, the midnight feasts.

One 10-year-old 'addict' described her reading experience to me in detail. Rachael was a particularly avid reader of these stories, but her account is in many respects typical. She started reading school stories when she was 9, and had been reading them compulsively ever since. Though no one had actively tried to prevent her from reading them, she was aware that they were not particularly approved of by parents or teachers; she herself didn't think that the stories were 'good', she wasn't sure that she even *liked* them, but nevertheless she returned to them almost obsessively. She had re-read each title in the *St Clare's* and *Malory Towers* series about twenty times. She was very conscious that the school stories did not represent 'real life', but she enjoyed them because the girls *did* things, and the things that they did were exciting. Significantly, although she read the stories often, her re-reading was selective; she skipped the bits that did not interest her, and the points she returned to were revealing: the rituals of opening and closure (invariably the 'first day' and 'last day' of term); the points where the order of the school is disrupted, its limits transgressed (the tricks, the sneaking out of the school at night); the rituals which assert the autonomy of the girls within the school (having their own studies and furnishing them). But Rachael's pleasure wasn't confined to the *events* in the stories. She particularly enjoyed the fact that, even on a first reading, she *knew what was going to happen*. She was extremely aware of the ritualistic conventions of the school story narrative: she could identify the recurrent stereotypes (the snob, the sneak, the comically inadequate 'Mamselle', the heroine who succeeds at everything and ends up as Head Girl) and the codes of the narrative itself. For example, she said that often at the outset one of the girls would say what a boring term it was going to be: you would then *know* that exciting things were going to happen, and this would be confirmed by a comment at the end of the chapter. When I looked at the books to verify this, I found that she was quite right.

There are two points of particular significance here. Firstly, part of the pleasure involved in reading school stories rests in the opportunity they offer the young reader to exercise a newly acquired skill: the ability to follow the structure of a narrative, recognise its 'clues', anticipate its development. The very formulaic and predictable nature of the school story, the experience of *knowing what's going to happen*, actively contribute to the enjoyment of the reader, to the feeling of being 'in control' of the reading process. There's a continual interplay between safety and danger, risk and control, in the pleasure which these stories offer. The almost invariable opening gambit of the school story – the first day of term – signifies *both* the movement out of the safe, normal, humdrum world of the family into the exciting, varied, turbulent world of the fantasised 'school', *and* the movement from the uncontrollable world of reality to the predictable, clearly defined world of fiction. The school story firmly addresses itself to the reader *as* fiction, demanding only that she share the desires it expresses, and its fictionality is quite transparent. For example, the moral code of the school story is apparently quite simple, but when you look closely it becomes clear that many of its 'codes' are in fact devices, subject to adaptation according to the demands of the narrative. The pervasive taboo against 'sneaking' is useful because it keeps the teachers *in the dark*, leaving action, responsibility, procedure and control in the hands of the girls, but this apparently inflexible taboo may be ignored when the narrative demands that the teachers be involved in the action. There is a similarly fine distinction between 'lying' and bending, or concealing, the truth, between 'cheekiness' and 'rudeness', 'naughtiness' and 'disobedience', 'loyalty' and 'blind devotion'. What matters, in fact, is not *what is done*, but *who does it*: whether the character concerned has the reader's sympathy, or the reverse. There's an interesting, if characteristically repellent, variation on this in Blyton's school stories, in her representation of 'foreign' or 'exotic' girls, like Carlotta (half-gipsy) in the *Malory Towers* series and Claudine (French) in one of the most popular stories, *Claudine at St Clare's*. Their consistently mischievous and subversive behaviour is simultaneously *celebrated* in the sense that it provides much of the 'fun' of the story, and *undercut* by being represented as a distressing result of origin, of ignorance of the 'English code of honour'. Carlotta and Claudine often dare to say and do what the other girls *want* to say and do; unlike 'bad' English girls, they are neither expelled nor fully tamed, but their actions are not imitable because you can't *choose* to be a 'foreigner'. The contradiction between the illusion of a rigid structure and inflexible morality, and the anarchy which actually reigns, is central to the appeal of these stories.

Her recognition of the stories' status as fictions allows the reader to read selectively, to suspend involvement or judgment where necessary. This seems to me the only way of understanding how Asian girls can enjoy these stories, and also important in explaining their appeal to white working-class girls, but there is a further point to be made in relation to the question of class. I would suggest, tentatively, that children of this age, perhaps especially girls, perceive class less as a specific distinction based on occupation and income than as a distinction between 'ordinary people' and 'snobs' (and perhaps 'rough people'). It is precisely this distinction which the school stories endorse: a pervasive stereotype is that of the 'snob' who boasts about her wealth, 'steals' other people's writing in order to impress her rich parents, or the girl who *pretends* to be wealthier than she really is, and steals or lies in order to maintain the deception. While the snob is sometimes represented as 'nouveau-riche', this is by no means *always* the case. Paradoxically, the effect of locating the novels within a sealed, self-sufficient class institution is to *efface* the question of class. While 'rough people' may lurk outside its walls, within the school to be in the same *form* is to be in the same *class*; to be part of the group is all that matters, and acceptance is represented as meritocratic, based both on 'proving yourself' as an individual and on sharing the 'common-sense' values of the group. While the scholarship girl from a poor home is often *rewarded* with an unexpected inheritance and/or the return of a 'dead' father who proves to be a 'gentleman', the stories nevertheless preserve the fiction that income doesn't *matter*, that to be poor but honest is better than to be rich and 'spoilt'. The stories address the reader, then, as part of a unitary group in which 'girlhood' is the significant factor, and it is of course in its configuration of girlhood that the appeal of the school story really lies.

III

The significant point here is that the school story presents a picture of what it is possible for a girl to be and to do which stands in absolute contradistinction to the configuration of 'femininity' which is to be found in other forms of popular fiction addressed specifically to women and girls. With the wealth of recent work on images of women in women's magazines, romantic novels, children's fiction and advertising, we are now familiar with the dominant models of femininity which work to define women in relation and in contrast to men, to confirm that woman's 'natural' base is the home, the family, the domestic.[5] Angela McRobbie's illuminating analysis of *Jackie* provides a particularly relevant example, since many of the older girls in my survey read it regularly.[6] A few read *Jackie* and school stories simultaneously, although some read the stories in conscious opposition to such magazines: 'Mostly for my age are love stories about really sickly sweet girls who never get greasy hair. And boys who are really good-looking and popular' – Lisa, aged 12, a school story 'addict'. Thirteen-year-old Kuldip's fiercely dissenting comment illustrates the other side of the argument, the 'scandal' of the school story: 'I didn't enjoy the books because it shows or gives a bad reputation for us girls. Especially the naughty parts it just shows us girls up. That's what I hate in these girls books. . . . I like to read girl magazines like *Jackie*.' This was an unusually severe criticism, but by the age of 13, most had 'moved on' from the school story to *Jackie, Tammy* and pop magazines like *Smash Hits*. A brief summary of Angela McRobbie's analysis will help to illustrate the difference between *Jackie* and the school story.

McRobbie argues that although the world portrayed in *Jackie* stories is an oddly empty one, populated by rootless young people in search of love, both stories and features nevertheless confirm the narrowness of women's role and prefigure the girl's future isolation in the home. Male and female roles are clearly separate and distinct. Boys *do*, girls simply *are*; a boy may be 'rough' and still irresistible, but to be a girl is to abide by the law, to *wait* passively, to be chosen, taken, loved, rescued. To be female is also to be isolated. Women are united by their femininity but divided by jealousy and sexual competitiveness; friends, even best friends, are not to be trusted, and the romantic relationship is the only relationship which matters and can provide fulfilment. Romance, fashion, beauty and pop stars provide the limits of a girl's concern; her personal life is a continual source of *problems*, but the problems can only be solved individually, in isolation, by compromise or acceptance. While she will almost certainly fail to meet the exacting standards men demand, she must 'work' continually, secretly, in the privacy of the home, to measure up: to disguise the faults in her appearance, to create the illusion of natural beauty, to fashion and re-fashion herself into the image which will secure her man.

The representation of 'girlhood' in the school story stands in almost total opposition to this ideology. In a world of girls, to be female is *normal*, and not a *problem*. To be assertive, physically active, daring, ambitious, is not a source of tension. In the absence of boys, girls 'break bounds', have adventures, transgress rules, catch spies. There is no taboo on public speech: in innumerable school stories, girls hold and address a tense, packed meeting. The ructures and rewards of romance are replaced by the ructures and rewards of friendship, and pop stars by idealised Head Girls. 'Pretence' and 'pretension' are questionable; mysteries are unravelled, codes broken, secret passages explored, disguises penetrated. 'Tricks' played on teachers replace 'tricks' of make-up; in place of diets, there are midnight feasts. Away from the family, girls are free; domestic tasks are invisibly performed. Clothes and appearances are of little significance in the unchanging world of the school, and to be beautiful is not an advantage. The exceptionally pretty and 'feminine' girl is represented as weak, frail, easily led, often vain. The heroine, on the other hand, is often 'lovable' for the very qualities which *Jackie* represses: she is often wilful, outspoken, impulsive, loyal to her friends. While the 'best friend' is the crucial relationship, *the group* is equally important: what matters is to be in the team, in the play, sharing a dormitory with friends. 'The group' itself has almost unlimited licence. The institutions within the school – clubs, teams, magazines – are initiated, organised and controlled by the girls themselves, sometimes by girls as young as 12. While the teachers are the ultimate arbiters, their presence is discreet and not infallible: the stock figure of 'Mamselle' represents the teacher whose power can be subverted, who is easily duped and teased. Other teachers smile secretly at the 'naughtiness' of the girls. The prefects, by contrast, have astonishing powers and influence; a 'bent' prefect can create havoc.

While some of these characteristics appear also in other forms of story popular amongst girls (pony books, stories of ballet or tennis 'stars'), the particular appeal of the school story is that it depends on no specialised interest or skill. Despite her ubiquitous success, the heroine is represented as 'ordinary' rather than exceptional; when she scores the crucial goal, writes the prize-winning poem, or saves the Head Girl from drowning, it is simply a reward for her energy and determination. It is a fantasy accessible to any girl who dreams of vindication, independence, freedom from constraint; a fantasy which combines the dream of autonomy and control with the freedom to be irresponsible within 'safe' limits.

The question that presents itself, then, is not so much why girls *read* school stories, as why they should be willing to give them up. How is it that girls relinquish the excitement and solidarity of the school story for the passivity and isolation of *Jackie* and the Mills & Boon romance? I want to suggest that while the school story *does* represent a subversive challenge to conventional representations of femininity, it *also* contains an implicit negation of that subversiveness, for the freedom it celebrates has clearly defined, and insuperable, limits.

IV

If we see ideologies of femininity in terms of a unitary, if overdetermined, progression towards passivity, domesticity and a reproductive role, then the representation of femininity within the school story clearly stands as an expression of resistance and subversion. The school story *makes sense*, however, in the context of an ideology which is just as pervasive and perhaps more insidious, since it embraces and normalises the contradictions in women's experience. The school story 'fits' into a configuration of female subjectivity which perceives it not as a smooth progression towards an unchanging goal, but as essentially and naturally fragmented: flexible, chameleon, infinitely adaptable and continuously adjustable. Within these terms, it is woman's task (and her desire) to create something orderly and smooth out of the unpromising and resistant material which is her physical and emotional self; to 'fashion' herself anew at the appropriate moment. Like Alice in Wonderland, if the house is too small or too large, she must change her size to fit it.

It was precisely this understanding of female subjectivity that the girls in my survey recognised when they said that they had 'grown out of' the school story. The reasons why they had enjoyed the stories were often still vivid in their memories, but they accepted that it was time to move on, to re-fashion themselves, to put aside childish desires. This is not to say that this process is necessarily smooth or easy, or even complete. Thus Violet Trefusis, recalling herself as a precocious and sophisticated upper-class schoolgirl at the turn of the century, remembers:

> The clock has been put back twelve years: I am fourteen, romantic, pedantic, mystery-loving. I haven't got over my stay in Florence: I allude to Verrochio, Donatello,

> Cimabue. I am deep in Marjorie Bowen – but not too old to surreptitiously enjoy L.T. Meade. (Letter to Vita Sackville-West, August 1920)[7]

The testimony of 13-year-old Rebecca in 1983 gives a more immediate insight into a similar conjuncture, all the more eloquent because barely articulated:

> They are sometimes funny but never boring. . . . I like the sports matches. They are exciting. Also on one book I have recently read 'Claudine at St Clares'. I liked it when she fell into the pool. Really I enjoy the whole book because I ~~find~~ found that I never ~~get~~ got bored with the stories. [And in tiny, cramped handwriting] But now I have stopped reading them as I have grown out of them.

This is not simply a question of succumbing to social pressure, for the temporal limits of the school story are defined by the stories themselves: they clearly locate the fun and licence they celebrate as a *stage*. In those stories which form a series, as the original girls grow older new little ones are introduced who now form the focus of the stories, who do the things their elders once did, in which the seniors take a vicarious pleasure while pretending to disapprove. The slang which the girls talk is a language which defines them as a group, which 'belongs' to them and is passed on from one generation to the next, used in resistance to the 'authorities' – but it is a language which has no currency beyond the schoolgirl world. Blyton's emphasis on 'naughtiness' clearly identifies such behaviour with childhood, only legitimate within the scope of 'the school'.

It is not simply a question of representing childhood as a 'golden age'. Sheila MacLeod's account of her girlhood reading of school stories, with which I began this essay, suggests a further point which is central to the appeal of these stories. The quotation is taken from MacLeod's analysis of anorexia nervosa, *The Art of Starvation*, in which she argues from her own experience that the anorexic is not motivated by the desire to be slim or sexually attractive, nor yet by an aversion to sexuality. Her refusal to eat is, rather, a bid for autonomy: a response to contradictory messages about the female body which leads her to believe that by starving herself, and thus delaying the physical effects of puberty, she is able to avoid growing up, to resist 'the burden of womanhood' and achieve control over her own identity. The logic would be impeccable, were it not that its ultimate conclusion is death.

In describing her own youthful addiction to the school story, Sheila MacLeod is not drawing any *literal* connection between anorexia nervosa and the boarding-school story, and it is certainly not my intention to do so here. Implicit in her account, though, is the relationship between the school story and the illusion of control which she so persuasively identifies as a central feature of anorexia, and I would argue that there is a further connection. For the crucial 'trick' of the school story is that, though set in 'a world of girls', it in fact evades the question of gender: the heroines occupy a position apparently somewhere *between* 'the masculine' and 'the feminine'. This is not exactly to say that they are 'androgynous'. When I asked Rachael to explain how the girls in the stories were different from the girls she knew, she began by saying, 'They're half girls and half boys', but then corrected herself: 'They're not like boys, they're *girls*, but they do things like boys.' The heroines in contemporary school stories are not so much 'like girls' or 'like boys' as *ungendered*: whereas the occasional tomboy will have an uncompromisingly boyish nickname like Bill or Tim, the central characters often have names or nicknames which can't precisely be identified in terms of gender: Nicky, Darrell, Aldred, Lawrie, Tish, and so on. The 'tomboy' and the weak feminine girl represent the oddities, the extreme limits: the average girl, the heroine, is suspended somewhere between the two.

This is particularly interesting because, while the present *readership* of the stories falls roughly between the ages of 8 and 12, the *characters* in the stories, including the most recent ones, are significantly older. Generally, the central characters in the stories are in the second to fourth year at secondary school: in other words, the age of puberty. Yet the onset of puberty, its physical effects, are nowhere in evidence. In Anne Digby's *Summer Term at Trebizon*, second-year Rebecca has a difficult term. Her life is dominated by three problems, all, as the narrative emphasises, beginning with M: Maths, her worst subject, Max, the new male maths teacher, and her name, Mason, which is the source of complicated difficulties. The disruptive effects of Max's Maleness within the all-female school are explored, but the other significant M – Menstruation – is entirely absent. That there should be no direct reference to menstruation or sexuality isn't surprising. The point is that the heroines remain as slender, as fleet-footed, as physically unaware of themselves, as they were as children. Bodies are not a problem; plump girls are extremely difficult for the school story to incorporate, and tend to be suspect. The physical and emotional changes which preoccupy girls of this age, and which signal their unequivocal entry into a female identity, are simply evaporated.

It seems to me that this fact is central to the appeal of the school story. The girls who read these stories are at an age when to be female is not obviously 'a problem'. At school, they are competing on equal terms with boys, are often more successful – yet they are constantly receiving cultural messages which make it clear that this will not always be the case. It's significant that a favourite 'trick' involves playing with time – turning the clock forwards or back. The stories hold out the impossible, Canute-like fantasy of a future in which the waves of time can be held back, a fantasy which cannot survive the material arrival of puberty. The gymslip, hallmark of the school story, is appropriate only for the slender, prepubescent body; the *St Trinians* films, designed for a voyeuristic adult audience, drew on the incongruity of the bosomy, physically mature female form bursting out of its gymslip. When breasts develop, menstruation arrives, and bodies become a source of secrecy and difficulty, the schoolgirl reader can no longer place herself within the school story; she is obliged to move on to the next stage, to a more unambiguously 'female' identity. Like anorexia, the school story represents a dream of control, an illusion of power, which contains its own termination, its own inevitable failure.

V

It is important to recognise that this has not always been the case. The school story as it exists at present is not simply an 'anachronism': it is a hybrid and deeply contradictory form which has retained some of the impetus of an earlier age while constantly evolving in response to new concepts of education and its relationship to women's role. If we are to understand the nature of the school story's current appeal, we need also to understand the ways in which it has departed from an initially feminist impetus, so I shall outline the major changes before discussing their implications.

School stories became established as a popular genre during the 1880s and 1890s. Many of the conventions still prevalent appear in the early stories: the ivyclad mansion behind high walls, the wilful and impulsive heroine, the stolen poem, the inadequate Mademoiselle, the central importance of friendships. The real precursor of the modern story, though, is to be found in the 'college' stories pioneered by L.T. Meade:[8] here we find the scholarship girl, the institution with its own codes, traditions and language, the emphasis on a new-found freedom, and a loving and elaborate portrayal of the girls' rooms which anticipates the later stress on 'dormitories' and 'studies'. These stories became popular during a period of intensive expansion in schools and colleges for women, a time when women's education, specially higher education, was an extremely contentious and widely debated subject.[9] The higher education debate is especially significant, not because it provided access to university life for a handful of women, nor simply because it provided a means of access to professions from which women had previously been excluded, but because it involved a re-definition of women's role and of the concept of 'woman' itself, in that it presented an obvious challenge to that ideology which confined middle-class women, at least, to the home and to the domestic role. The 'college' takes on a symbolic significance in stories for girls (clearly related to the exceptional numbers of single women in this period) through which the writers directly counter current arguments against the changes in women's education and celebrate an understanding of women's role as, within clearly defined limits, *plural*: narrative devices, especially the friendships, distinguish between the shy, poor, industrious scholarship girl who is destined for *work* and the romantically fascinating, wealthy, wilful girl who is destined for *marriage*, but equally validate each through the closeness of their relationship. Two of the most popular early writers of the school and college stories, Sarah Doudney and L.T. Meade, were both members of the progressive and fervently feminist women's club, the Pioneer, to which many leading feminist writers also belonged.[10]

The early stories, then, were clearly feminist in their impulse, though it is a feminism specifically of its period, a feminism which emphasises social purity, women's moral superiority, the importance of self-sacrifice and religious devotion.[11] In these early novels there is a persistent *celebration* of women's newly found access to knowledge, in which the young women perceive themselves as pioneers with an obligation to pass on their knowledge; the pleasure of learning for its own sake is always balanced by an emphasis on its *usefulness*, on the necessary relationship between the knowledge acquired in the college and its currency in the outside world, and the college stories often show their young heroines moving on to settlement work in the East End of London. The intensely romantic friendships which characterise these novels are closely linked with the joys of learning, and also depend on a secure concept of gender difference, of 'womanliness' perceived as a state so absolute that once achieved it is secure, and which can only be achieved by and through the models presented by other women. There are many idealised teachers who have consciously *chosen* to abjure marriage in order to devote themselves and their lives to the education of girls, and for whom their pupils feel a strongly romantic affection, such as Miss Thornhill in Sarah Doudney's *When We Were Girls Together*:

> That mouth always seemed to Jennet the loveliest that she had ever seen; the smile that haunted the full, red lips was indescribably dreamy and sweet. To her, Una Thornhill, with her deep blue eyes and creamy skin, had the looks of an enchantress, and 'The Enchantress' was

> the name by which she called her in thought, little guessing that by this very name Miss Thornhill had been really known in other days. . . . The peculiar charm of eyes and smile which had 'enchanted' many world-worn men and women, now won the hearts of the most impressionable schoolgirls, and achieved more conquests over stubborn wills than Miss Sand could ever boast of having gained.[12]

L.T. Meade's *The Girls of Merton College*, clearly inspired by Girton, shows such a relationship from the teacher's point of view. Jocelyn Silence, the college principal, is (remarkably but symbolically) the first girl to have been born into the 'House of Silence' for a couple of hundred years. Noble-looking, with soldierly bearing and 'eyes like the softest brown velvet', she has been inspired by Dorothea Beale to devote her life to the education of girls. The chapter which describes her first meeting with Katherine, the brilliant scholarship girl heroine, is highly emotional and ritualistic:

> Miss Silence felt a sort of tingling coming down to the very tips of her fingers as she considered what this girl might do for the college, for the life there, for women generally. She trembled with pure pleasure at the thought of seeing her.[13]

Katherine's role as acolyte is underscored when she receives a ceremonial kiss and serves her 'Head Mistress' with tea: 'I am hungry,' says Miss Silence, 'be sure you serve me well.'

The school story continued to have an appeal for a younger, more 'bohemian' generation of feminist writers, like Evelyn Sharp, member of the 'Yellow Book' circle, socialist, and, later, militant suffragette.[14] Sharp's very funny story, *The Making of A Schoolgirl* (1897), presents itself as a debunking of the 'priggishness' of earlier stories, but in fact employs many of the familiar conventions: romantic friendships, idolised teachers and dizzy enjoyment of learning.

The shift which took place early in this century can be most clearly seen in a novel written for adults, Clemence Dane's *Regiment of Women*, which created a considerable stir when it was published in 1915. Set in a girls' high school, the novel traces the destructive effect of Clare, a cool, highly competent and ruthlessly ambitious teacher, on two younger women. One, the motherless schoolgirl Louise, becomes infatuated with Clare; when her affection is not returned, she becomes unbalanced through overwork and overstrain, and finally kills herself. Louise's passion for Clare is represented as 'innocent' though excessive, and Clare herself represses all emotion, but the novel nevertheless has an extremely strong atmosphere of 'unhealthiness', and that unhealthiness is firmly located in the hothouse, highly charged atmosphere of the single-sex girls' school. Clare is *dangerous* because she usurps the place of the mother and exploits her position of power; cold, 'warped', sterile, she provides an 'unnatural' role-model in her choice of career over marriage and motherhood. Now, Clemence Dane was later a regular contributor to the feminist journal *Time and Tide*, a member of the Six Point Group, and moved in 'sapphic' circles in the 1920s;[15] her novel is not simply the product of anti-lesbian, anti-feminist propaganda. I would suggest that it's indicative of a shift in progressive and feminist thought of the period, which perceived the distinction between marriage and work as oppressive for women, and which, in arguing for a recognition of women's sexuality, was dubious about the model presented by the 'spinster' teacher.[16] The single-sex school and college no longer stood as an unambiguous symbol of advancement for women; the form is increasingly taken over by writers who are either ambivalent about feminism or actively opposed to it. The school story increasingly turns in on itself, and there is a shift of emphasis from the school as a source of *knowledge* to the school as a source of *fun*. Teachers are not idealised 'role-models', but remote one-dimensional figures, 'frozen' in time and place; lesson-time is play-time. Whereas the early stories saw the time of education as an 'oasis' which was both rewarding in itself and crucially *related* to life afterwards, the twentieth century increasingly represents the school as a *refuge* from the real world, an *escape* from knowledge.

There is a marked shift also in the representation of friendship. Relationships between the girls in the stories become steadily less passionate, but perhaps because schoolgirl attachments were exempted from early studies of lesbianism and perceived as a 'normal' phase, the change is gradual.[17] It is directly resisted by Angela Brazil, who continues to represent her schoolgirls as 'in love' and 'at white-hot heat'.[18] The influence of the boys' public school may be a more significant factor in the emergence of a new pattern, exemplified by the Anti-Soppist Society formed by the girls in Dorita Fairlie Bruce's 'Dimsie' stories of the 1920s; the rules of this society forbid its members to give flowers to teachers or seniors, to sleep with a senior's hair ribbon under her pillow, or to kiss anyone at all during the term 'unless absolutely obliged to'.[19] In the modern school story, friendship between girls of the same age remains extremely *important*, but as a matter of comradely loyalty, based on shared interests and characteristics. They are no longer romantic love affairs, crucial elements in the girl's moral and intellectual development, or a means of defining her future role in society; they are static mirrors which find their most perfect expression in the popularity of the 'twin'. What remains is the schoolgirl 'crush' on an older girl, still a significant feature in Antonia Forest's stories in the 1940s and 1950s, and residually in more recent stories.[20] This romantic attachment finds expression as a courtly and chivalric devotion, especially in protecting the older girl from the machinations of less scrupulous prefects. The importance of this is that it firmly locates the crush as a 'phase'; the older girl has already passed *through* this phase, so it can't be reciprocated and must rest at heroine-worship from a distance.

These changes are important because they are both drastic and incomplete; the result is a form which can be simultaneously reactionary and subversive. The stories retain a residue of their original feminist impetus, in that they offer a positive and active identity for girls, an emphasis on comradeship and shared female identification, but the changes I've identified work to narrow the period in which such an identity is practicable to an increasingly limited 'stage'. Whereas the early stories expressed a broad concept of girlhood which extended from 10 to 20 and appear to have appealed to a similarly broad readership, the modern school stories locate the ending of girlhood at puberty. The 'time of your life' is getting shorter.

Equally significant, though, is the way in which the school story has become divorced from 'real life'. The early stories were 'fantasies', in that they described a dream which could only be realised by a small number of readers, but it was a dream which was related to feminist aims, which saw access to knowledge as access to power, and the experience of school or college as a crucial preparation for the public and private life of the 'New Woman'. In the modern story, the school behind its walls is neither microcosm nor formative experience, but another place, suspended in time, complete in itself.

VI

The popularity of the school story demands that we confront the questions of 'realism' and 'relevance', for it is precisely *because* the school story has had an increasingly tangential relationship to 'real life' that it continues to have an appeal for young readers. Some of the girls in my survey explained the discrepancy between the stories and their own experience by suggesting that the novels were set in the past, 'in the fifties', but most showed a more sophisticated awareness of the relationship between literature and life, and of the difference between 'realism' and 'reflection'. Many emphasised *both* that the stories were 'true-to-life' and 'realistic', *and* that the schools, the girls and the teachers in the stories were unlike the ones they knew in life. These points are not as incompatible as they may seem. The girls who enjoyed school stories were not seeking an experience which mirrored their own: Rachael, for example, thought that the stories in Blyton's *Naughtiest Girl* series (set in a mixed school, with younger characters) were 'better' than the boarding-school stories because they were more like her own life – but she didn't *enjoy* them as much, and rarely re-read them. Similarly, other school story 'addicts' enjoyed the *Grange Hill* television programmes, which are set in a mixed comprehensive school, but had no desire to read the books which are based on the series.

Girls read school stories during the complicated period of transition from the 'motherly' world of the primary school to the bigger, more anonymous, more competitive world of the secondary school, and on the edge of the transition from 'girlhood' to 'womanhood'. The messages they are receiving in 'real life' – from home, school and the media – are often contradictory. Girls may be simultaneously urged to compete, to pass exams, to aim for the world of work, and to define themselves in terms of the domestic role; to see their power as located within the family, while accepting a subordinate position within that family; to see their sexuality as a source of power which must also be 'passive' and 'innocent'.

The school story takes the familiar pieces of the jigsaw – family, gender, school, friends, lessons, rules – and puts them together in a different way, making a picture which is more brightly coloured, more sharply defined, less complex than its real-life original. In its re-assemblage of lived experience, the school story also re-assembles the ideologies which inform those experiences, offering the possibility of a positive female identity not bound by the material or 'the possible'. Central to the school story, for example, is the fantasy of escape from the family, yet many of the girls who particularly enjoyed school stories commented that they would not like to go to a boarding school themselves because they could not bear to leave their families, would hate the feeling that they were being 'pushed out'. It's not that they were deceiving themselves; the simultaneous desire to be within the comfort and the secure identity offered by the family, and to escape the constraints of that same identity, is a real contradiction which can only be resolved on the level of fantasy. Located in an impossible time – the age of puberty in which puberty never happens – and an impossible place – the fantastic dream of a school which has no relationship with the world beyond it – the school story offers its young reader the possibility of resolving the contradictions in her life without ever needing to confront them directly.

The difficulty here is not so much that this resolution is 'ideological', nor yet that it expresses contradictory desires, for it is in the nature of fiction to do so. It is, rather, that the school story is most 'relevant' when it seems most 'unreal'. The 'time of her life' which the schoolgirl heroine enjoys, the time of puberty-and-not-puberty, can never be realised by the reader; asked to recognise that the stories cannot be *good* because they are not *realistic*, she may come to accept that the desires they allow her to express – for fun, freedom, friendship and a life unconstrained by gender difference – are also 'unreal'. As the schoolgirl reader 'moves on' to the alternative fantasies offered by romantic fiction, by *Jackie* and *Smash Hits*, female subjectivity itself becomes identified with pleasure deferred, with an endless succession of impossible dreams.

Acknowledgment

I would like to thank Rachael Carpenter, Chris Foley, Lesley Leak and Hilary Minns for their help with research into girls' reading, Mary Harron for some stimulating conversations about the school story, and Simon Frith, Angela McRobbie and Cathy Urwin for reading and commenting on an earlier draft of this piece.

Notes

1 Sheila MacLeod, *The Art of Starvation*, 1981, p.42.

2 See Mary Cadogan and Patricia Craig, *You're a Brick, Angela! A New Look at Girls' Fiction from 1839 to 1975*, 1976, especially the introduction and Chapter 3. There is a similar account of Meade's novels in J.S. Bratton's *The Impact of Victorian Children's Fiction*, 1981, pp. 201–7.

3 Cadogan and Craig, *op.cit.*, p.200.

4 The questionnaire was distributed in July 1983 to a first-year class in a mixed comprehensive school, a second-year class in a single-sex comprehensive, and a small random sampling of girls in a mixed primary school. All three schools were in predominantly working-class catchment areas. It is not my purpose here to present a sociological analysis of girls' reading, and the sample is clearly too small to be definitive, but some further details may be of interest to future researchers.

In the first-year class, four girls out of fifteen came into the category of 'addict' (i.e. those who had read all of the *St Clare's* and *Malory Towers* series at least twice, and in some cases five or more times, and who had also read school stories by authors other than Enid Blyton). This seems an exceptionally high number, and was in striking contrast to the second-year class, only one of whom approached the 'addict' classification, although many had read several school stories and were clearly familiar with the genre. However, the second-year girls were noticeably more distanced from and critical of the school story –

all, including the ex-'addict', emphasised that they had now 'grown out of' these stories – and it does seem possible that they had already censored their own memories of their reading.

There were few Afro-Caribbean girls in the three schools in the survey, and none in my sample, so I am not able to comment on whether the school story also has an appeal for Afro-Caribbean girls.

Quotations in the text are taken verbatim from the girls' answers to the questionnaires, but spelling has been 'normalised'.

5 See for example Janice Winship, 'A woman's world: *Woman* – an ideology of femininity', pp.133–54 in Women's Studies Group, *Women Take Issue, 1978*; Judith Williamson, *Decoding Advertisements 1978*, and Cammilla Nightingale, 'Sex roles in children's literature', pp. 141–53 in Sandra Allen *et al.*, *Conditions of Illusion*, 1974.

6 Angela McRobbie, *Jackie: An Ideology of Adolescent Femininity*, 1978.

7 Violet Trefusis to Vita Sackville-West, 23 August 1920. Reproduced in Philippe Jullian and John Phillips, *Violet Trefusis: Life and Letters*, 1976.

8 See for example L.T. Meade, *A Sweet Girl Graduate*, 1891, *The Girls of St Wode's*, 1898, and *The Girls of Merton College*, 1911, and also Alice Stronach, *A Newnham Friendship*, 1901, and Mrs G. De Horne Vaizey, *A College Girl*, 1913. There is a brief discussion of these novels by John Schellenberger in 'Fiction and the first women students', *New University Quarterly*, Autumn 1982, pp. 352–8. The extremely popular and prolific L.T. Meade (1854–1914) wrote over 250 novels, mostly for young readers. Her school stories include also *A World of Girls*, 1886, and *Betty, A Schoolgirl*, 1894.

9 For fuller details see Joan Burstyn, *Victorian Education and the Ideal of Womanhood*, 1980.

10 Mona Caird, Sarah Grand, Menie Muriel Dowie and Lady Florence Dixie were all members of the Pioneer Club in the 1890s. Sarah Doudney (1843–1926) was a popular and well-respected writer of stories for girls. Her school stories include *Monksbury College*, 1872, and *When We Were Girls Together*, the latter serialised in 1885 in *The Girl's Own Paper*, to which Doudney was a frequent contributor.

11 For fuller details see Constance Rover, *Love, Morals and the Feminists*, 1970, Chapters 6–9, and Olive Banks, *Faces of Feminism*, 1981, especially Chapter 6.

12 Sarah Doudney, *When We Were Girls Together*, 1886, pp. 161–2.

13 L.T. Meade, *The Girls of Merton College*, 1911, p. 45.

14 See Evelyn Sharp's autobiography, *Unfinished Adventure*, 1933.

15 See *Time and Tide*, the feminist journal founded by Lady Rhonnda in 1920. For Dane's friendship with Violet Trefusis, see Victoria Glendinning, *Vita: The Life of V. Sackville-West*, 1983, p. 110, and Julian and Phillips, *Violet Trefusis*, p.193. Lillian Faderman speculates that Dane may herself have been lesbian, but sees *Regiment of Women* as the product of internalised lesbian self-hatred. (See Lillian Faderman, *Surpassing the Love of Men*, pp. 341–3 and 392.)

16 The journal *The Freewoman*, 1911–1912, published several articles on this theme; see also Dora Russell, *Hypatia*, 1925, and Clemence Dane's own *The Women's Side*, 1926.

17 See for example Havelock Ellis, 'Appendix B. The School-Friendships of Girls', in *Sexual Inversion: Studies in the Psychology of Sex*, vol. 2, 1897, revised edn 1928, and Sigmund Freud, *Dora*, p.95 (first English translation 1925).

18 Passionate friendships are pervasive in Brazil's stories, but see for example *A Patriotic Schoolgirl*, 1918, and *Loyal to the School*, 1921.

19 Dorita Fairlie Bruce, *Dimsie Moves Up*, pp. 39–40.

20 See for example Antonia Forest, *Autumn Term*, 1948. There is a faint echo of the 'crush' in Anne Digby's *Summer Term at Trebizon*, 1979, but it is emphasised that Pippa's relationship with Rebecca is like that of an 'older sister'.

7

'Listen, how the caged bird sings': Amarjit's song

CAROLYN STEEDMAN

Introduction

Several years ago I was working in a primary school in a provincial city – a northern city, a working town – that year without a class, a 'remedial' teacher, a teacher for 'language development'. About half the children in the school spoke English as a second or third language, and under these circumstances I saw Amarjit, a 9-year-old Punjabi girl, every day, when she came to my room as part of a small group of children who received extra help with reading and writing. We thought vaguely that she had problems, difficulties with reading (staffing levels were still generous then; I doubt that anyone now could afford to think that she had a problem); she was in fact, in the process of becoming bilingual. Terminology has moved on in the last few years, and in some cases is more helpful now than it was then. Four years ago Amarjit was, in the jargon, 'a second language learner', a label that confirmed her as being in possession of some irritating and elusive inadequacy. Born here, speaking the local dialect, she was a child who didn't need to be taught to speak English, but who failed in some mysterious way to write English adequately, to measure up to the norm on reading tests, to demonstrate the requisite quality of imagination and the proper degree of promise.

It has become clearer over the years since the incidents described in this chapter took place that this reaction of mild irritation and exasperation shown towards the written productions of a child like Amarjit, and towards the inadequacies of her reading aloud, was only a heightened version of a much more general attitude towards the intellectual efforts of working-class children in schools. Part of the purpose of this chapter is to outline a history of this attitude, and to find Amarjit's place within it.

But more than this, this chapter is designed to show that

Amarjit was not the passive inheritor of her own history, nor of the pedagogical narrative designed to explain her position within it. Briefly, she confronted it, used it, exploited it, entered into it her own experience. What happened was that the child used a reading book she had borrowed from school to make up a song. That is what the following pages are about: a child's artifact made out of the materials she had to hand – a reading primer in a second language, set in the mythic European past, and her voice.

An act of transformation like this can be seen as an act of play, in the same way as reading and writing are play, a way of manipulating the symbols of a social and emotional world, and of abstracting meaning from a particular reality.[1] Children will do this where they find themselves, and with what is available to them at the time, in school, out of school, in the brief respite from picking stones from a windswept Cambridgeshire field in the 1860s.[2] Play is a way of understanding the world without becoming involved in it, a means of 'assimilating reality to the ego without the need for accommodation'.[3] The particular value of what Amarjit did lies only in there being evidence of the process, in the text that she made her song from, and in a recording of her voice.

But there may be more to it than this. Amarjit's song was the production of dislocation (a working-class child, whose family came from a rural Indian background, an industrial city, working England of the late 1970s); but at the same time it represents a journey through dislocation to a powerful synthesis. For us as adults, it can serve to reveal the historical circumstances that the child found herself in, and in this way help us read the undrawn map of our own displacement. And perhaps the song served something of this function for Amarjit herself, allowed her to know the topography of her disjuncture, to use an act of play to discover a social and political world and to work out what it implied for her future. What Amarjit thought she was doing when she made up her song was to practise her reading; but what this chapter is concerned with are the *effects* of this conscious effort, and the place where the by-products of her invented method of reading aloud permitted her to examine and accommodate the meaning of both a linguistic system and a social structure.

I was impressed by the child's song, and made a tape of it which I played – foolishly I know now – at morning assembly. Some children laughed. Neither they nor their teachers thought very much of Amarjit's production. That's the story.

March 1979: Amarjit's song

The group that Amarjit was a member of arrived one Friday morning, and she produced from her folder the book she had taken home the day before. It was *The Green Man and the Golden Bird*, a book in the 'Hummingbird' series by Sheila McCullagh.[4] 'I like this book. I really like this book,' said Amarjit. 'I love this book. I don't read my reading book. I sing it in bed at night.'

The portion of the text that she had chosen for her song was where the children's mother buys a caged golden bird in the market, and her daughter begs her to let it go: 'The song is so sad I can't bear to listen to it. The bird wants to get out and fly away.' 'Don't be silly', replies the mother. 'That bird cost me a lot of money.' Amarjit had quite simply set the words to music of her own composing. She sustained the melody over a considerable portion of the book, and with some skill dealt with the difficulties of incorporating the irregular rhythms of prose in regular melody. The tune is sad, distant; it reminded me at the time of some Northumbrian folksongs.

Amarjit seemed quite clear about which musical tradition she was operating in. When I had recorded the song, I asked her if I could take the tape home to ask a musician I knew if there were any influences from Indian music in the song. She said I needn't bother, because it was English, she knew it was English. But I did take the tape home, and the tune was notated. It was apparent at the time that Amarjit must have used a good deal of implicit and intuitive knowledge of Punjabi and English in the composing of her song, and that she had used a written text, and her translation of it into musical composition, to practise the language she was acquiring, just as nine years before her infant babbling had been her practice in her first language, Punjabi. She chose as well a hallowed place of safety for her enterprise: children's chosen environment for reading seems to be their bed,[5] and earlier than this, bed is the place of their pre-sleep monologues.[6] At the time, Amarjit's song made clear to me that in learning a language children can, and do, make powerful steps to become effective and competent. In this case her song seemed to be providing Amarjit with practice in the timing and intonation of a second language. What *precisely* the child was up to only became clear much later.

Equally striking at the time was her choice of text. Amarjit composed her song out of a portion of the story that deals with the question of possibilities: that a bird might fly, might be made free. These possibilities were narratively and stylistically rooted in the present: the restrictions that a mother places on a child's desire to act; the price of the bird. At some level, the text she contemplated in such a sustained way allowed her to think about the difficult linguistic relationship of the present and the conditional, of what is, and what might be, not simply as a syntactic matter, but as a social and emotional question too.

Most languages, and the way children are taught to read them, makes the understanding of tense sequence difficult. English tense sequence for example, demands the sophisticated manipulation and re-ordering of function words such as 'will', 'would', 'might', 'did', 'do' and 'used'. At a time when children are still being taught to pay close attention to individual words when reading, the verbal and written responses asked of them demand the ability to manipulate strings of words according to meaning through time. Amarjit was learning to do this in both Punjabi and English. It seemed likely that she used this story – and many others – to help herself with this task, for stories are themselves hypotheses, leading from an easily comprehended present – the interrelation and reaction of people to each other in dialogue – through different states of time. It is the desire of the moment, the yearning expressed in the present ('the bird wants to get out and fly away') that predicate hypothetical and conditional states of affairs, and in this way make linguistic structures based on 'might' and 'perhaps' comprehensible. That Amarjit read herself in those particular lines, saw her own position between what is, and what might be, was obvious; but the transformation of imagery that she achieved, the operation of a culture that she witnessed in her reading of the narrative only became apparent later on.

A few days after I had recorded her song, I played it to half the school in morning assembly. There had been a plan to have a friend of Amarjit play the notated tune on her recorder, but it proved too difficult for a beginner to master in so short a time. I explained that I would go back to the story of David and Goliath that another teacher had delivered to the children in assembly the week before, and get everyone to think about how a shepherd who possibly couldn't read and who almost certainly couldn't read music learned to play so well that he could please a king. I was going to suggest, I told Amarjit, that it was because he did something like she did: heard a story that he liked and made a song out of it.

I hated doing assembly. Clause 25 of the Education Act of 1948, which directs that each school day open with a corporate act of worship, places these burdens on those of us who know that one tacit reason for our occupying a particular position in the school hierarchy is to relieve colleagues of this awful burden. I had a senior post in that school, and if someone had written my job description, taking assembly would have been listed. It is difficult to explain these matters to outsiders: who among those who read these pages except for teachers will have as atheists to propagate Christianity as part of a job of work, and to engage in matters of conscience that are so dreary, so old-fashioned and so unimportant? If some of us unwillingly take part in a system that disseminates the Judaic-Christian myths, then much of it has to do with our understanding that at one level such propagation has absolutely nothing to do with the ideas that are embodied in these re-tellings. I knew as well as everyone on the staff did that all gatherings of the school together, assemblies, hymn practices, sponsored walks, are for the adults involved like plonking the kids in front of the telly at home, putting your feet up, letting the mind drift, the ease of not being responsible. In 'Shooting an elephant' George Orwell explains what it felt like to earn a living by acting as the administrative tool of a despised ideology – as a policeman in Burma in the 1920s,[7] and I found there an expression of my feeling of bored oscillation between resentment and obligation when faced with the duty of taking assembly. But this is too grand a comparison for what is, in primary schools, only like doing dinner duty with God thrown in. And it is harder than that. It would be easier to resist telling children what one doesn't believe if it wasn't also clear that those who do not understand the metaphors of a culture are denied access to power: the pleasure of knowing, structures of thought, interpretive devices. And this giving of access to the symbols of a culture would in its turn have been more gratifying if I hadn't also been taking part in a system of genteel racism that ended every 'multicultural' assembly with a rendering of 'Jesus friend of little children'.

On the day in question, the day I played Amarjit's song in assembly, the recorded song filled the hall, and the children started to laugh. I remember telling myself in a moment of fine, mad, panic that it was all right, that this was just the Fish and Chips for Supper Effect, the laughter of recognition and release that Leila Berg encountered when she read some of the first Nipper books to London schoolchildren.[8] I smiled fixedly and reassuringly at the assembled, and the laughter died away, ordinary England, obedient to a glance.

But it wasn't release and liberation at all. It was the laughter of confusion and embarrassment – because of the plain, unadorned voice, because Asian children weren't often performers at assembly in that school, for many reasons, which this chapter will attempt to outline. I have returned many times to that cold hall, to that assembly, and indeed, in many narratives that I have made out of the incident that I describe here, it has become the focus of my attention, the point of the story. There is still a subterranean account here that goes like this, in which I read rejection in the faces of teachers and children in front of me, believe that some of my colleagues think that I am comparing a 9-year-old Asian working-class girl with a reading problem to David the King, make an unspoken yet still quite improper act of identification with Amarjit, tell the head three days later that I won't do assemblies any more, that I'll pull my weight some other way, and everyone in the staffroom thinks that getting out of obligations is the desired end of making a great deal of fuss about absolutely nothing at all. But that is the wrong narrative. The point was the song; and the dual concerns – investigation of a language system, and of a social system on Amarjit's part – that it revealed.

Birdsong

The portion of the text that Amarjit was recorded singing is as follows:

> It was a very beautiful song, but it was a very sad song, too. 'Let the bird go!' cried Redigan. 'Do let it go! The song is so sad, I can't bear to listen to it. The bird wants to get out and fly away.' 'No, no!' said her mother. 'Don't be silly, Redigan. That bird cost me a lot of money. You must take it to your grandmother. She lives all alone. She likes wild things. She can listen to the golden bird singing.' 'But the bird sings so sadly,' said Redigan. 'The bird sings beautifully,' said her mother. 'You and Colin must set out early in the morning and take the bird to your grandmother.' She put the red cloth back over the cage, and the bird stopped singing. Colin and Redigan got up early next morning and set off to see their grandmother. Colin carried the cage with the bird, and Redigan carried a basket of cakes. They had a long way to go. Their grandmother lived in a little house on the other side of the green hills. Grandmother had a bad leg and she couldn't walk very far. But she was very happy in her little house. There was a big bush of roses in her garden. She had a cow and six brown hens. The cow came to the door every day to be milked, and the hens lived under an apple tree in the garden. Colin and Redigan went to see their grandmother every week, and took her a basket of cakes and fresh bread. They always wanted to go and see her. She told them stories, and gave them apples and cakes to eat. She fed the birds every day. All the birds in the woods came to her garden, and she was never lonely. She was so happy that she made Colin and Redigan happy too. . . .

On the tape, her voice grows tired, and she stops here,

though she may have sung much more alone in her bed at night. Yet she was quite certain about where she wanted to start, three pages into the narrative, with the beautiful, sad song. The rest of *The Green Man and the Golden Bird* rehearses an old theme, in which the golden bird, released from its cage by accident, protects Redigan and her brother from various dangers. The elegiac simplicity of the opening pages, in which the ideas of restriction and freedom are presented, does not provide the overall structure of the story. It seems that Amarjit took from the text precisely what she wanted, and left the rest.

'Of all the creatures . . . that women writers use to stand in, metaphorically, for their own sex, it is their birds who have made the most impression on me,' remarks Ellen Moers in *Literary Women*. She speculates on reasons for this choice, on the littleness of birds, the ease with which they can be tortured by small boys, their half-promise of exotic, sensual delights. But the two most arresting hypotheses that she puts forward are the self-containment and self-indulgence of the bird's song, and at the same time, its representation of confinement, its encapsulation of the yearning for 'the wings of liberty': 'from Mary Wollstonecraft's *Maria* – to Brontë's *Jane Eyre* – to Anne Frank's *Diary of a Young Girl* – I find that the caged bird makes a metaphor that truly deserves the adjective Female . . . a way for the imprisoned girl-child to become a free adult'.[9]

Out of eight years of teaching I have brought away half a dozen tape recordings of children – always girls – singing; and they represent many occasions when the clatter stopped, the room fell silent, a child sang. Some of these recordings are of academic interest, for instance, a rendering of the ballad 'Lord Randal', called 'Henry my son', learned from a Glaswegian grandmother by a 7-year-old and which appears in none of the major collections of British or North American folksongs.

It is well known among folklorists and anthropologists (less well known perhaps, among child linguists and educationalists) that the speech play – the catches, jokes, rhymes, riddles and skipping games – of 7-, 8-, and 9-year-olds speaking their first language demonstrates a spontaneous interest in its sound system. Like all theories of development, developmental linguistics has been constructed in a highly specific way. It is, for a start, generally concerned with young children, children under school age, and it has been reluctant to absorb the findings of other disciplines concerning children's language, such as anthropology, which is, in any case, concerned with language use of older children. What is more, the corpus that informs the theories of language that are transmitted to schools is based on the linguistic development of monolingual children. There is little explanation within these everyday theories of what bilingual children might be up to in performing particular language functions, and there is a tendency to equate the performance of children like Amarjit with that of much younger monolingual children, even to think of them, half-consciously, as babyish or backward.

For instance, most children master the phonological system of their first language by the time they are 2, so the 8-year-old repeating and reversing strings of sounds in speech play is not *practising* anything in a way that a baby could be said to be practising when she babbles; the 8-year-old is rather rehearsing a long-possessed skill.[10] At 9, Amarjit was rehearsing Punjabi in this way; but also, at the same time and for slightly different purposes, she explored the phonological possibilities of a second language – of English. Her song served her as a quite specific piece of practice in English; but it also allowed her to explore the poetic possibilities of the language. If children in the process of becoming bilingual set themselves the dual task of rehearsal and delight – and the evidence is that some of them do[11] – then it cannot be equated with an earlier period of *first* language acquisition, but must be seen developmentally in its own right.

The elaborate formality of Amarjit's translation from text to song indicates her conscious involvement in this process of language acquisition. What is more the social and psychological *content* of the song was something that she, as a 9-year-old, was deliberately trying to confront and understand. Amarjit elaborated speech play in a second language by using its musical system, and this technique she employed can be seen as a search for a more sophisticated and rigorous means of linguistic exploration than speech play itself provides, for the musical system of a culture can operate as a more abstract representation of its linguistic system.[12] 'The comparison of melodic structure and linguistic intonation patterns' has rarely been investigated,[13] but it is this comparison that is needed in considering Amarjit's song. It has been argued that it is this relationship that accounts for the typicality and appeal of certain melodic systems, for instance that

> the peculiar, inimitable evenness of the ska beat may be closely related to the fact that the Jamaican dialect of English is . . . extremely 'syllable timed' – that is, each syllable takes up very much the same amount of time, unlike dialects of southern English, in which the stressed syllables are markedly longer than the others. . . .[14]

Most of the dialects of English spoken in Britain are in fact stress-timed:

> this means briefly, that the main stresses in an utterance will fall at approximately regular intervals, no matter how many 'weak' syllables intervene. . . . In individual words too, there is a characteristic main stress. . . .[15]

Learning the timing of a new language is one of the many tasks facing the child becoming bilingual.

Punjabi, which was Amarjit's first language, has a very strong *tendency* towards syllable timing. The poetic system of Punjabi represents in a heightened form the half-way position that it occupies along the continuum of syllable-timed/stress-timed languages, for the system rests on the combination of long and short syllables. In this way it is unlike, for example, the poetic system of an extremely syllable-timed language like French, where the sheer number of syllables is what makes a poetic unit. A particular feature of the Punjabi poetic system is the freedom it gives to the poet to lengthen and shorten syllables for rhetorical effect. The notion of stress can be imposed upon a basic syllabic system in a formalised way. The poetry and rhymes that Amarjit knew – the songs, rhyming games and cradle songs of the Punjab – formalised and elaborated the tendency in everyday prose towards stress-timing.[16]

When Amarjit turned the prose of her reading book into a song, it was possibly her familiarity with Punjabi verse that gave her the extraordinary confidence and facility that she displayed in the contracting and lengthening of phonemes.

Her song offers linguistic evidence, that adults can take from her production, of the way in which a child employed her knowledge of one language, and the musical system that was based on it, in acquiring another. The song offers a clear example of a child performing a linguistic device that is known among bilingual children (though rarely witnessed to such a sustained degree): that of mapping the phonological system of a first language on to a second.[17] But more importantly than that, it offers evidence of a child creatively using her knowledge of two language systems, for highly practical purposes, and for the purposes of delight, both at the same time.

Song, pedagogy and social learning

Children, then, use song for their own developmental purposes, and always, their purposes have been appropriated by adults. The German educationalist and founder of the kindergarten movement, Friedrich Froebel (1782–1852) was convinced that the traditional songs of childhood could be 'converted into a systematic form for the unfolding of the child's mental and corporeal powers',[18] and set about showing how in highly formalised books of songs for use in schools. All those who impose upon children the task of labour, who gather them together and tell them what to do, are oppressed and irritated by their noise.[19] Like all mothers, primary schoolteachers know that the noise of children can, quite simply, send you mad, and the song is one way of harmonising the noise, of making it pleasing. It serves the useful function, as well, of bringing tears to the eyes of those who know that it is proper to be touched by childhood.[20]

Beneath the plaintive and appealing music of children's voices raised in song lies the subterranean image of little girlhood, the isolated, original song of young Mary Wollstonecraft that Ellen Moers noted, the chant of the story told to oneself. It is easy to see the song as an acceptable form of female expression, for it harmonises the original voice into cultural phrasing, and frequently prevents the content from actually being heard. Amarjit's song was made from the portion of her book that dealt with the themes of restriction and isolation, the desire to be free. But it occupies a novel position within the hidden tradition of little girlhood outlined above, for she moved inquiringly and confidently between the two cultures she had access to in order to find an original voice.

It is a commonplace within various theories of primary education that a child's own experience must be a starting point for learning, and recent elaboration of this theory within the field of multicultural education would emphasise Amarjit's alienation from her reading book, the distance of her own experience from its fairy-tale Germanic setting, the blue-eyed blondes who people its pages.[21] But what Amarjit did in fact, was to occupy, take hold of, and transform the set of metaphors she encountered in its pages; for what she found there was most profoundly herself.

Amarjit's poetic and practical interest in the sound system of English, and the way in which this was exemplified in her song, has already been outlined. This interest in phonology is connected to another that children display when manipulating language in verbal play: the formal rehearsal of adult roles, particularly those of sexual and marital relationships. There is evidence from the anthropological study of speech play in children across many cultures that suggests that investigation of the social and sexual world is a primary concern of children from 7 to 12.[22] It is the argument of this section that her song gave Amarjit the means to explore the world of adult intention and purpose that surrounded her, by permitting her to consider an adult sexuality, and its perceived implications for her future. Children who are in the process of becoming bilingual may well combine both concerns in their speech play: Amarjit provided herself with practice in the phonological and intonational system of English and with an understanding of the process of her own socialisation.

It became clear from conversations with Amarjit's friends over the next year that an understanding of the economic basis of their existence was a dominant feature of the girls' understanding of themselves – as indeed it may well be for all working-class little girls, though the part that economic relationships and children's understanding of them plays in the growth of the sense of self rarely enters into normative accounts of child development.[23] The conversation with children that provided me with the most insight into the metaphoric order that Amarjit transformed in making her song was held with four 10-year-old children (three girls and a boy) a year after Amarjit made her recording. In what follows, and in considering the children's discussion of weddings, babies, boy children and implicitly, the dowry system, though it is never directly mentioned, it is important to remember that what the children's words reveal is *their* understanding or the social and sexual future that awaited them, not an *account* of that social and sexual system.

The children were detailing the celebration and party giving that surrounds the birth of a boy child in the Sikh community: 'when somebody gets a girl,' commented Ravinder Kaur[24] matter-of-factly, 'nearly all the ladies get sad. When they have a little boy, they're happy. . . . They cry, when they have a girl. . . . ' This reaction to her own sex was formalised in the telling; she, a dearly loved child, presented it as a ritual that had a learned explanation. But in their account of parties and celebration, the children struggled to understand something of themselves:

> first it's at home, a gudwara;[25] then it's a party – two weeks later it's a party. Then when he has his teeth they give another party for the teeth, so it's a real good celebration for the boy. . . . Girls don't usually have parties . . . they're silly having parties for girls because boys are – they think boys are more important than girls.

The children hovered between the adult formulation, and the economic unit of the known self:

> the boy has to have his wedding very specially. He does. Because the boy is going to get married . . . and the parents have to give the girls some special things . . . the other parents don't have to give the boy anything, so he's very lucky.

It was in fact the only boy who was present during this

conversation who produced a formulation of the clarity that Amarjit achieved when she composed her song. Not bearing the same emotional relationship to the economic system that the girls did, Jatinder Singh, after twenty minutes of speculative listening, looked up from his writing and announced:

> I know why girls don't have parties. When girls are grown up and they get married, they are going to go away from their home. . . . If they're a boy, they just stay in that place, and the girl's got to come to that place.

Girls were, indeed, costly items. Don't be silly Redigan. That bird cost me a lot of money. . . .

A year before (and a year younger than the children talking here), Amarjit had explored the same theme. The imagery she took from her book, and her manipulation of it, allowed her to dwell on both economic value and economic restriction. The metaphors she was able to use allowed her not only the idea of 'the wings of liberty', but also, by permitting direct comparison between the expensive bird and herself, allowed her to move beyond the traditional European usage of this image, as outlined by Ellen Moers, and to see the flight to freedom overshadowed by restriction.

It seems likely that the *cost* of the bird in the story was the feature that Amarjit most wanted to dwell on, for its price expressed most clearly the contradictions of the adult role she was trying to confront. By dealing with the bird's price she drew on another set of cultural referents, separate from those outlined by Ellen Moers, and saw herself as both valued and resented, the costly item that would inevitably disappear from the home, its flight sought out and seen as inevitable, its resting place fragile and insecure.

In 'A daughter: a thing to be given away', Penelope Brown and her colleagues have described the structural and economic foundation in Punjabi Sikh society for the emotional attitudes that Amarjit was trying to learn and assess. In describing the external features of a social organisation which puts women 'at the service of men', and in which, having no economic or social alternative, women are inexorably drawn into marriage, they outline the dangerous emotional territory that the young Punjabi bride must traverse, the enforced flight from a loving and protecting mother to a mother-in-law:

> As a mother-in-law, a woman who has herself been subordinate in her husband's household becomes more powerful with age and the adulthood of her sons. Her own natal kin ties gradually become less and less important, and her interests become irretrievably connected to those of her husband. . . . It is in her interest to repeat these patterns with her new daughter-in-law. New brides pose a threat of potential breaches of family solidarity – they have to go through the dangerous process of aligning their interests with those of strangers and breaking the ties with their natal families. A mother in her turn must let go of her daughter. There are many Punjabi proverbs and sayings about daughters which illustrate this point:
> 'She is a bird of passage'
> 'Another's property'
> 'A guest in her parents' home'
> 'A thing that has to be given away'.[26]

The words of Redigan's mother in the story, where she tells the child she is foolish for wanting to let the bird go, may have been seen by Amarjit as the traditional preparation of daughters by mothers for a harsh future: 'A mother knows what her daughter's life will be like, and it is her duty to prepare her for it.'[27] If this was the case, then the image of the flight to freedom turns in upon itself, the daughter's going viewed resentfully, because of the wasted expenditure involved in rearing a bird of passage.

The isolation and privacy in which Amarjit made her song probably allowed her a deeper insight into the ideas she was dealing with than the children quoted above were provided with. However, it is difficult to compare the effects of individual composition with a discussion, the function of which the children involved understood to be to explain to someone who did not know – or did not know very much – about the mechanisms of their culture.

Invisible children

I am further from Amarjit now. Five years ago I knew her – not uncomplicatedly, but clearly – as a female child, a working-class little girl, an Indian whose family history lay in the small farming area between Amritsar and Jallunder. Her individual history represented a new version of the long tradition of change and migration within English society, the borders of cultures traversed, communities unknown to each other linked across great distances by a million individual journeys, the shift from country to city that carried its own resonance 'between birth and learning', that showed 'history active and continuous: the relations . . . not only of ideas and experiences, but of rent and interest, of situation and power; a wider system'[28]. Indeed, to see Amarjit within this half-hidden tradition was the only honest interpretation I could find for the difficult and contradictory relationship between a white woman teacher and a black child in racist, late-twentieth-century Britain.[29] It was possible then to see Amarjit occupying the position of nearly all working-class children in schools: seen as falling short of some measure of 'real' childhood, somehow lacking, inadequate. It was quite clear, as Maureen Stone was to write, that 'black children are a section of the working class in Britain, and whatever is true of the working class generally, it is also true of [them]'. In *The Education of the Black Child in Britain* she went on to say that she saw

> the social structure as operating through schools to reinforce the low status of black pupils. The use of social psychological theories to 'explain' lower class and/or black achievement in schools, I regard as an unwillingness to relate social psychological theories to the wider historical, sociological, political and economic factors operating in society, both in terms of working class children generally, and of black children in particular.[30]

It is the argument here that these theories of linguistic and cultural deprivation that teachers are implicitly expected to work with in primary schools, and the much deeper set of social beliefs and relationships upon which they are based, dictated much of the indifferent response to Amarjit's song.

However, the last five years or so has seen the emergence of a set of ideas within the field of multicultural education that seems to offer an alternative to the hopelessness of these various theories of deprivation. The idea of multicultural education is seductive, offering as it does items of culture, lists of minority group habits and beliefs that can be learned in order to understand children like Amarjit.[31] In many ways what this means is that over the years, the child has been distanced into something exotic, and it is much harder to see her now plain as a poor working-class Asian child with a reading problem. One specific result of the dissemination of multicultural theories is the clear expectations that some schools now have of the creative achievements of minority group children: even at the time Amarjit would have made more sense in school if she had painted an elephant, or a temple – something Indian – rather than making her own meaning out of a tale in the European tradition.

Developments within the theory and practice of multicultural education, and the prescriptions that have been passed on to schools in the past few years,[32] can serve to lay bare a rarely discussed contradiction that operates in the lives of children and teachers. The contradiction centres on the question of experience – children's expertise – its use in classrooms, and its incorporation into reading, curriculum and learning material. This question is, in its turn, a reflection of a much longer history of relationships within the primary school which, once uncovered, could be used to show how the pedagogy designed to encompass Amarjit's experience actually rejected its creative expression. The position of this child within the school system highlights a much wider absence of children's experience from the form and content of their learning.

It is a commonplace within radical critiques of popular education that 'the history of formal education in this country has not generally reflected the culture of the mass of the people',[33] and that given this, 'it would be quite unrealistic to expect schools to cater to the cultural needs of a black minority of the working class when they have demonstrated their inability or unwillingness to cater to the cultural needs of the majority white culture.'[34] Maureen Stone is writing here of children of West Indian origin in British schools, children who are often assumed to have 'no culture' at all. Children like Amarjit, on the other hand, can be seen to represent an exotic 'high-culture'. The well-worn cultural markers of tourism and cookery books are an entirely unthreatening permanent form of the cultural exotic: children can paint temples and list the fourteen great gurus, cook samosa in the classroom and demonstrate the tying of a sari because none of this has anything to do with the processes of history and politics, and completely ignores the fact that 'children as they grow create for themselves a living culture out of the elements of the various existing cultures to which they have access'.[35] This is precisely what Amarjit did in making her song; but the educational theory designed to support her in fact denied her this act of transformation.

In spite of the strategies designed to support her, children like Amarjit do not exist within our educational system. She exists legally, of course, in that she possesses a birth certificate and a passport, and her name is written in many registers of the state. But in school, where pedagogical practice and assessment is constructed on the evidential base of many studies of child development, the experience of minority group children is nowhere entered into the records. In 1963 the Newsons explained why 'immigrants' were to be excluded from their study of childrearing practices in Nottingham:

> we were primarily interested in normal babies in ordinary family situations. For this reason we deliberately excluded from our sample a number of cases . . . all illegitimate children and all children known to have gross disabilities . . . Children whose parents were recent immigrants to the country . . . for the purposes of the study the picture could only be confused by their inclusion.[36]

And the Bristol Language Development Study, which was set up in 1972 to study the role of language and parental attitudes in the transition from home to school, and on which an enormous amount of educational practice and assumption is based, specifically excluded 'children with known handicaps, those in full-time day care and those whose parents did not speak English as their native language'.[37]

The absence of children like Amarjit from such studies is only a heightened version of the absence of working-class children in general from the psychological, psychoanalytic and linguistic evidence which supports our mid-twentieth-century understanding of what childhood *is*. This understanding of childhood has been evolved over the last two hundred years, and is based on the experiences of a limited number of middle- and upper-class children.[38] It is this understanding which, in its turn, informs the longitudinal studies from which Amarjit is so conspicuously absent. Her physical absence is a metaphor for a wider absence of working-class children, for though children from social classes 4 and 5 are, of course, present in these surveys, the *idea* of the child with which they are observed and questioned makes it easier to define working-class childhood as an inadequacy, a kind of pathology. In his book *All Things Bright and Beautiful*, Ronald King notes the strained disjuncture between how a child *ought* to be, and how she actually *is*, in her teacher's eyes. He records teachers' definitions of a statistical minority of children, those of the professional middle classes, as 'just ordinary children', whilst the vast majority, those of the working class, are defined as not normal children, odd or peculiar in some way.[39]

This day-to-day emotional and social relationship between some teachers and some working-class children in school makes it difficult for those teachers to provide the sympathy and empathy with the child that is the central feature of our official educational ideology of child-centredness.[40] It is difficult, for example, to think of mothering, or treating as one's own, children whose real mothers are defined as inadequate.[41] The history of state schooling, in fact, and the theories about what it could do for working-class children that have been developed within it, provides a centrally available image of working-class children in classrooms of such children lacking something, falling short somehow, of some measure of 'real' childhood.

By the end of the nineteenth century, the school saw itself as a place where working-class children might be compensated for belonging to working-class families.[42] In the early years of state-aided education schools were seen as places that make up for the absence of morality and discipline in working-class homes;[43] the innovation of early childhood education at the beginning of this century was to see that children might be physically and emotionally compensated for their disabilities.[44] The infant-nursery school saw compensation in terms of cleanliness and love, whilst more recent developments in the idea of education as compensation have dealt in terms of cognitive and linguistic deficit. By filling working-class children with rich experiences, schools may hope to fill the emptiness, compensate the child for the 'noise, crowding and physical discomfort' of her home, 'in which the usual (i.e. middle-class) parental role of tutor and guide is largely lacking'.[45]

Amarjit, a working-class child who spoke two languages, found herself being schooled within a set of theories that had added her bilingualism to the checklist of disadvantages that marks the deprived child. The history of this attitude towards bilingualism has not yet been written, but it is possible to pinpoint landmarks of dissemination. In 1967, for example, the Plowden committee recommended that Educational Priority Areas be identified, and that certain factors be taken into account when resources were allocated. Bilingualism was added to a list that included the presence of mentally and physically handicapped children in an area, the number of parents receiving state benefits, domestic overcrowding, and so on.[46] When Educational Priority Areas were finally set up in 1972, having a first language that was not English was rejected as a measure of deprivation;[47] but the Plowden report had by then been very widely circulated and discussed among teachers, and there is some evidence that the notion of bilingualism as disadvantage is still strong in schools. When the 'Social Handicap and Cognitive Functioning in Pre-School Children' Project was set up in 1975, teacher groups working with the project defined a socially handicapped child as 'one whose home background may be that of a one-parent family . . . of a large low-income family; with the father unemployed; with one member of the family chronically sick; a child left with untrained help before or after school; the only or younger child of elderly parents; or *from a home where the language spoken is different from that of school*' (emphasis added).[48]

There is now, in the mid-1980s, a considerable body of literature that underlines the cognitive advantages of bilingualism,[49] and this literature shows in general, as Amarjit's song does with great specificity, that the more a child knows about one language, the more she can transfer that knowledge to acquiring and understanding a new one.[50] Within this set of theories, Amarjit can be seen as a privileged learner, because of her age and the objective understanding of language as a system that age brings, and because, by accident, she found a means of manipulating and transforming the meanings that two linguistic systems presented her with. But the idea that bilingualism confers certain advantages on children has not yet become common currency in schools.

There is as yet no adequate way of talking or writing about the restrictions that are placed upon children by these theories of class and intelligence. Brian Jackson, reporting from a multiracial reception class in the midlands in 1978, did find a way, but only at the difficult expense of blaming the adults who taught the working-class and minority-group children he spent a year with. He pointed out that in a city where the majority of the people are rooted in a working-class culture, a sense of that culture is quite absent from the school:

> teachers simply do not know about the children's homes, backgrounds, pre-school years . . . the child simply doesn't make sense in school. Many of a teacher's difficulties arise because she is governed by one cultural perspective . . . [the] universe of early childhood, mixed cultures and the home itself is almost invisible . . . my reports of a child's domestic life only a few hundred yards away were like the afterwork tales of a traveller from unknown lands. Such images as teachers had of home life . . . were ludicrous folk caricatures which are . . . painful to record.[51]

In this situation there is a whole network of common-sense arguments about deprivation to provide a teacher with comfort: 'she can then either fall back on deficit theories – "What can you expect?" – or simply pass over the matter.'

Assembly

The recorded song filled the hall and the children started to laugh. There was no way of imagining, on their part or their teachers', what could have been a good and acceptable piece of work from Amarjit. Transfigured somehow, moved to the other side of town, a child without her history, someone else, perhaps she could have had a school acknowledge her learning as effective, and thus have come to understand the implications of her own insights. The sense of power, the intellectual pleasure of knowing that something has been worked out, was, of course, denied to all the children in that cold hall.

Amarjit's song provided her with practice in the timing and intonation of English, and meditation upon the social circumstances that provide the substructure for the construction of linguistic hypotheses. What Amarjit wanted to think about was change, about now, where the bird is caged, and about a future, in which the bird is free. Her movement towards understanding hypothetical and conditional states of affairs, the connections within time of the present and the future, between what is, and what might be, was based on her identification with the bird's current desire. Amarjit, reading her book, watching herself:

> The song is so sad
> I can't bear
> to listen to it.
> The songbird wants
> to get out and fly away.
>
> No, no, said her mother
> Don't be silly, Redigan.
> That bird
> cost me a lot of money

Notes

1 Sixth Report of the Children's Employment Commission (1862), PP 1867, vol.16, p.132. David Vincent, *Bread, Knowledge and Freedom: A Study of Nineteenth Century Autobiography*, London, Methuen, 1982, pp.89–92, p.107.
2 L.S. Vygotsky, *Mind in Society*, Cambridge, Mass., Harvard University Press, 1978, pp.97–9.
3 Jean Piaget, *Play, Dreams and Imitation*, London, Routledge & Kegan Paul, 1954, pp. 89–104.
4 Sheila McCullagh, *The Green Man and the Golden Bird*, St Albans, Rupert Hart-Davis, 1976.
5 Margaret Spencer, 'Handing down the magic', in Phillida Salmon (ed.), *Coming to Know*, London, Routledge & Kegan Paul, London, 1980, p.54. See also Carolyn Steedman, *The Tidy House: Little Girls Writing*, London, Virago, 1982, pp.85–109, and Vera Southgate *et al.*, *Extending Beginning Reading*, London, Heinemann, 1981, pp.188–9.
6 Ruth Weir, *Language in the Crib*, The Hague, Mouton, 1970.
7 George Orwell, 'Shooting an elephant' (1936), in *The Collected Essays, Letters and Journalism of George Orwell: An Age Like This*, Harmondsworth, Penguin, 1970, pp.265–72.
8 Leila Berg, *Reading and Loving*, London, Routledge & Kegan Paul, 1977, pp.87–8; *Fish and Chips for Supper*, London, Macmillan, 1963.
9 Ellen Moers, *Literary Women*, London, The Women's Press, 1978, pp.245–51.
10 Mary Sanches and Barbara Kirshenblatt Gimblett, 'Children's traditional speech play and child language', in Barbara Kirshenblatt Gimblett (ed.), *Speech Play*, Philadelphia, University of Pennsylvania Press, 1976, pp.65–110, especially p.105.
11 Sabrina Peck, 'Child-child discourse in second language acquisition', in Evelyn Hatch (ed.), *Second Language Acquisition*, Rowley, Mass., Newbury House, 1978, pp.383–400.
12 John Lyons, *Introduction to Theoretical Linguistics*, Cambridge, Cambridge University Press, 1968, pp.19–20.
13 Robert A. Hall, 'Elgar and the intonation of British English' (1953), in Dwight Bolinger (ed.), *Intonation*, Harmondsworth, Penguin, 1972, p.285.
14 Johnny Copasetic, 'Rude boys don't argue', *Melody Maker*, 19 May 1979, p.41.
15 Roger H. Flavell, *Language Users and Their Errors*, London, Macmillan, 1983, p.55, p.17.
16 I would like to express my thanks to Dr Christopher Shackle of

the School of Oriental and African Studies, University of London, for the information he gave me about the poetic system of Punjabi and the artistic and domestic culture that supports it. For a description of the wider poetic system into which that of the Punjab fits, see S.H. Kellogg, *A Grammar of the Hindi Language*, London, Kegan Paul, 1938, pp. 546–84.

17 Susan Ervin Tripp, 'Is second language learning like the first?', *TESOL Quarterly*, vol.8, no.2, June 1974, p.124. Jules Ronjat, *Le Developpement du langage observé chez un enfant bilingue*, Paris, Champion, 1913, pp.17–35.

18 Bertha Maria Marenholtz-Buelow, *Women's Educational Mission: Being an Explanation of Friedrich Froebel's System of Infant Gardens*, London, Darton, 1855, p.15.

19 'You see,' said a farm labourer's wife whose children laboured in one of the smaller domestic industries in 1867, 'their little spirits get so high, and they will talk to the last, and that is aggravation.' Sixth Report of the Children's Employment Commission (1862), PP 1867, vol. 16, p.89.

20 'I always like to hear them sing at their work,' said a Birmingham button manufacturer, employer of many children, in 1864. 'It makes the work go . . . sweet again . . . good often arises from it to the grown-up. . . . Last winter I stood outside in the cold and listened to them, and they all sang carols in the shop. . . .' Third Report of the Children's Employment Commission (1862), PP 1864, vol.22, pp.104–5.

21 See Hazel Carby, 'Multi-culture', *Screen Education*, vol.34, Spring 1980, pp.62–70, especially p.67, for a discussion of popular multicultural education. See also Barry Troyna, 'The ideological and policy response to black pupils in British schools', in Anthony Hartnett (ed.), *The Social Sciences in Educational Studies*, London, Heinemann, 1982, pp.127–43, for the legislative base of multicultural education. See Bob Dixon, *Catching Them Young* (2 vols), *Volume 1: Sex, Race and Class in Children's Books*, Pluto Press, London, 1977, for an assessment of children's reading material within the theory; and for the role of children's experience within 'multiculturalism' see R. Jeffcoate, 'A multicultural curriculum: beyond the orthodoxy', *Trends in Education*, vol.4, 1979, pp.8–12.

22 Karen Ann Watson Gegeo, 'From verbal play to talk story: the role of routines in speech events among Hawaiian children', in Susan Ervin Tripp and Claudia Mitchell Kernan (eds), *Child Discourse*, New York, Academic Press, 1977, pp.67–90. Kirshenblatt Gimblett, op. cit., pp.65–110. Brian Sutton Smith, *The Folkgames of Children*, Austin, University of Texas Press

for the American Folklore Society, vol.24, 1972, pp.485–90.

23 Steedman, op. cit., pp.122–31.

24 For the naming system of the Sikh community, see A.G. James, *Sikh Children in Britain*, London, Oxford University Press, 1974, p.24 or W. Owen Cole and Piara Singh Sambi, *The Sikhs: Their Religious Beliefs and Practices*, London, Routledge & Kegan Paul, 1978, pp. 113–14.

25 See James, op. cit., pp.30–52, and Owen Cole and Singh Sambi, op. cit., pp.112–13. The children used the word for the place where the Sikh scriptures are kept, that is, the temple, or a room in a private house set aside for worship, to describe the ceremony itself.

26 Penelope Brown, Marthe Macintyre, Ros Morpeth and Shirley Prendergast, 'A daughter: a thing to be given away', in Cambridge Women's Studies Group, *Women in Society*, London, Virago, 1981, pp.127–45, especially pp.129–35.

27 Ibid., p.132; and not of course, only in Punjabi society: 'because of their social position and the demands that go with it, mothers, who are themselves second-class citizens, are in the unenviable situation of having to raise their daughters to step into their shoes . . . it is the job of those who are themselves in a subordinate position to prepare the next generation of girls to take their place', Luise Eichenbaum and Susie Orbach, *What do Women Want?*, London, Michael Joseph, 1983, p.52.

28 Raymond Williams, *The Country and the City*, St Albans, Granada, 1975, p.17.

29 Carby, op.cit., p.69:

> a white woman teacher . . . may care about the position of black women and want to learn about them, understand them, and teach them. Nevertheless, it would be important that she should recognise the implications of white womanhood for black womanhood, clarify what are the social relations with those she teaches. . . . The conflict-ridden duality in the pedagogic role will remain unperceived if teachers . . . are too uncomfortable or complacent about their own anti-racism.

30 Maureen Stone, *The Education of the Black Child in Britain: The Myth of Multiracial Education*, London, Fontana, 1981, pp.61–2, p.35. See also Ken Worpole and Dave Morley, *The Republic of Letters: Working Class Writing and Local Publishing*, London, Comedia, 1982, p.104.

31 Amrit Wilson, 'You think we've got problems', *New Statesman*, 13 November 1982.

32 See for example Louis Cohen and Lawrence Manion, *Multicultural Classrooms*, London, Croom Helm, 1983.

33 Stone, op. cit., p.69. Stuart Hall, 'Education and the crisis of the urban school', in John Raynor and Elizabeth Harris (eds), *Schooling in the City*, London, Ward Lock, 1977.

34 Stone, op. cit., p.69.

35 Alan James, 'The "multicultural" curriculum', in Alan James and Robert Jeffcoate (eds), *The School in the Multicultural Society*, London, Harper & Row, 1981, p.23.

36 John and Elizabeth Newson, *Patterns of Infant Care in an Urban Community*, Harmondsworth, Penguin, 1965, p.262.

37 Gordon Wells, *Learning Through Interaction: The Study of Language Development*, London, Cambridge University Press, 1981, p.5. See also J.W.B. Douglas, *The Home and the School*, Glasgow, MacGibbon & Kee, 1964; R. Davie, N. Butler and H. Goldstein, *From Birth to Seven*, London, Longmans, 1972; K. Fogelman, *Britain's Sixteen Year Olds*, National Children's Bureau, London, 1976; J. Essen and M. Ghodsian, 'Children of immigrants: school performance', *New Community*, vol. 7, no.3 1979, pp.422–9.

38 Steedman, op. cit., pp.85–6; p.110.

39 Ronald King, *All Things Bright and Beautiful? The Sociology of Infants' Classrooms*, Chichester, Wiley, 1978, p.102, pp.110–26, pp.89–95. See also Rachel Sharp and Anthony Green, *Education and Social Control: A Study in Progressive Primary Education*, London, Routledge & Kegan Paul, 1975, pp.137–65 and *passim*, where many working-class children are called 'peculiar' or 'odd' by their teachers.

40 For a brief account of this ideology as an *official* one, see Maurice Galton, Brian Simon and Paul Croll, *Inside the Primary Classroom*, London, Routledge & Kegan Paul, 1980, pp.33–5.

41 See Cyril Burt, *The Backward Child*, London, University of London Press, 1937, pp.126–8; Joan Tough, 'How shall we educate the young child?', in Alan Davies (ed.), *Language and Learning in Early Childhood*, London, Heinemann, 1977, pp.77–8, and Wells, op. cit., p.263, for the development, in the modern literature of deprivation, of the assumption that the mother is the more guilty partner in the production of the child's disadvantage.

42 Audrey Curtis and Peter Blatchford, *Meeting the Needs of Socially Handicapped Children*, Walton-on-Thames, Nelson, 1981, p.16.

43 Report of the Commission Appointed to Inquire into Popular Education, PP 1866, vol.21 (Part I), p.28, p.114, p.539. Jo Manton, *Mary Carpenter and the Children of the Streets*, London, Heinemann, 1976, pp.81–96.

44 Nanette Whitbread, *The Evolution of the Infant/Nursery School*, London, Routledge & Kegan Paul, 1972, pp. 53–80.

45 John R. Edwards, *Language and Disadvantage*, London, Edward Arnold, 1979, contains a useful survey of post-Second World War theories of cultural, social and linguistic deprivation.

46 Department of Education and Science, *Children and Their Primary Schools* ('The Plowden Report'), London, HMSO, 1967, vol.1, pp.57–9.

47 A.H. Halsey, *Educational Priority* (4 vols), 'EPA problems and policies', vol. 1, London, HMSO, 1972, pp. 43–53.

48 Curtis and Blatchford, op. cit., p.19.

49 Wallace E. Lambert, 'The effects of bilingualism on the individual: cognitive and sociocultural consequences', in Peter A. Hornby (ed.), *Bilingualism: Psychological, Social and Educational Implications*, New York, Academic Press, 1977. Jane Miller, 'How do you spell Gujerati, Sir?', in L. Michaels and Christopher Ricks (eds), *The State of the Language*, Berkeley, University of California Press, 1980, pp.140–51.

50 Ervin Tripp, op. cit., pp. 116–20. Jane Miller, *Many Voices: Bilingualism, Culture and Education*, London, Routledge & Kegan Paul, 1983, pp.6–7, pp.143–52.

51 Brian Jackson, *Starting School*, London, Croom Helm, 1979, p.100, p.136.

8

Constructing motherhood: the persuasion of normal development

CATHY URWIN

> The modern mother takes for granted that she will have the advice of experts and will not have to rely on the advice of her mother. The previous generation of mothers may not necessarily be the best advisors of the present generation. This is not to belittle the enormous support which grandmothers can give. . . . But the modern mother is less convinced than her predecessors that her mother knows best. (Hugh Jolly, *Book of Child Care: The Complete Guide for Today's Parents*, London, Sphere, 1981, p. 1)

Given that women's social position and motherhood are so commonly equated, it is perhaps obvious that the differentiation between public and private spheres described in previous chapters implies changes not only for women as homemakers but also as mothers. This apparent expansion in women's responsibilities has brought with it a steady production of prescriptions which circumscribe the maternal role. This production has been supported both by the development of scientific knowledge of child health and development and by the emergence of social regulatory apparatuses concerned with the well-being of children. These apparatuses, as Donzelot[1] suggests, have contributed to the production of the modern family as a site for intervention and the reproduction of dominant ideologies. One consequence of this has been a general tendency to define the role of the mother in terms of assumptions about children's needs and propensities.

In this chapter I shall be concerned with the present and recent past, and with factors contributing to contemporary notions of mothers' responsibilities over the first two or three years of their children's lives. Using material obtained from interviewing forty mothers of infants, I aim to illustrate in particular the influence of certain ideas from the psychology of child development not only on current orthodoxies on what mothers 'should' do but on women's own aspirations and desires. In my analysis I use a critical application of the concept of 'normalisation', associated in particular with the work of Foucault, Donzelot and other post-structuralist accounts.[2] This concept rests on the argument that, over the historical period we are concerned with in this book, the birth of practices of surveillance, which are ostensibly concerned with identifying deviance, has depended on forms of knowledge facilitating the production of categories or parameters for differentiating 'abnormal' from the 'normal' (the sick from the healthy, the mad from the sane, the imbecile from the possessor of normal intelligence, and so on). In this process the construction of norms has become a basis for regulating the rest of the population. Crucial to this is a shift of strategy which involves not only the isolation of deviants but the introduction of forms of prevention which support particular orthodoxies and effectively 'police' entire populations.

Here I shall illustrate the effects of such normalising apparatuses and the orthodoxies they support by looking in particular at such now-routine social practices as infant testing and check-ups with the doctor or health visitor, and at what John and Elizabeth Newson have described as 'the cult of child psychology'.[3] The latter refers to the explosion of books, pamphlets and magazine articles, published in apparently ever-increasing numbers, which is mainly directed at first-time mothers and is concerned almost exclusively with infancy and the pre-school years. The former refers to social practices which have also flourished in the post-war years under the rubric of 'prevention' or early detection. These include practices associated with ante-natal care, post-natal check-ups on the mother's health and also regular checks on the baby's development. Initially these check-ups usually take place in ante-natal or baby clinics or at the GP's. As the baby gets older they are backed by routine visits from health visitors who are assigned to particular mothers and babies, visiting them at home from shortly after the babies are born. Both health visitors and doctors rely crucially on the notion of a normal course of development and the use of standardised baby tests to assess babies' developmental progress, in order to pinpoint children who are not achieving particular milestones within the average age range.

As such these practices are concerned with the early detection of deviance, and I shall not discuss here how they have been established, nor the question of whether or not they are effective in what they are designed to do, for instance, to pinpoint children with particular problems. Rather I am concerned with how they may function in the construction of mothering more generally, with seeing their impact in relation to other sources of support, guidance and information on child development which may be available to women. Using what the particular women interviewed told me about their experiences of pregnancy, childbirth and the ensuing months, and about their aspirations, difficulties and conflicts, and how they thought things had changed since they were brought up, I shall illustrate firstly how both the normative account of development and the power relations which these practices imply may operate to define not only what development should be but the mother's role in promoting it. Secondly, looking at the books and pamphlets read by these women, I shall also indicate how the normative view of development and an image of an almost totally child-centred mother is reinforced by contemporary child care literature. Like the practices themselves, this appears to be increasingly drawing on psychological studies which see developmental concomitants of 'social deprivation' in terms of maternal failure, contributing to new orthodoxies on the role of 'normal' mothers. In doing so I want to suggest that the social practices and current orthodoxies may have powerful effects in defining women's roles as mothers by giving specific content to their desires, aspirations and daily work and by occluding alternative options. But while the concept of normalisation is particularly useful in revealing this relation, I shall also argue that this effectiveness depends on specific economic and material circumstances. Furthermore I shall illustrate how any explanation for how or why women themselves collude in this process must take account of subjectivity. In this case, it becomes crucial to understand the particularities of their desire to bear children in the first place.[4] Finally, I shall describe some of the inconsistencies and contradictions felt by these women in relation to these practices and the dogma they support, and how, for some of them, relationships with other mothers could provide possibilities for resistance, enabling them to see development differently and re-evaluate their own positions.

An interview study

It is important to stress from the outset that the women interviewed do not constitute a representative sample in any orthodox sense and that they were originally contacted and interviewed for quite other purposes. I was setting up a longitudinal study of social relationships which may develop between babies of the same age. I wanted to work with pairs of infants who would see each other outside the context of the study. To this end I put an advertisement in two local free weekly newspapers, distributed to every house in Cambridge and the near vicinity. Headed by the caption 'Do babies make friends with other babies?', this advertisement explained that 'a psychologist' in the university wanted to contact mothers of babies, between four months and 2 years of age, who saw another baby of the same age, or within six weeks of the same age, frequently and regularly, with a view to setting up a study on the development of communication between babies. The advertisement stressed that the mother of each baby's 'friend' should also be interested in being involved, and gave an address and telephone number.

The response to this advertisement was staggering. After the eightieth mother (representing eighty pairs and 160 mothers) had written or telephoned within the first few days, I had to explain, regretfully, that the contact phase of the study was now closed. Since I had initially assumed that, given the hegemony of the nuclear family, babies in our culture do not on the whole have the opportunity to 'get to know each other', it became necessary to know what lay behind the phenomenon of infant friendship, or their mothers' interest in this possibility, who these women were, and why they had applied.

I therefore carried out relatively informal but structured

interviews with the first twenty pairs, representing forty mothers, who fulfilled the criteria for the longitudinal study which I intended to carry out with a small sub-group. It was in the context of this interview that what lay behind the phenomenon of 'infant friendship' rapidly became clear. The babies became friends because their mothers had become friends first. Three-quarters of the women interviewed were first-time mothers, many being in their early twenties, but some in their late twenties or early thirties. Alternatively, they tended to be women whose older children were at least of school age, if not adolescents, the baby representing 'a second family'. This was due to the fact that many of the women had met in ante-natal classes, and sought out the contact afterwards. Or else they had met in hospital, or were near neighbours on nodding terms until getting pregnant around the same time drew them together. In very few cases were the mothers close friends before their babies were born. The general story, repeated over and over again, was that there was an initial drawing together through being 'expectant' and 'expecting'; making contact with other pregnant women helped them to locate and understand their own experience. After the birth of the babies, the relationships acquired new functions. Almost invariably the mothers stressed that the first weeks had been much more difficult, much more anxiety-provoking, and much more tiring than they had anticipated. It was in this context that renewing contact with another mother going through similar kinds of things was invaluable. Apparently it was far more reassuring to have another mother say, '*I* don't know what you should do. Isn't it awful?' than any amount of expert reassurance of the sort, 'Never mind, my dear, your anxiety is natural. Some babies are like that.' The discovery that other mothers had similar problems did not, of course, make them disappear. But it enabled them to re-evaluate their own competence. As the babies got older their mothers continued to meet, going shopping together, or spending time in each other's homes, talking about their preoccupations or more tentatively discussing other problems.

This advertisement, then, had reached pairs of women who could be described as being part of a culture of mothers and babies, on their own during the daytime. As might be expected from the way they had been contacted, the women interviewed were predominantly middle-class, judged by husband's occupational status.[5] But this was not entirely so, and very few of the people replying to the advertisement were connected with the university. There were many women living on council estates or in council flats, or in rented accommodation in surrounding villages. With the exception of one Asian woman, all the women interviewed were white. Though one woman was living with a man who was not the child's father, and three women were pregnant before getting married, all were married at the time of interview and regarded themselves as relatively settled. Many families were in the process of buying their first houses. Although money was not plentiful, and several mothers referred to the uncertainty of the job situation and threat of unemployment, they were, on the whole, managing to live reasonably comfortably. At the time of interview only one husband, a lorry driver, was out of work, but was expecting to get employment shortly.

As far as occupations themselves are concerned, amongst the men there were several sales representatives or managers, and many of the men were associated as designers or engineers with a local electrical company. Other occupations included lorry driving, train driving and work for the Post Office. Amongst the women, virtually all of them had been working before their babies were born, either full- or part-time, as secretaries, in clerical or shop work, or in nursing and teaching predominantly. There were also two nursery nurses.

What was striking here was the predominance of traditionally 'female' occupations amongst the women. These are generally taken as being compatible with part-time work, associated with maintaining the full-time job of mothering. Consistent with this, very few of the women were working at the time of interview, and even those who were did so only on a part-time basis. The part-time workers included one academic, who was doing a little teaching for her department and trying to keep her research going. Her child was minded by a neighbour during this time. Another woman returned to her old job, as a personnel officer, on a mornings-only basis, making use of a local day nursery. Otherwise, the paid work consisted of occasional shop work, an evening or so a week working in bars or restaurants, and occasional half-days helping out at their old places of work, or doing bits of typing at home. Equally striking, on being asked specifically about it, few of the women expressed the desire for more work at the moment, although some admitted that they missed the company, doing something different, and the money. Occasionally they referred to the loss of independence. One mother, whose pregnancy was unplanned, had intended to go back to work, with the insurance company where she was a secretary, once she had the baby, but then found she did not want to. The mother whose child was in a day nursery reversed her decision in the opposite direction, in the face of a lot of opposition from her own parents. She had found the first six months at home with the baby extremely difficult and had decided that she was not a 'natural mother', and had been very much happier with the child since returning to work part-time.

Within this group of mothers, this situation was an exception. In most cases, giving up work was consistent with what they had intended before their babies were born, and the majority of conceptions were planned. Where they were not planned, staying home to look after the baby was consistent with what they had 'always thought' about becoming mothers when they grew up. As far as the future is concerned, in virtually all cases, the mothers wanted their children to go to nursery schools before going to school proper. Here they emphasised the need to help them get on with other children and to become more independent. Although there was a general expectation that they would go back to work eventually, this was generally expressed in terms of 'when the children have all gone to school'. Since they were in most cases intending to have more children this was a long way off. Here, too, in speculating they stressed that what work they did would need to be compatible with school hours: 'I wouldn't want them to come home to an empty house.'

The majority of these women, then, had actively decided not to work. Although the conditions of recruitment suggest they may be an unusual sample, it is revealing that, in a current interview study looking at the expectations of adolescent girls, Prendergast and Prout[6] found that the girls interviewed generally assumed that they would give up work in order to look after their children, even if they returned later. Here, this was justified by reference to what has been a dominant orthodoxy on children's needs since the post-war years, one which stresses the importance of mothers' constant contact with their babies as necessary for the latters' emotional development. This normative view of mothers' responsibilities Riley attributes to popularised versions of post-Kleinian psychoanalysis, and in particular to the work of Bowlby and Winnicott.[7] Thus, in giving reasons for not working now, many of these women emphasised their babies' emotional needs – this was 'the time when they needed their mothers most' – illustrating how theories initially based on clinical cases or forms of pathology have contributed to defining the role of the normal mother. But it is important to stress that here statements like this were not expressed as pieces of dogma which could be evaluated and accepted or rejected. Nor was there any indication that such reasons were given solely for my benefit. Rather they were put forward as statements of what the mothers believed themselves. For example, they stressed how they would feel 'awful' leaving their babies, and that they would feel guilty for not doing the right thing by them. Interestingly, several women commented that they did not like the idea of 'handing the baby over to someone else', the implication being not simply that they would be failing their children but that there might be competition for the infants' affections. That is, another caretaker could pose something of a threat. But while these reasons for not leaving their babies may appear negative, the majority of women asserted positive advantages of being at home. Having a baby was something that they had worked for and planned for, and they were determined to get as much as possible out of it. This was expressed in such terms as: 'I feel I want to enjoy them when they're young', 'They grow up so quickly', 'I wouldn't want to miss out', and 'I quite liked my job, but I'm not a career woman.'

By and large, then, these were women for whom children were desirable. The having of them was seen as part of a long-term fantasy of family life in which children were a centrepiece and in which there were considerable pleasures and satisfactions associated with the maternal role. Many stressed the importance of fathers being actively involved, though individual mothers' accounts of fathers' contributions varied from observations like, 'He takes her on the swings at the weekends', to 'He'll do whatever I do, when he's here.' But in practice, given that most fathers were out throughout the day, the major responsibilities for child care fell on the mothers. With very few exceptions, no mother said that she wanted her husband to do more than he already did. Here there were indications that they had found or sensed that the positive gains which they had expected to accompany being mothers could be undermined if their husbands took too much responsibility.

These women, then, had approached motherhood with expectations which were on the whole positive, and in managing child care had reached a state of relative equilibrium with their husbands. At the time of the interview, in my judgment, they were managing to cope reasonably well and their morale was relatively high. This is in contrast to the groups of mothers described by Brown and Harris[8] and Oakley,[9] for example, who have documented a high incidence of depression in young mothers. But this does not mean that these women had no problems. Several referred to periods of weepiness and a feeling of let-down after the birth of the baby, and a few to phases in which they had been relatively severely depressed, though they tended to put that period in the past. Here, discussion of their previous experience and expectations and the support they had received in the early months revealed powerful but contradictory implications of regulatory practices.

Support from family, friends and professionals: producing normal development

Despite their desires to both have children and to become mothers, like mothers interviewed in other relatively contemporary survey studies such as Gavron's[10] and Hubert's,[11] few of the women felt that they had had much experience with babies before they had had their own. Exceptions included women with very much younger brothers and sisters, or whose training and work had brought them into contact with small children and babies. Mrs Davis, for instance, insisted, 'Well I *was* a trained nurse!' Feeling 'ignorant' about it all was a major reason why virtually all the first-time mothers attended ante-natal classes. Most women had found these helpful, in teaching them how to relax, and in preparing them for the birth. But the most important benefit stressed was the opportunity of meeting other women in the same situation, which had of course proved particularly important afterwards. Of the classes themselves, several women complained that, apart from lessons on bathing the baby, everything was geared towards the visit to the hospital. As one mother put it, it was as if that was the bit that mattered rather than being prepared for what to expect at home.

A lack of preparation for what it would be 'really' like was one reason these mothers gave for early difficulties. As previously mentioned, all the first-time mothers were far more anxious and exhausted through the first months than they had anticipated. Here the pain came not only from finding it difficult to cope, but from feeling that they were failing in some way. For instance, Mrs Williams, who had worked for several years as a laboratory technician before having her baby, who had cried a lot and slept badly in the first weeks, said, 'The whole time you think you're failing. Especially, you know, if you've had a job that you've been able to cope with quite competently. You can't believe that a baby – that you can't cope with *that*' (her emphasis). It was then that she went on to talk about the importance of discovering that other people were similarly finding things difficult.

> 'It's only when they get bigger, or when you happen to call on someone and they are in a very bad state, that you realise that other people are going through it too. Because everyone is isolated in their little units. I remember once going to see Sally [whom she had met in ante-natal classes], and she was in exactly the same state. And we had both been locked in our own houses, not believing anybody else could be so bad.'

This contact and mutual discovery provided the basis for their friendship. There were of course potentially many other sources of support besides other mothers. As Gavron[12] found, most of the women interviewed felt that the arrival of the new baby changed their relationship with their own mothers, sometimes substantially. Some referred to feelings of neediness or helplessness and to how they themselves had wanted 'mothering' again in the early weeks. In almost all cases frequency of contact between daughters and mothers had increased on the baby's arrival. This was not without problems, particularly if there were conflicts between these mothers' views on child rearing and their own parents', as I will discuss in the next section. But as far as support was concerned, though some mothers said that they would ring their own mothers over specific worries, especially in the early months, support on a day-to-day basis was only realistic if their parents lived locally.

Here it is relevant to ask what sort of guidance these women could obtain from professionals such as doctors and health visitors. A few mothers said that they had always had 'a very good relationship' with their doctors, which meant that they were not unwilling to approach them over specific problems. More generally, however, unless the baby was obviously ill, or all other channels had been tried, they were loath to contact their doctors specially. They had to rely instead on the routine check-ups at baby clinics and on the fact that, in the course of being asked standard questions about feeding, sleeping, 'any other problems?', and so on, there was an opportunity for raising questions and receiving some advice and/or reassurance.

As to why it was difficult to approach the doctor, it emerged that part of the problem was an unwillingness to 'bother' him or her, especially if the matter turned out to be trivial. For instance, Mrs Cox, an ex-secretary with adolescent children as well as the new baby, commented, 'If I'm concerned I usually ring my mother. I wouldn't go to the doctor over everyday things. I'm never quite sure if I should be going or not. I'd feel a bit of a fool.'

The problem of negotiating the boundary between sickness and health, or in knowing how to define a problem as 'serious' or 'trivial', has been commented on in sociological studies of doctor-patient relationships generally.[13] Here the difficulty was that going to the doctor seemed to presuppose that there were clear symptoms which the mother could specify or articulate, which might indicate a medical problem. The implication of having to accept a medical definition was particularly clear where mothers discussed the difficulties in talking to their doctors about their *own* problems, rather than their babies'. Unless there was something demonstrably wrong, like trouble with stitches after an episiotomy, it was extremely difficult to raise anxieties or worries which they themselves did not understand. As Mrs Williams pointed out, it is very difficult to admit to being unable to cope if it is the feeling of failure at not coping which is what is really unsettling you.

Similar problems arose in relation to health visitors, the most generally accepted source of professional advice for more everyday matters. Here I am thinking of anxieties over several broken nights' sleep in a row, rashes which might indicate 'illness', 'teething' or 'allergies', the baby being sick after feeding, or over whether it was 'time' to move the baby on to this or that. Few were unreservedly positive about health visitors, though some could give examples of where they had been particularly helpful; for instance, in suggesting changes of diet which would stop the baby putting on weight too rapidly. Exceptions included a young woman who had become pregnant unintentionally, and who was living with her husband's parents until very shortly before the baby was born, when the couple were provided with a council flat. She recognised that she had been given special treatment by her health visitor, which she was very ready to accept at that time. Otherwise, the reservations about health visitors again centred on the difficulties of obtaining help if the anxiety or nature of the problem could not be specified. This itself contributed to the sense in which advice or reassurances often felt like platitudes. For instance, as Mrs Daw, a train driver's wife who had given up her work as a clerical assistant, put it, 'Like it all comes out of a book, you know.' Comparatively few women contacted their health visitors outside routine calls or visits to the clinic, and a surprisingly large number of women complained that their health visitors did not 'have children of their own'. The implication intended here was that someone who did not have children could not really understand what they were going through. Whether they were right or wrong about this, they clearly felt that the service they had received was alienating or insufficient. For instance, Mrs Daw, again, talked about difficulties associated with her child's feeding problems.

> 'They haven't got time for you. If you try to say you've got a problem, they'll listen. But they haven't really got time. They're in too much of a hurry. Whether it's because there's too many babies per health visitor or what, I'm not really sure. But they just don't have a very good attitude towards things. I mean – I think if a mother's got problems and is very upset, I used to say *can* you help me, and she would say, there's nothing I can do. I mean, she would listen, but she wouldn't help me think of things to do. So I had to do it on my own. And as I say, I could have done with help really.' (her emphasis)

Health visitors will, of course, vary in how sensitively they do their work. But they do not in general terms provide the individual support and the unique solution which Mrs Daw's comments imply that she is missing. The problem here may at least in part relate to the position of the health visitor within the social regulatory apparatus. From this perspective, one of the health visitor's major responsibilities is to monitor the baby's development and its management with a view to pinpointing problems which may lead to later deviance or pathology. These may be problems in the emotional relationship between the baby and the mother, for example, or the presence of a physical handicap. Under these conditions an apparently 'off-hand' attitude becomes comprehensible. For instance, in the health visitor's terms a particular mother and baby may well be 'doing fine', irrespective of what the mother herself may feel. Moreover, in saying that a particular problem is one which will 'sort itself out', the health visitor may well be attempting to be reassuring, and making an honest statement about the limits of her knowledge. Of course, the pain here is due to the fact that the 'problem' for the mother may not be the presenting difficulty *per se*, but what she feels or thinks about it, and her own sense of helplessness. Similarly, even if it were possible to freely express one's anxieties in an interview with the family doctor, it is not clear that this context can provide a productive way of dealing with them. Being reassured that they are 'natural' and therefore normal, will not, in itself, make them disappear, even if it trivialises them. The alternative of a diagnosis of 'depression' offers little consolation for a sense of failure.

Given the relative lack of contact between these women and their doctors, and the cynicism expressed towards health visitors, one might be led to conclude that these practices concerned with detecting the 'abnormal' and the professional dogma associated with them have little effect, particularly if there are opportunities for relying on other mothers. But this is not so. Firstly, regular check-ups in which the baby's developmental progress is assessed through routine questions and standardised tests contribute to defining the course which development should take, and also what constitutes a problem. Here, the fact that some problems may go unvoiced, or fall through the net, does little for the mother's confidence or sense of adequacy. Secondly, the focus of these practices is almost entirely on the baby, or the mother in relation to the baby; her independent status as a woman is discounted. As I have indicated, the implications of this are particularly clear when women attempt to raise anxieties about themselves. These are either pathologised, or evoke reassurances which feel empty. It also means that the mother is likely to defend herself against this anxiety by acting in whatever ways are necessary to ensure that at least the child's development conforms to the norm. It is not surprising, for instance, that tangible evidence that the baby is developing satisfactorily could provide considerable reassurance, not only about the baby but about the mother's own competence. As I shall illustrate later, the counterside of this, of course, is that slow or aberrant development is the mother's own fault. Here some mothers noted that their health visitors were likely to make these assumptions explicit. For example, Mrs Robbins, an ex-secretary married to a solicitor, explained why she was loath to contact her health visitor by stressing that the latter had said to her, 'I know *you're* all right.' The implication here is that there are other mothers, and other families, who are not 'all right' and that Mrs Robbins knows about them. For her, then, to contact her health visitor would mean that she herself was a 'problem' case.

These normalising apparatuses, then, may not only help define what constitutes the developmental norm and the role of the mother as central to producing this. They also invoke or invite comparisons between individual children and mothers and between social groups. For instance, a woman may become motivated to define herself in opposition to the 'problem family' or the 'depressed mother'. But such effects are not independent of material circumstances and other sources of expectation and aspiration. Moreover, here their functioning already presupposed that these women were concerned to do their best for their babies. I have already illustrated that they both regarded children as desirable and held particular expectations about the maternal role. Probing these in greater depth, these mothers' accounts indicated substantial shifts in emphasis compared with what they knew or remembered of their own parents' practices and beliefs. The impact of developmental psychology was particularly evident here, and again this hinged on particular notions of normal development.

On being involved with the baby: some differences across generations

Despite their professed ignorance or lack of experience, all the women revealed long-standing ideas about the responsibilities of mothers, even if these were not clearly articulated. For instance, 'doing one's best' by the baby seems to presuppose the belief that what one does has some effect. All the first-time mothers were adamant that what parents do 'makes a difference' to children's development. Interestingly, the six mothers whose older children were at school or approaching adolescence tended to be far less certain. This uncertainty seemed to have come through having learned that 'you have to work something out with the child', 'they're all different', and 'you can't predict'. But it also reflected the sense in which the world outside the family was felt to be outside the parents' control. For example, some mothers pointed to the 'dangers' of influence from other children, or to the fact that 'teenagers are exploited nowadays'. Alternatively the answer might reflect the incomprehensibility of the process of growing up, or a resigned acceptance of their own limitations and lack of power. More generally, the specific nature of what these women were trying to achieve and how they saw their own contributions was particularly apparent in responses to a question which I put to all the mothers: Did they think the ways in which they were bringing up their child or children were similar to or different from the ways in which they had been brought up? This question generally interested or intrigued these women. As one of them put it, 'It's the eternal question, isn't it?' In some cases it was not something that they had thought about before. In other cases, they had had to confront it directly, in the face of criticism from their own parents, or in order to assert that they wanted to do something differently. But there was a surprising degree of generality in the differences that were stressed. The principal difference asserted was that mothers nowadays, or parents generally, 'spend far more time with their children than they used to'.

Here, of course, they were referring to their own lives and priorities. But in so far as they were also reflecting on other mothers they knew, again their assumption that 'more time' is spent with children nowadays may in fact be correct. American evidence, for instance, suggests that, despite the availability of labour-saving devices and decrease in family size over the last half-century, the total time spent on domestic tasks has remained stable, but that an increasing proportion of this time has been spent on child care rather than on cooking and cleaning.[14] Land[15] suggests that since the war a similar pattern has emerged in this country. A number of observations given by these women were directly congruent with this evidence. For instance, references to the availability of household appliances which made housework easier, such as 'my mother never had a washing machine', were used to support the assumption of 'more time with the baby nowadays'. Alternatively differences in material circumstances might be emphasised. For example, Mrs Jones, a secretary, explained the implications of the fact that her parents did not have a house of their own. 'They were living with his parents; so I think she had to keep us out of the way a bit.'

It does not, of course, necessarily follow that having more time or more space should imply a greater involvement with the baby. But sometimes these constraints on their own mothers' availability were used to explain differences between the mothers and themselves, which might otherwise indicate failure on the part of their own mothers. For example, Mrs Light, a teacher who had also worked in a day nursery, and who had worked for several years before having Anna, now seventeen months, reconstructed her own early childhood years:

> 'I think when I was this age [seventeen months], my mother had a much more difficult situation because she had me in the first year of her marriage and she was living at home, looking after her father and brother because her mother had died. So she had three men all doing shift work and me as a baby. I think she had a pretty tough time, actually. I think she did have a pretty good neighbour who used to help. And I think I was a pretty demanding baby. Used to cry a lot. *That was probably because she was tired out and over-anxious I should think*. I think anyone would be in that sort of situation.' (my emphasis)

The implication here was that her own crying as a baby was due to her mother's non-availability. This is an expression of maternal culpability which we have come to associate with the influences of psychoanalytic ideas on infants' emotional needs since the war, as mentioned previously. Mrs Light goes on to illustrate what she takes to be more general differences in 'attitudes' to things, pointing to specific changes in child care practices since her mother's time.

> 'She had me potty trained when I wasn't much bigger than Anna. I know she sort of thinks I should be putting Anna on the potty regularly, things like that. . . . When

> she [Anna] was little I couldn't bear to leave her to cry. But my mother said, you know, leave her. It's only *natural* for babies to cry. But I always felt I couldn't. Although I must admit I gave in in the night, but that wasn't anything to do with my mother. It was only because the doctor suggested it – I would never have naturally left her to scream. It seems cruel.' (her emphasis)

The appeal to what is 'natural' to support two opposing courses of action, leaving the baby and not leaving the baby, is interesting, as is her reliance on the sanction of the doctor to whom, as she had told me earlier in the interview, she had gone for advice about Anna's sleeping problems after being turned off by her health visitor's 'casual' attitude. She was one of the mothers who stressed a 'good relationship' with her doctor. Though most women felt that fashions had changed, some of the middle-class women could pinpoint changes in orthodoxy more precisely. Here they signalled in particular a shift away from rigid disciplinary strategies. For instance, 'There was that man, who was it, Truby King? My mother was telling me', 'It was routines and regimes everywhere, playpens and straps', and 'It was all, put them in the pram and shove them down the garden.'

These comments reflect changes in dominant orthodoxies presented in child care literature since the post-war years, a change which the Newsons have discussed in terms of a move from medical hygienism to greater permissiveness.[16] In some cases, the women interviewed seemed to have become aware of shifts in emphasis through their professional training as teachers or child care workers. In other cases it reflected conversations with their own mothers which had arisen as they confronted differences in what their daughters were doing, conversations which were often emotionally complex.[17] But as far as current orthodoxies were concerned, Mrs Barker, a teacher, explained the situation thus: 'I think we want to be more *involved* in our children's development. We want to see it more. And of course, we're so much more theoretical about it all than they were. They were so much more instinctive about it really' (her emphasis).

The question now is, what did this involvement consist of? In terms of the actual practices which contributed to being 'more involved' here what was particularly stressed was the idea that, compared to their own mothers, mothers nowadays spent more time 'playing with' their children. In this sample, this emphasis on play ran across all social classes. It was justified in terms of both getting something out of the process of mothering, for themselves, and the presumed benefits for the child. These were more or less explicitly articulated in such terms as, 'It helps them learn things', 'It's the quality of attention you give them, isn't it? I mean it's not just a question of being around all day', 'It's what they need at this stage, lots of one-to-one attention' and 'The more you put in, the more you get out – I feel I'll reap the benefits later.' Second, perhaps, to questions of responses to crying, playing with the baby was the area in which most differences to their own mothers were articulated. Mrs Light, for instance; said, 'I think they were more ladylike in those days. I can't imagine, you know, I don't think people in those days *did* sit down on the floor with their children with bricks and things' (her emphasis).

Mrs Cox compared her mother and herself like this: 'My mother wouldn't have had the idea that playing with the baby makes any difference, really. She never played with me. She would occasionally do a puzzle, play with cards or ludo. But they were more grand occasions. Something that happened occasionally.'

Thus, spending more time with the baby implied giving him or her more attention, the medium for which was play. Where has this idea come from, and how has it attained a purchase on what these mothers feel they should do? The importance of children's play is not, of course, a new idea. It is associated in particular with the child study movement of the end of the last century,[18] the Montessori movement, and more recently, as learning through action, and it has contributed to the adoption of Piagetian theory into primary school practice. The idea that play is the child's own mode of expression and discovery seems to emphasise the child's engagement independent of adult support. But as Steedman[19] and Walkerdine[20] have both pointed out, although the teacher does not instruct, she is not inattentive. Indeed, primary school teaching practice has itself been influenced by the psychoanalyst Winnicott's[21] idea that one of the functions of the 'good enough mother' is to be available to provide a place of safety for the child's creativity to unfold through the process of play itself.

The fact that a theory of mothering has been incorporated into teacher practice may partially account for the interchange of ideas from teaching to mothering, a process which is explored in Clarke's and Walkerdine's chapters in this book. But these mothers' comments imply a much more active role, on their part, in structuring the child's activities as well as simply being available. It was not, after all, simply a matter of being around all day. The source of this emphasis, I suggest, is to be found in developmental psychology of the 1960s and early 1970s and the social conditions in which it was produced. This demonstrated, firstly, the importance of environmental enrichment to institutionalised children.[22] This emphasis went beyond the assertion that more attention should be given to such children by caretakers, an emphasis which was a liberal response to Bowlby's and others' claims as to the devastating effects of early separation.[23] Rather, using assumptions originally derived from Piaget, it was argued that the characteristic retardation in cognitive development found in institutionalised infants could also be prevented by harnessing their 'intrinsic motivation', through using mobiles and so forth, to increase their opportunities for learning through action.[24] The idea that it was possible to prevent cognitive retardation, seen in terms of progress through Piagetian stages and standard developmental norms, by intervening early became central to the headstart and poverty action programmes which flourished, in particular, in America.[25] Now, however, the aim was not, simply, to promote infants' intrinsic motivation, but to forge a bridge between correlations taken to indicate a link between impoverished homes and lack of parental involvement, and poor school performance and high drop-out rates. The method was to harness or direct the talent of mothers. The rationale for this was originally based on differences produced in laboratory studies, which were read as lack of 'child-centredness' or 'attunement to the child' on the part of working-class mothers.[26] Though the artificiality of these experiments has since been criticised, this has not counteracted a continuing outgrowth of studies of mother-infant interaction which seek to pin down the contribution of the normal mother to her baby's cognitive development.[27] This has led to the reification of certain parenting skills involved in promoting learning through play, a process which, perhaps more aptly than he realises, the psychologist Bruner has described as 'scaffolding'.[28]

The idea that the normal mother can function as a 'tutor' or pedagogue is so central to many contemporary intervention programmes with socially disadvantaged children that it is not surprising that, even in cases where the mothers emphasised similarities rather than differences between themselves and their own mothers, in cases where their mothers had been particularly supportive, for instance, the educative role of the mother should emerge in answers they gave to other questions in the interview. For example, all the mothers were asked about any favourite toys their babies might have, and about the rationale behind choosing particular toys for them. Here, again running across all social classes, there was an emphasis on toys that would not only give pleasure, but would be educational. Moreover, the notion of 'educational' was linked not, simply, to preparation for school but to the idea that there is a normal sequence which defines what the child would and should be ready for, and when. Thus, the mothers stressed that they would choose toys which were appropriate to their babies' particular developmental stages. The word 'stimulate' occurred frequently, even in working-class mothers, and was assimilated to broader values and priorities. Like mother love, 'I believe in it.'

These answers suggest the impact of developmental psychology not only on how these women saw their children's development but also on how they thought they should spend their time with their babies. They also illustrate how knowledge originally produced with the aim of intervening within a disadvantaged group has contributed to general orthodoxies. But it might be argued that here the mothers were particularly constrained by the fact that they knew that I was a psychologist, such that they gave me answers that they presumed that I wanted to hear, to reflect some accepted definition of good motherhood. But while the source of this definition would itself be interesting – how, for instance, would they know what I wanted to hear? – several mothers themselves pointed out to me that nowadays toys for babies and pre-school children frequently have the 'appropriate' ages marked on the boxes, indicating what the baby was 'supposed' to be ready for, and that shops like Mothercare organise their displays accordingly. The equation between play and education is further demonstrated locally through the presence of a branch of 'The Early Learning Centre' in Cambridge, a toyshop which stocks toys largely designed for the under-5s who are generally either at 'playschool' or at home with their mothers.

It is still important to consider how these women may have come by these ideas. On being asked about this, the women were in fact fairly vague. For example, there were frequent references to 'it's all around you'. On the other hand many of the teachers and nursery nurses acknowledged the influence of both their work experience and their training. They also suggested the influence of television – 'There are ideas you pick up from the telly, you know' – and magazine articles and colour supplements – 'Things you've read, casually, sometime, you forget it, but it perhaps comes out later.' There were also, of course, child care books.

In the next section I examine in some detail publications which these women used or referred to. Here the influence of developmental psychology is particularly evident and the notion of normal development is presented explicitly. As I shall show, this implicitly reinforces the impact of regulatory practices and at the same time constructs the normal mother.

Child care books

Apart from attending ante-natal classes, many of the first-time mothers read books on pregnancy and childbirth. They felt the need to 'understand everything that was happening to me'. Here the most popular book was Gordon Bourne's *Pregnancy*. In many cases this was read over and over again as 'thoroughly sensible'. It does indeed give an account of what may happen to them through the various 'stages' of pregnancy, pinpointing in a fairly reassuring fashion possible points at which things may go wrong. For these women, the positive value was that it went over things that they had not understood or there had not been time to grasp at the ante-natal check-up with their doctors, and answered some of the questions which they did not know how to ask.

Of literature on child care itself, many women mentioned the pamphlet given out routinely at the hospital after the birth. Prepared by doctors, it includes information about what little babies can be expected to do as well as guidelines on feeding, sleeping and weight gains, and on how to establish a settled routine. Though the tone reflects that it is written from a position of authority, it aims to be reassuring, emphasising the need for mothers to find their own way and the considerable variation in what is normal in babies. If in doubt, consult your doctor. Nevertheless, despite an acknowledgment of variability, the final page includes a table of behavioural items, age-linked, of the sort that go into developmental tests. Here the assumption is that parents, too, can be actively involved in early detection. Some mothers had kept this pamphlet and gained considerable pleasure from checking off items as their babies passed. This procedure was not entirely unproblematic, as I shall show later.

Otherwise, most of the first-time mothers had one or more books which at some time they had consulted regularly, and sometimes read several times over. The mothers with older children were more inclined to rely on working things out, or on what they had already learned. They also had less time. Although Mrs Cox, for instance, had 'always meant to get a book', 'somehow I've never got around to it.' There was a striking similarity in the books which the mothers had bought or had been given. Although there were a few sheepish or embarrassed references to 'Dr Spock',[29] the most popular were Hugh Jolly's *Book of Child Care*, Penelope Leach's *Baby and Child* and the St Michael *Complete Book of Babycare*, sold through Marks and Spencer. No mother had only Dr Spock or Hugh Jolly; they seemed to feel the need to supplement the book by 'a doctor' with something 'more general'. Mrs Walker, the academic, for instance, suggested that her two books were 'good antidotes to each other'.

These particular books are amongst the most popular on the market, and a preliminary survey suggests that they reflect changes in the way in which advice has been presented over the last twenty years or so, over which time there appears to have been a greater input from psychology and a greater emphasis on mothers as part of a consumer market. Though the contributions to the St Michael *Complete Book of Babycare* are largely written by doctors, the editor, Barbara Nash, was formerly associated with *Mother* magazine, under the auspices of which the collection was originally published in hardback. The popularity of the book is no doubt related to its glossy packaging and copious illustrations, which depict romantic images of mothers and babies and happy couples; they play precisely on the desirability of motherhood.

Despite variations in presentation, as I shall show, there are many similarities in the content of these books. As to why these women read them, they were occasionally consulted over particular problems, though the general tendency here was to rely on consulting parents or friends. Some women would 'read ahead' in order to think about how to move on to potty training, and so on. But more generally, they chiefly functioned as a check for themselves that their babies were doing the right thing. For instance, Mrs Smith put it as follows:

> 'I found even the pamphlet they gave you at the hospital helpful. I was reading it again and again. It helps just to put your mind at rest. I think you just need something to reassure yourself. Then I found the Penelope Leach book which I think is excellent. I like reading it. I like reading books about babies anyway. But I think if there's no one around, like mother or somebody, as in my case, you need something. I need something, anyhow.'

Similarly, Mrs Taplow, the personnel manager who had returned to work part-time:

> 'Apart from the ante-natal classes, which were preparation for birth, really, the only thing I'd got to prepare myself for motherhood was Penelope Leach.

> You read that from cover to cover. Now I look at it to see that Carol [her child] is developing at the appropriate – well. It's all I've got to go on is what Penelope says. According to her she's doing things in advance of her age and I look to see what the next development thing is. And really to keep an eye on her development. That things are going the way they should be. It's all I've got to go on.'

Given these particular women's investments in having children and becoming mothers and the terms in which they have described differences between their own upbringing and current aims and practices, in examining these books it is immediately obvious why they have such appeal. In many ways they provide, on the one hand, just what the mothers wanted to hear on the importance of the early years and the parents' contribution. For instance, Hugh Jolly[30] introduces his book in these terms:

> If we were 'mothered' well by our parents we have at least a head start on those whose intellect is the same but whose childhood experiences were less happy. The early years of life are the most vital in laying down an individual's future pattern, both as regards whether he [sic] achieves his full intellectual potential and whether he is sufficiently secure and well rounded as a personality. Since these early years are so vital, is there any need to argue the need for child upbringing to be a subject of study, in books and other media, for all parents?

He goes on to emphasise, as do the other books, the considerable amount of knowledge which is now available to us, such that 'Today's parents are probably better at bringing up their children than any previous generation. They are more aware of the importance of the early years and, knowing this, they are more concerned not to make mistakes!'[31]

But despite this onus of responsibility, the message is none the less that being a parent is one of the most fulfilling experiences that life has to offer. As the St Michael book puts it,

> What may be learned in these pages will, in our view, help to prepare every parent for what is, after all, the most important and most fulfilling role offered to any human being – that of being mother or father and therefore responsible for the physical, mental and emotional and spiritual development of a brand new human being.[32]

Now in spite of this reassurance, there is no denial of the fact that mothers may experience considerable problems and anxieties. But here, the message is that learning about babies' development, and being prepared for what will happen next, will lead to greater understanding, and greater freedom from anxiety. It will also lead to greater rewards in becoming parents. For example, drawing on psychological knowledge, Hugh Jolly asserts that learning to understand the baby's behaviour in terms of developing skills and personality will enable 'today's parents' to get away from mechanical explanations, to escape the rigid rules of earlier generations. Penelope Leach's style is less obviously didactic. Having discussed the problem of 'sexist language', speaking as a 'mother' rather than a 'family doctor', she nevertheless appeals to similar principles:

> The more you can understand her [the child] and recognise her present position on the developmental map that directs her towards being a person, the more interesting you will find her. The more interesting she is to you the more attention she will get from you and the more attention she gets the more she will give you back.[33]

What these books offer, as suggested in the mothers' own explanations, is a considerable amount of information not only on generally defined 'problem areas', but also on the 'stages' of normal development or the kinds of behaviour which children of different ages can typically be expected to show, whether in motor development, in play with objects, in language, or in 'making friends'. Coupled with this are exhortations on the importance of 'stimulation' and 'attention', and of doing things with your baby. There is advice on how to choose age-graded toys, and how to play with the baby in age-appropriate ways. From Penelope Leach there are suggestions as to how to get over your problems with playing with your child. Hugh Jolly adds to his Preface to the third and most recent edition of his book, 'I have also enlarged the chapter on play since I am now aware that many parents are worried because their toddlers or older children won't play without them. I have explained why this behaviour is normal.'[34] There are strictures against playpens as impediments to natural curiosity,[35] and perhaps unsurprisingly, St Michael has found it necessary to include a whole section on how to avoid 'overstimulation'.[36]

The congruence between the content and orientation of these books and what the mothers said about their own aims and views on how things have changed is clear. The obvious explanation for this would be that the books were the source of these beliefs and ideas. But this relationship is not a simple one. There was no necessary correspondence between the books used by particular mothers and the examples they gave, for instance, and indeed some of those who were most vehement on the nature of changes and the importance of 'being with' the child were ones who had not used any particular books at all.

Rather, I suggest the popularity of these books related to the fact that they appealed to fantasies or feelings which these women had already experienced, and were congruent with ideas which they already held, however ill-informed. Firstly, given these women's desires for children, and the expectation that child rearing will enhance their own sense of completeness and productivity, the message that this is, 'after all, the most important and most fulfilling role offered to any human being' is precisely what they want to hear. Secondly, through ante-natal classes, routine check-ups and later checks on the babies' development, they were already prepared to think of their babies' development in terms of relative progress through or deviation from a universal norm, for which they might take credit or feel responsible. The disenchantment or disappointment they may have felt with doctors or health visitors does not detract from this. Rather, for the relatively well-educated mother it becomes even more important that she herself should understand and have access to the wisdom of child development.

These mothers, then, could find themselves in the text, which at the same time provided criteria through which their babies' normality could be made explicit. Given the expressed need for reassurance, the evident pleasure gained from seeing or anticipating the 'next stage', and the mothers' investment in contributing to this progress, one might stress positive advantages of publications like these, especially since they apparently free mothers from the need for expert guidance. But, in the first place, it is still the same body of specialised knowledge which sets the terms of development. Secondly, these terms themselves are not unproblematic. The notion of 'normal' development is based on what children everywhere can be expected to do at around the same age. Paradoxically, it does not apparently entail anything in addition to what anyone could see if they looked at children around them; anyone can see, for instance, that children generally begin to crawl and walk somewhere around the end of the first year or the beginning of the second. Indeed the development of infant tests and developmental norms appears as a particularly clear example of the translation of 'what everybody knows' into scientific opinion. But although the process seems innocuous, in the process of producing stages of development not only are aspects of development reified and others occluded[37] but the production of the 'norm' through which individuals are assessed in relation to a population implicitly invokes comparisons. One baby is implicitly compared with other babies, and one mother with the next. Of course the process of comparison, whether it is between one's own baby and other babies or his or her place on the development chart, can engender considerable pleasure and pride if the child is advanced. If the opposite is the case, the mother is likely to feel considerable anxiety and guilt. And here a reminder that there are variations in what is 'normal' will not necessarily reduce anxiety if this message is at the same time coupled with a stress on the important role played by the parents.

It is not surprising, then, that even women who had stressed the value of these publications could have problems using them. Mrs Freeman, for instance, a young woman who had been doing clerical work before getting pregnant and getting married, describes how she eventually went to the doctor because she was worried that her baby was 'a bit slow to sit up'. 'I didn't exactly think there was anything wrong with him. But I kept thinking there was something I should be doing that I wasn't doing. That it must be my fault. I think it was that that was worrying me, really.'

Given the emphasis on the importance of 'stimulation', it is hard to see how the conclusion that the mother is responsible can be avoided. This emphasis on stimulation was not, of course, without problems in itself, particularly for those mothers who 'understood' its importance, but who nevertheless found it difficult or tedious to play with the baby. For instance, Mrs Cox:

> 'Sometimes it bothers me a bit that I'm not doing enough. I'm sure I didn't play with Shirley enough, being my first one. . . . I mean, just have her up when she's awake. Play with her with bricks and puzzles and things. Some mums do seem to *enjoy* sitting down and playing and doing things with the children and not worrying about whether the housework gets done. Where I'm more inclined – I hope I don't put the housework first. But I like to be reasonably straight *before* we start playing. . . . I think other mums *enjoy* it! Perhaps that's said to ease my guilty conscience. I don't know.' (her emphasis)

By invoking comparisons between babies, and by emphasising the parents' contribution, these publications are, of course, at the same time inviting comparisons of parenting skills. They are thus helping to produce a normative account of the parental function, the effects of which are perhaps all the more subtle because of the way in which they appear to bypass the role of the expert.

But there is more to constructing the mother than simply emphasising the normal course of the baby's development and the mother's role in promoting it. The previous discussion of contacts with doctors showed how difficult it was for the mothers to raise anxieties about themselves as women, as opposed to women defined in relation to their children. This conflation is equally apparent in the child care literature. It thus reproduces the asymmetry of the mother-doctor or mother-health visitor relation which at first it appears to circumvent. It is achieved through an emphasis on child-centredness which collapses the needs of the mother and the baby, such that the former are totally written out. The two, as it were, become one. This results in a compelling but in fact completely illogical conclusion, as is epitomised in Penelope Leach's advice on how to deal with one's own conflicts and anxieties as a mother. Again the message is, learn to understand the baby:

> So taking the baby's point of view does not mean neglecting your, her parents', viewpoint. *Your interests and hers are identical.* You are all on the same side; the side that wants to be happy, to have fun. If you make happiness for her, she will make happiness for you. If she is unhappy, you will find yourselves unhappy as well, however much you want or intend to keep your feelings separate from hers. . . . This book . . . will not suggest that you do things 'by the book' but rather that you do them, always, 'by the baby'. (my emphasis)[38]

The only way in which one can argue that the needs of the mother and baby are 'identical', of course, is by totally discounting the needs of the mother as an independent person altogether.

But nowhere is the discounting of the mother as a person in her own right more apparent than in discussions of mothers working outside the home. The inclusion of this as an issue for discussion in child care books reflects the extent to which this is generally regarded as a problematic or contentious area, as the comments of the mothers interviewed implied. Here the aim of the discussion appears to be to reveal how incompatible is working outside the home with the view of mothering which this literature is intending to present. Penelope Leach, for instance, aims to deal with this problem by demonstrating the value or importance of mothering as 'work', and begins in an apparently comforting way, with a discussion of the bind of guilt, described as 'the most destructive of all emotions'.[39] But the solution which is then offered, however, is to listen hard to the *baby's* signals indicating need: 'whatever you are doing, however you are coping, if you listen to your child and to your feelings, there will be something you can actually *do* to make things right' (her emphasis).[40] Thus, listening to the baby is not only supposed to clarify what the mother should do, but it also gives the erroneous impression that this will somehow make the mother's guilt disappear too. From here, Leach goes on to illustrate the value or importance of mothering as 'work'. Child-centredness, it is admitted, imposes constraints. But mothers' priorities none the less are made indubitably clear:

> Bringing up a child in this flexible, thoughtful way takes time and effort. It involves extremely hard work as well as high rewards. But what worthwhile and creative job does not? Bringing up a child is one of the most creative, most worthwhile and most undervalued of all jobs.[41]

Like Leach, St Michael[42] similarly asserts the value of mothering as a worthwhile job of work. Opening a section entitled 'Working mothers' with a subtitle in the form of a question, 'Do you need to work?' it goes on:

> There is a saying: 'If you educate a man you educate a person, but if you educate a woman you educate a family'. All babycare and childcare experts know that this is true and that a child needs his [sic] mother because, however incompetent she may believe she is, she is her child's first teacher. Sadly there is an idea in circulation at the moment that to be a mother is to be a second rate citizen; that worthwhile work and opportunities to use education and talent only exist outside the home, away from the family. Nothing, however, is further from the truth. The better educated and more talented the mother, the more fortunate the child.

There is here an implicit appeal to the idea of the mother as a 'natural' teacher on the one hand, and the idea that she may need training on the other. From here St Michael thus proceeds to construct the mother's work, through the image of the child-centred mother as pedagogue,[43] the image which many of these mothers were putting forward themselves.

> A mother who appreciates that her child has five senses and a mind that needs stimulation, and who makes a point of showing and naming everything for him [sic], speaking to him, singing to him, reading to him and generally teaching him and bringing the world to him while he cannot go to the world, is performing the most marvellous and worthwhile job life has to offer. *Such babies become the brightest and most alert.* (my emphasis)

Here the language of enrichment programmes and early intervention has been used to produce an account of normal mothering which precludes the possibility of work outside the home, an effect which may be all the more pernicious because the literature appears so innocuous. For any woman in doubt about whether she wants to or should attempt to work, such a message may be hard to resist. For most of the women here, this was not yet an issue: they had already decided to be at home, even though in practice some found that they missed work in many ways. Again, I suggest the appeal and power of these books is that they reinforce or perpetuate fantasies which women may already hold. By providing reassurance, knowledge and practical suggestions, and by constantly stressing the rewards, they present the view that not only is mothering a desirable and worthwhile job of work, but one in which it should be possible to be thoroughly satisfied and fulfilled. By implication a woman who does not find this has failed to grasp how it should be done. At the same time, the account precludes particular options or alternatives for women which might, for example, increase their relative independence and their economic power within the family and outside of it. In this sense the construction of the normal mother feeds into and perpetuates the values and constraints of the traditional nuclear family.

Concluding discussion: some positions of contradiction

In this chapter I have aimed to illustrate how particular ideas from developmental psychology have entered into the constitution of contemporary motherhood, affecting not only orthodoxies on what should be done, but what women may actually believe. To the emphasis on mothers as central to the completion of infants' emotional needs, which we have come to associate with normative appropriations of psychoanalysis such as Bowlby's work, we now have an orthodoxy which stresses mothers' contribution to infants' intellectual and social development as well. I have suggested that this orthodoxy is not only prescribed through regulatory apparatuses such as those which operate through medicine and social welfare, but also through child care literature which women read of their own volition. In both cases they have effects in the constitution of motherhood, firstly, by prioritising a sequence of stages in 'normal' development, to which the mother's contribution is, in fact, ambiguous, and secondly, by linking this to an emphasis on the importance of stimulation and enrichment provided by her. The impenetrability of the account rests heavily on the ways in which the needs of the mother, her independent interests, her conflicts in defining her own priorities are rendered inaccessible through the emphasis on child-centredness, which itself is reinforced through practices which view the health of women as mothers or potential mothers rather than as women.

The emphasis on pedagogic aspects of mothering is, of course, not new, as is demonstrated in several chapters in this book. Here, I have suggested that the source of the contemporary emphasis is the notion of environmental enrichment which flourished in the 1960s and 1970s, which is itself inextricably tied to notions of social and maternal deprivation and the prevention of social deviance. Now, perhaps, it is entering the priorities of the general population. Given the political climate of the 1980s one must find this alarming. Not only does the emphasis on child-centredness reinforce the notion that women's place is in the home, but if mothers are accepted as children's first teachers, it becomes relatively easy to develop this into an argument for, for instance, a reduction in nursery school placements, thus perpetuating the subjugation of women as mothers further.

However I have stressed that normalising effects such as these should not be understood as being imposed on women as if they play no active part. Moreover in using the interview material it is again important to emphasise that I was working with a sample who, by definition, were likely to find their babies' development interesting. They were also coping relatively well emotionally and, on the whole, living in relatively stable economic and familial circumstances. Indeed, it may well be that the child-centred approach espoused by Penelope Leach, for example, can only gain hold or purchase where there is some minimum level of material security. For instance. Booth[44] has vividly described the cynicism and disillusionment evoked in working-class mothers living in extreme poverty in Glasgow as the result of an intervention programme which gave central importance to 'teaching' mothers how to 'play' with their children.

With respect to the women interviewed here, I have suggested that the power of the normalising apparatus is achieved not through a simple coercion but through more subtle ways in which it pulls on desires and fantasies which women already hold. These themselves are related to how they have come to see the world and their own position. But even though these women had chosen not to work, it was not the case that the attempt to conform to the normalised image of motherhood presented no conflicts or contradictions for them. It was, after all, the recognition of their own needs, or the discovery that something had been discounted, which drew them together in the first place. Furthermore the particular practical solution to the problems of being a mother at home which these women had found was at least taking them out of their houses. In this study I had come into contact with a contemporary form of neighbourhood sharing in which to some extent the women were transcending familial boundaries.[45] That is, in spending time with each other, their patterns of child care were cutting across what have been assumed to be the usual methods, in which babies are either looked after at home *en famille* or at a child minder's or nursery. While it may be that forms of sharing and companionship have always been fundamental to coping with motherhood, here it is important to ask, whether these social relations with other mothers provided these women with a basis for viewing their own situations differently, and what this implied for the notion of normal development?

Given this emphasis on inter-generational differences, discussed previously, it is not surprising to find that these women stressed that relationships with other mothers were as important, if not more important, than their own parents in influencing or crystallising their own priorities. As one mother put it, 'you sort of *compare* yourself.' Here some mothers give examples of how they had attempted to emulate other mothers whom they admired. Alternatively, they could also identify how reactions of the sort, 'I wouldn't let my child do that', crystallised their own beliefs, making them conscious of their own assumptions. Here, three women, a teacher, a nursery nurse and a secretary in an insurance firm used references of the sort, 'I've seen the sort of damage it can do', to point explicitly to the clear consequences for children of being 'deprived' at home, thus defining themselves by opposition.

Given the emphasis on comparison, unsurprisingly friendships with other women were not without problems. For instance, some women referred to differences of opinion which they tended to keep quiet about in order to avoid overt friction. In many cases, too, contact with other mothers was kept sharply divided from family life, which remained the priority. The women would meet between the hours of 9 and 4, when their husbands were at work, and before it was time to prepare the evening meal. They did not meet in the evenings or at weekends. Rather, the friendships helped to sustain them through the day time, the supportive network making a difficult job relatively pleasurable, or an impossible job possible.

In such cases, the friendships helped to maintain, rather than challenge, the women's position in the home and their function in the family. However, in other cases more intimate friendships enabled individual women to gain the confidence for greater independence, or at least to challenge a particular ideal of family life. Here, for instance, several women referred to their 'husband's idea' that theirs would not be a 'proper family' if they were not at home looking after the children, ready to look after their husbands when they returned. Mrs Carter, a young woman, newly married, who had done 'all sorts of jobs' on leaving school, put her struggle with her husband like this:

> 'It means a lot to him, this idea of the family. He thinks I should be happy to be at home all day, looking after her [the baby] and waiting for him. Whereas I can't survive like that. I know I'll want to be doing something different with my life, though I don't know what.'

Now, after more contact with other mothers, she acknowledged the importance of at least being able to begin to talk about this.

More generally, the talk with other mothers enabled some women to discover that their own feelings of ambivalence about their situations, and towards their babies, were not so peculiar or abnormal as they feared. For instance, it was through talking to other mothers that Mrs Taplow came to the conclusion that 'maternal instinct' was a myth. She commented facetiously on what a relief it was to discover that she was not alone in being rendered nauseous by the smell of babies' dirty nappies, and gained the confidence to discount Penelope Leach on the issue of returning to work. Unsurprisingly, the changes in perspective on their own situation were generally less radical than this. Nevertheless, it was clearly a major factor contributing to the relatively high morale, enabling many women to adopt a cheerful cynicism. This was reflected in bits of advice which I had asked all of them to give to an imaginary prospective mother. 'Get yourself a baby carrier and get out of the house', 'Remember that you matter too', 'Find someone you can drop in on for cups of tea' and 'Two against two is an awful lot better than one against one!'

As far as the mothers' ideas about development were concerned, again regular meetings with another baby of the same age were not without problems. Comparisons between how each of them was doing seemed inevitable to many women and had to be handled sensitively. Either 'you keep quiet when your baby does something new even though you're pleased about it, or the mothers would reassure each other, if one baby was fast in one thing, the chances are he or she would be slow in something else.

But there are other possibilities, apart from overt or covert competition and reassurance. Some mothers found ways of confronting the problem more directly. Here more open discussion of differences in rate and changes in which baby was in front could reveal inconsistencies or contradictions in the notion of normal development and the role of the mother in promoting it. This contradiction was well expressed by Mrs Eliot, who eventually participated in the longitudinal study.

> 'You know all these "stages" of development, that children are all supposed to go through? Well I've been thinking. If children everywhere are all supposed to do the same things at round about the same ages, what difference does it make, anyway, *what* I do?!'

Mrs Eliot's friendship thus helped her to crack the normative image presented in the child care literature. More generally, these mothers' comments suggest that, on the one hand, this kind of supportive network may, for some women, help to cement rather than confront their emotional investments in the traditional family. On the other hand, there are indications that patterns of child care evolving as practical solutions to problems of child care for mothers at home can generate a re-evaluation of the position of women as mothers, and new ways of seeing babies' development. In either case it is imperative to write in this aspect of women's contemporary history and experience and to move at the same time towards alternative accounts of the construction of motherhood. This perhaps should take as a starting point the production of desire for children in its historical specificity, and must include an analysis of processes which promote or militate against women's relations with other women.

Acknowledgment

The research described here was supported financially by the Margaret Lowenfeld Trust. I am particularly indebted to Dina Lew for help with collating data.

Notes

1 J. Donzelot, *The Policing of Families.*
2 The thesis of normalisation is perhaps most clearly developed in M. Foucault's *Discipline and Punish*, though his *The Birth of the Clinic* is also relevant here. See also C. Gordon, 'The normal and the biological, a note on Georges Canguilhem', Donzelot, op.cit., J. Henriques *et al.*, *Changing the Subject*, and N. Rose, 'The psychological complex: mental measurement and social administration'.
3 J. and E. Newson, 'Aspects of childrearing in the English-speaking world'.
4 For other critiques similarly arguing both the utility of the normalisation concept and limitations with it, see for example P. Adams, 'Family affairs', and Henriques *et al.*, op.cit.
5 As in most sociological surveys, I used the Registrar General's index of social class. However this scheme is particularly unsatisfactory in describing the class position of women which is defined exclusively in terms of the social position of men; the father's occupation defines the class status of the unmarried woman, and the husband's occupation the class position of the woman who is married.
6 S. Prendergast and A. Prout, personal communication.
7 D. Riley, *War in the Nursery.*
8 G. Brown and T. Harris, *Social Origins of Depression: A Study of Psychiatric Disorder in Women.*
9 A. Oakley, *Women Confined.*
10 H. Gavron, *The Captive Wife.*
11 J. Hubert, 'Belief and reality: social factors in pregnancy and childbirth'.
12 Gavron, op. cit.
13 See for example P. Atkinson, 'The reproduction of medical knowledge'.
14 A. Leibowitz, 'Women's work in the home'.
15 H. Land, 'Who cares for the family?'.
16 J. and E. Newson, op.cit.

17 The Newsons, op. cit., discuss the complicated feelings which changes in expert opinion can provoke in the previous generation.

18 For some account of this movement, see Riley, op. cit., and V. Walkerdine, 'Developmental psychology and the child-centred pedagogy: the insertion of Piaget's theory into primary school practice'.

19 C. Steedman, 'The mother made conscious'.

20 Walkerdine, op. cit., and this volume.

21 D.W. Winnicott, *Playing and Reality*.

22 See M. Rutter, *Maternal Deprivation Reassessed*, pp. 81–94.

23 Ibid.

24 See for example B. L. White, 'An experimental approach to the effects of experience on early human behavior'.

25 See F.G. Horowitz and L.Y. Paden, 'The effectiveness of environmental intervention programmes'.

26 Ibid.

27 See B. Bradley, *The Neglect of Hatefulness in Psychological Studies of Early Infancy*, for a critique of mother-infant interaction studies.

28 J.S. Bruner, 'Learning how to do things with words'.

29 B. Spock, *Dr. Benjamin Spock's Baby and Childcare.*

30 H. Jolly, *Book of Child Care: The Complete Guide for Today's Parents*, p. 1.

31 Ibid.

32 B. Nash (ed.), *The Complete Book of Babycare*, p. 5.

33 P. Leach, *Baby and Child*, p. 9.

34 Jolly, op. cit., Preface.

35 For example Jolly, op. cit., p. 272.

36 Nash, op. cit., p. 216.

37 There is, for instance, scant reference to aggression in young babies, and to the possibility that it may be 'normal' for babies to show signs of rejecting their mothers. See Bradley, op. cit., and also Walkerdine, this volume.

38 Leach, op. cit., p. 8.

39 Ibid., pp. 14–15.

40 Ibid.

41 Ibid.

42 Nash, op. cit., p. 161.

43 Ibid.

44 T. Booth, personal communication.

45 See for example E. Ross, 'Survival networks: women's neighbourhood sharing in London before World War One'.

9

On the regulation of speaking and silence: subjectivity, class and gender in contemporary schooling

VALERIE WALKERDINE

> As I found my own voice in analysis, droning on day after day, it gradually took the place occupied for so long by the schools. One day it was inevitable that I should cease to be a schoolgirl. (Catherine Clement, 1983, p. 187)

> [We argue that] the structure of the social system and the structure of the family shape communication and language and that language shapes thought and cognitive styles of problem-solving. In the deprived family context this means that the nature of the control system which relates parent to child, restricts the number and kind of alternatives for action and thought that are opened to the child; such construction precludes a tendency for the child to reflect, to consider and choose among alternatives for speech and action. (R.D. Hess and V. Shipman, 1965, p.869)

The family and the primary school are sites for the regulation and production of the modern conception of the individual. In this chapter I want to explore, in a preliminary way, some aspects of current practices, concentrating on how the power to speak and conflict have been regulated and understood. In particular I shall be concerned with the idea of the rational independent, autonomous child as a quasi-natural phenomenon who progresses through a universalised developmental sequence towards the possibility of rational argument. This 'normal development' is taken to be facilitated by a sequence of cognitive development on the one hand and language development on the other, both being viewed as depending on the presence of the mother. The previous chapter examined how normal development is central to the regulation of contemporary mothering. Here I shall explore the connection between the family and the school, examining these as sites in which individuals are understood as being actively produced. In particular I shall focus on some contemporary effects of historical shifts from overt regulation of the population to apparatuses of covert regulation which depend upon the production of self-regulating, rational individuals. Such accounts of normal development seek to describe all children and all families. But since normalisation hinges on the detection of the pathology, the targets of intervention continue to be the poor, the working class and ethnic minorities. In such practices, the position of women as mothers and teachers is central and strategic. As I shall show, psychoanalysis is doubly implicated here. On the one hand aspects of psychoanalysis have been crucial in the regulation of sexuality, passion and the irrational. More recently, normalised accounts focusing on the mother's role have made women the object of the production of a maternal nurturance, understood as the guarantor of the rational subject. However, I shall seek to go further than a simple deconstruction of the productive power of modern apparatuses. As the previous chapter demonstrated, intertwined in modern practices are the workings of desire, which suggest a complex subjective investment in what I shall call 'subject-positions'. These positions, given in the relations of the practices themselves, are not unitary, but are multiple and often contradictory such that the constitution of subjectivity is not all of one piece without seams and ruptures. This means that we can examine those very practices and ruptures as sites of production of subject-positions and of either potential coherence or fragmentation. Utilising some insights from a re-working of certain concepts adapted from Lacanian psychoanalysis and Freud's analysis of mechanisms of defence[1] I shall suggest how it might be possible to re-work existing explanations in order to examine the production of class and gender relations within and between existing practices. In doing so, I hope to illustrate how relations of power and desire interpenetrate the complex workings of apparatuses for the production of subject-positions, and how those positions, in their contradiction and multiplicity, are lived. In doing so I shall suggest that the modern conception of the rational, contained in logocentric discourses, sets up as its opposite an irrational. This is invested in and understood as the province of women, who must contain it at the same time as being responsible for its removal in their children. A crucial consequence of this analysis is a re-working of conflict and its relation to language. The achievement of rationality becomes, in part at least, understood as the transformation of conflict into rational argument by means of universalised capacities for language and reason.

Speaking and silence: the transformation of conflict into discourse

As we sketched out in the Introduction to this book, and as several chapters have already demonstrated, classic studies within feminism examining silence have concentrated on 'finding a voice'. Here, feminism was understood as providing both a place and power to speak. In this context, silence has been understood as both repression and resistance.[2] A refusal to speak was taken as a psychic repression, or a suppression of the articulation of forbidden discourse. 'Speaking out', in this sense, is seen as the articulation of a difference, in contrast to its repression which is seen as a deviance, illness or absence. However, as earlier chapters have illustrated, the issue of silence and speaking is not a simple matter of presence or absence, a suppression versus enabling. Rather, what is important is not simply whether one is or is not allowed to speak, since speaking is always about saying something. In this sense what can be spoken, how and in what circumstances is important. It tells us not only about its obverse, what is left out, but also directs attention to how particular forms of language, supporting particular notions of truth, come to be produced. This provides a framework for examining how speaking and silence and the production of language itself become objects of regulation.

I shall begin by drawing on Michel Foucault's classic study, *Discipline and Punish*.[3] Here he charts the emergence in the nineteenth century of modern techniques of surveillance of the population showing how the development of apparatuses and technologies of regulation were crucially dependent upon the newly emergent 'sciences of the social'. The regulation of conflict (of crime, pauperism, deviance as pathologised) is central to such sciences and technologies. Here I can do no more than signal some crucial displacements which followed from this. However, it is particularly important that from the outset a regulation of conflict and rebellion was aimed at the poor, at a population newly contained in towns and cities.[4] At first such regulation involved overt surveillance and attempts to inculcate 'good habits'. But in the problems associated with such overt practices covert self-regulation became favoured. That children who were so obviously watched and monitored might still rebel, for example, remained a continuing problem. In transformations relating to pedagogy, love became the basis of techniques designed to avoid problems associated with overt surveillance. Now the aim was to produce citizens who would accept the moral order by choice and freewill rather than either by coercion or through overt acceptance and covert resistance. But this investment of love in the child occurred in conjunction with other transformations which, as I shall show, are particularly important to understanding the regulation of speaking and silence. For example, the emphasis on caring nurturance located in women was also central to the medicalisation of their sexuality.[5] The latter itself involved a regulation of passion and, in the process, a displacement of irrationality. The heralding of the rational, the production of the bourgeois citizen capable of reasoned argument, was itself made possible through new knowledge and practices, producing the irrational through an opposition. Reclaiming irrationality, speaking out, then, cannot be simply a release from repression, nor as a new freedom, the power to speak, but must be understood in terms of the relations of its own production.

The natural was produced in those practices which proclaimed its possibility. As Jacqueline Rose has argued in this volume, it is centrally important to deconstruct the claims to truth of that natural reason and language. Thus, there is no liberation of a repressed voice so much as a new natural language which was made to speak itself, and the absence of which became a pathology. It is particularly evident in the regulation of those practices surrounding the family and school. Here the production depends upon the positioning of women as mothers and teachers, who provide the 'facilitating environment'. Women become guardians of the irrational: their love becomes nurturance. They ensure the production of individuals who are self-regulating through the powers of rationality. Not swayed by irrational forces and free from conflict, they are to become the free agents of bourgeois democracy who will, by choice, accept their place in the new order and will not rebel. As I shall show, the regulation of conflict becomes centrally its displacement on to rational argument, crucial to which has been the production of theory and practices centring on a naturalised sequence of child development. Through this means the child becomes the target of interventions destined to either facilitate the 'natural' emergence of rationality or understand its absence as (ab)normal, pathological, therefore to be corrected by a variety of medical, educational and welfare agencies. Central here is the idea of an autonomous agent, who attributes feelings to him- or herself and does not feel an excess of passion or conflict. Such an agent is a citizen who, as in the humanist dream, sees all relations as personal relations, in which power, struggle, conflict and desire are displaced and dissipated.

My aim in this chapter is to begin to explore how the practices operating in schooling, and in the family, position the participants. They aim at producing an autonomous and rational individual, who is class- and gender-neutral, while at the same time ensuring that these categories assume a built-in deviance, a problem to be dealt with and corrected. In contrast to a view which aims at the liberation of individuals from repressive forces, I shall go on to indicate how the regulative features of practices themselves, in providing multiple sites for the creation of subject positions, also create a complex machinery of desire.

The subjects of schooling

The school, as one of the modern apparatuses of social regulation, defines not only what shall be taught, what knowledge is, but also defines and regulates both what 'a child' is and how learning and teaching are to be considered. It does so by a whole ensemble of apparatuses from the architecture of the school to the individualised work-cards. Here I am concentrating on modern primary school practices which relate specifically to the development of the child-centred pedagogy.[6] These practices depend centrally upon a conception of learning and development as individually paced, counterposing this to any instruction of the class as a whole. Knowledge is defined in terms of experience and activity: in the words of the Plowden report, 'concepts to be acquired, not facts to be stored'. In general terms, the pedagogy is individualised and conceptions of the child and of knowledge both depend upon a naturalisation of a conceptual apparatus of structure. Knowledge, understood as concepts, is acquired and produced through the development of an active learner, who develops 'at his own pace', by actively incorporating experience. This itself is defined in relation to an environment which is taken to consist of a world of objects. The teacher does not actively teach, indeed *must* not teach, but must passively become part of the facilitating environment which observes and monitors the sequence of natural development.[7] In this way, the very pedagogy itself produces the possibility of individualisation.

These taken-for-granted assumptions have a complex history involving the production of a range of systems of categorisation which, on the one hand, are claimed to be universal, and yet at the same time produce differences and effects on class and gender lines. Central to claims to universality are certain truths located in the body. At least since Descartes, reason has been located in the body. The Cogito and the rational individual (of property, wage-labour, etc.) form the centrepiece of a variety of interlocking practices. But, the body in question is not any body. Over the historical period dealt with in this book, women's bodies became understood as incapacitated for reason. Hystericised and medicalised, they were capacitated for reproduction of the species, not the production of knowledge. Women's bodies were both the place where the production of reasoning beings as children was assured and yet a constant source of danger. For example, educating women inasmuch as it might adversely affect their productive capacities, was discouraged as endangering the future of the species.[8] Women had therefore to become both the producer of reason through child rearing, and its opposite. Passive, receptive and nurturant femininity became the obverse of reasoning or masculinity, itself made possible through active exploration. However, a constant threat was the intrusion of the irrational. Medicalisation of women's bodies became a surveillance of passion, of an active sexuality. As Catherine Hall points out, it was bourgeois women, confined at home as guardians of the moral order, who ensured the safety of the reproduction of children, whose path towards rational adulthood was assured by their presence, a presence at once cold and hygienic. All active desires of women were thereby transformed into a cool, calculating and passive nurturance. At the same time the pathologisation of passion, activity, on the part of the women regulated their fitness for motherhood.

From this century many examples could be given of how women's sexuality and their fitness for maternal nurturance become the object of interlocking apparatuses and technologies. An obvious one is in the decision-making process which may operate in child custody cases.[9] Here my concern is with those interventions which firstly relate the promotion of natural reasoning to language, and secondly link mothering to the production of both.[10] In each case what is vital is that the links hinge on various notions of 'deprivation', as discussed in the last chapter, and position the mother in relation to the child in very specific ways. Correlatively, this argument was linked to assumptions about the management of conflict in relation to socialisation practices in home and family.

In primary schooling we can uncover a remarkable congruity in the positioning of the teacher and assumptions about the mother who must provide the 'facilitating environment' for the production of rationality. The teacher was to become a passive observer, watching the unfolding of development. Like mothers, teachers' passivity is vital to the possibility of children's activity. Teacher training for primary schools has developed in relation to the amplification of women's capacities for maternal nurturance.[11] Women, who previously had been prohibited education on the grounds that it would endanger their reproductive capacities, were now allowed to train as teachers, producing an effect whereby women could safely be educated in as far as it made possible the staffing of the caring professions. This effect is still present as even a minimal examination of current statistics on women's entry to higher education and employment will show. But if passive, nurturant femininity was necessary to produce active learners, in this respect, the education of girls as 'children' represents something of a problem. Modern conceptions of child development understand children as active, enquiring, discovering. Yet that activity also defines an active masculinity in which passive femininity is its obverse. The Plowden report for example, consistently transposes 'child' into 'boy'.[13] By definition, active childhood and passive femininity exist at the intersection of competing discourses. For girls, therefore, their position as children must remain shaky and partial, continually played across by their position as feminine. Conversely, for boys masculinity and childhood work to prohibit passivity. And in both cases passion and irrationality are constantly displaced.

But it is in the understanding of silence and the management of conflict that these contradictions are particularly apparent, and in which the issues of class are to be foregrounded. If the normal child is self-regulating, any overt conflict, a failure of reason, will be displaced on to pathology. Yet the pathologies are different for different discourses, for example those regulating the normal child (male) and normal femininity.[14] What is crucial therefore is both the truth of the normal and the pathologisation of its obverse.

Both the family and the school are sites of an array of practices in which the covert regulation of the population is aimed for. These practices depend upon the revelation of conflict, of power relations, of aggression, but also in its dissipation. This dissipation is the responsibility of women who, in humanist developments of psychoanalysis and child development, nurture, free and aid autonomy. There is no overt policing and monitoring but a covert regulation through which passion is transposed into feelings, the irrational into the rational, power into interpersonal relations, and conflict into aggression. But this move towards self-regulation depends not only upon an active learner who develops through action on objects. It also depends upon the medium of argument, language, which itself emerges naturally through a sequence of development. Speaking and silence therefore become normalised as the facilitation of a universal linguistic system. Silence is pathologised as absence, for, although language is natural it develops only if facilitated by a family (or more particularly mother) who interacts, extends, elaborates the utterances of the child. Silence is a pathology if the school and family simultaneously permit and celebrate the possibility of speech.

Talk about it: the incitement to discourse

This emphasis on language did not immediately fit easily within the child-centred discourse. The pedagogy of experience and natural development eschews all texts. It is founded upon 'doing'. The action upon and interaction with the world is, in the post-Plowden climate of the late 1960s and the 1970s, an object world. Denied as a social space in its own right, the classroom is an 'environment' where a number of children may experience together. In this respect, at first talking was subsumed to 'doing'. It was only following the impact of structural linguistics on studies of children in the 1960s and 1970s that an emphasis on language became implicated within the child-centred pedagogy. For this talk had to be dissociated from the passive regurgitation of the 'old' system of overt regulation and passive remembering. Talk became an aspect of freedom, of the facilitation of language, which unfolded almost of its own accord in the right conditions. Language development as a naturalised system was thus added on as an extension of child-centredness, an addition to the production of rationality. Studies of the failure of urban education in the American ghettoes became studies of the environmental facilitation of natural language. While mothers were implicated, teachers everywhere began to be taught how to talk to children. They learnt to extend and expand utterances. Language was categorised into functions and its presence checked and monitored. In such practices, although texts as textbooks had been the object of ridicule, they began to re-enter the scene. But they were not the same texts. Nothing could enter below the baseline of an unsullied natural experience. Thus texts had to build upon natural language and 'tell it like it is'. Children could create their own texts in their own words. And those texts which were produced were to be explication of the everyday experience and language of, particularly, inner-city children. They were taken to represent reality, not to intervene, and therefore went alongside a view of facilitation which apparently existed outside of any regulation.[15] Like natural reason, natural language was allowed, permitted, desperately facilitated. It is therefore very difficult to understand such practices as regulative. Regulation had gone underground.

In such a climate of enablement an absence of language and of reason can be nothing but a pathology, and its cause must lie in the environment itself, the centre of which was the mother.

The family as causal

The mother and child are both caught in the play of practices for ensuring the possibility of self-regulated, rational and autonomous subjects. Women, I suggest, in the necessity to ensure a stable, nurturant and facilitating environment, are the price paid for autonomy, its hidden and dispensable cost. Some feminist accounts of women's psychology have taken up this point, wanting to extend autonomy to women. But if we understand independence and autonomy as something denied to women, then, like the work on silence and repression, we tend to assume a model of liberation from oppression and repression in which women can be set free to take their place as fully-fledged individuals. Indeed, some accounts of women's psychology present this as a kind of re-birth, like a butterfly emerging from a crysalis. But, might we not emerge as individuals only to be further implicated in the patriarchal and logocentric tradition which proposes the bourgeois individual as guarantor of the new order? Here I want to take a rather different approach, examining firstly how woman and child have been coupled in the production of the autonomous child in the practices of home and school. If individuality depends on the presence of naturalised language and reasoning, its absence is pathologised. After all, if development is natural its absence is a very fundamental absence in that which permits or facilitates the very centre of human development itself. From here, it is not just the absence of language which is pathologised. The normal woman is invested with a nurturance which is naturally given by the workings of her reproductive system, which amounts to a capacity for facilitating and enabling the natural development of children. Far from being passionate, this love is platonic. Passion and activity are pathologised. It follows that resistance to rationality in the form of any expression of conflict becomes an excess, a pathology, the cause of which is the mother. In this process the failure of overt regulation, the obvious resistance manifested in crime, poverty or threatened anti-establishment uprising is removed from social relations to become established as an aspect of the psyche. The declared failure of overt practices of regulation in this historical period forced another, and more covert, tactic. This itself has involved a further double shift particularly significant in the regulation of women, as the infant's relationship with the mother, or more particularly, the bourgeois mother, confined in the home, is understood as the basis of conflictual behaviour. Between the two world wars, Melanie Klein posited an innate tendency to aggression to account for conflict, observable as a struggle between love and hate, which was fuelled by primitive desires or instincts, directed towards the mother. Liberal practices designed to facilitate the letting out of aggression through play, in play therapy, child rearing and in schooling, relate to this approach. But this emphasis was followed by another shift as post-Kleinian psychoanalysis focused more on maternal nurturance and the actual bodily presence of the mother as against destructive fantasies. These moves marked the location of the mother firmly in the home, to be responsible for the ensuring of self-regulation through nurturance. That is, self-regulation was made possible through the toleration of the presence and absence of the mother, understood as the child's overcoming frustration.

Conflict has thus been firstly located causally within the family, laid at the door of the mother, and finally shifted to an experience of frustration. In all of this, as in all subsequent humanist developments within psychology, the relational dynamics, the regulation of practices themselves, become 'feelings' which are experienced as attributes which individuals must learn to recognise, for example, frustration as their own irrationality, their own feelings. And additionally, as rationality is separated from irrationality, fantasy becomes secondary to an 'adjustment to reality', the pinnacle of logocentrism. Power and desire are therefore both crucially absent from this framework.

Rationality as a regulative device

In the shift from overt to covert regulation, then, a capacity for language has been linked to natural reason, and conflict has been individualised, reduced to feelings or a mastery of frustration. The production of self-regulating individuals now depends crucially on how conflict is managed between parents and children. At the centre of explanation of maternal deprivation in relation to pedagogy lies the absence of 'reasoned argument' as a control device in working-class mothers. Regulative devices of other kinds, such as threats or smacks, are simply taken to be pathological. If reasoning is natural, then the problem becomes mothers who do not foster it. Classic studies such as that of Hess and Shipman[16] utilise the early work of Basil Bernstein to legitimate their claims. It is important that both Hess and Shipman and Bernstein point to evidence of the presence of language (that is, that working-class children 'have' language), but for different purposes. Hess and Shipman, unlike Bernstein, treat purpose as synonymous with presence. They fail to recognise what comes over again and again in their own research and other studies of this ilk: that differences in regulative devices have to be understood in relation to distinct practices. In one very telling piece of evidence presented by Hess and Shipman mothers were asked to say how they would prepare their young children for school. I reproduce it below:

> 'Suppose your child were starting school tomorrow for the first time. What would you tell him? How would you prepare him for school?' One mother, who was person-oriented and used elaborated verbal codes, replies as follows:
> 'First of all, I would remind her that she was going to school to learn, that her teacher would take my place, and that she would be expected to follow instructions. Also that her time was to be spent mostly in the classroom with other children and that any questions or problems that she might have she could consult her teacher for assistance'. 'Anything else?'
> 'No, anything else would probably be confusing for her at her particular age.'

They then go on to discuss the potential value of the mother's contribution to the child:

> In terms of promoting educability, what did this mother do in her response? First, she was informative; she presented the school situation as comparable to one already familiar to the child; second, she offered reassurance and support to help the child deal with anxiety; third, she described the school situation as one that involves a personal relationship between the child and the teacher; and fourth, she presented the classroom situation as one in which the child was to learn.

They then go on to exemplify the opposite position by reference to a second mother:

> A second mother responded as follows to this question: 'Well, John, it's time to go to school now. You must know how to behave. The first day at school you should be a good boy and do just what the teacher tells you to do.'

And they comment:

> In contrast to the first mother, what did this mother do?

> First, she defined the role of the child as passive and compliant; second, the central issues she presented were those dealing with authority and the institution, rather than with learning; third, the relationship and the roles she portrayed were sketched out in terms of status and role expectancies rather than in personal terms; and fourth, her message was general, restricted and vague, lacking in information about how to deal with the problems of school except passive compliance.[17]

The oppositions are clearly set up here by Hess and Shipman. In their terms the first mother personalises the relationships, suggesting security and warmth. The second mother reveals to her child an overt system of regulation. This is identified as harmful. This process is well illustrated by Turner's[18] summary of social class differences in disciplinary techniques produced in the mid-1960s.[19] Where everywhere middle-class parents are identified as more 'permissive' in relation to children's transgressions and disobedience, they also 'provide more warmth and are more likely to use reasoning, isolation, show of disappointment or guilt-arousing appeals in disciplining the child.' Working-class parents, on the other hand, 'are more likely to use ridicule, shouting or physical punishment in disciplining the child, and to be generally more restrictive.'[20] Permissiveness in child rearing is thus associated with an absence of coercion, an absence of overt regulation which is seen as punitive, and harmful. As in the child-centred pedagogy, freedom is taken to be this absence, in which reasoning prevails. But what this identification of absence as deviance conceals is the movement towards covert regulation of conflict, which everywhere aims at its displacement on to self-regulation through reasoning and 'internalised reactions to transgression'.[21]

The practices of regulation pinpointed in the extracts set out each of the danger spots of the production of the autonomous individual: the presence of the mother, her facilitation of natural language, the personalisation of emotion and its displacement from overt conflict on to rational argument. Thus, working-class mothers are themselves pathologised and responsible for the pathology in their children by going out to work; regulating their children through overt displays of positional power, there is little personalisation and an absence of expansion of language and reason as a regulative device. These absences and the presence of the 'wrong' attributes provide evidence necessary for the intervention of medical, welfare and educational agencies to correct the pathology in a variety of ways.

John and Elizabeth Newson, in their studyof 7-year-olds in Nottingham,[22] make clear some of the conditions necessary to the covert regulation of conflict and the production of autonomy. Although they make clear the illusory nature of choice, by pointing both to the fact that some conflict between parents and children is necessary and to the 'engineering' of willingness by covert means, they are trapped within a permissive discourse. This understands power only as overt regulation and therefore psychically harmful:

> Some conflict between parent and child is almost inevitable: it arises because parents require children to do things, and this interferes with the child's autonomy as a person, with wishes and feelings of his own. In disciplinary conflicts, by definition, we have a situation where certain individuals exercise their rights as people of superior status (in age, power and presumed wisdom) to determine what younger and less experienced people, of inferior status, may or may not do. If the child complies willingly of course (even if his willingness has been engineered by offering him the illusion of choice) his self-esteem can be kept intact: but whenever he is forced into an unwilling compliance by the threat of sanctions, whether these be pain inflicted or approval withdrawn, he will inevitably suffer in some degree feelings of powerlessness and humiliation.[23]

They make it clear that autonomy relates to the regulation of conflict. Feelings are attributed to the child and parental power or authority is understood to be bad. Overt regulation, in the form of threats, compliance and sanctions, produces 'feelings' of powerlessness and humiliation. These are clearly to be avoided. It is an 'illusion of choice' which seems the key here to what they recommend. The child must experience him-(sic)self as in control, as the author of his intentions, of free will, independence – autonomy. Thus, any practice which might inhibit that illusion is frowned upon.

But the problem with reducing powerlessness to a 'feeling' is that it becomes a property of the person. The child is therefore not helpless or powerless before the practices and authority relations which position him: s/he feels powerless. Such feelings can be overcome by means of an 'illusion of choice'. The child will thus experience 'himself' as empowered, free, in control. S/he will not therefore recognise the regulative chains of the practices in which s/he is positioned and is able, and moreover willing, to accept 'his' lot, adapt to reality, deal with frustration: in short become a self-regulating, democratic citizen. But in so far as 'he' 'experiences frustration', 'feels powerless', and so forth, these feelings are pathological. And what is more we can locate both a cause – failure of maternal nurturance of the correct kind – and a remedy – some process of re-presenting that nurturance, some therapeutic practice. Powerlessness can hardly be recognised as an effect of regulation in those practices in which power itself is denied.

But from a different position power and powerlessness can be understood as aspects of the regulation of practices themselves and not as unitary or simple possession.[24] If we examine in more detail what working-class mothers are taken to do, it becomes evident that to some extent they expose the fraudulence of choice. In doing so, these mothers constantly present their children with power and regulation. They may persist in telling their children that 'they cannot have everything they want'. They remind them that for a variety of tangible reasons, they do not have the choice, a central component of the bourgeois order which is continually held out to them as a possibility. So working-class mothers, in making it clear that children cannot 'just ask and get', that money is scarce, their time is limited, etc., shatter the illusion. But, such shattering is difficult to live if dreams of fulfilment – of constant presence, constant happiness – are proffered as reality. Difficult to live too, if other practices depend for their operation on that choice.

Thus the pathologisation of overt regulation produces a truth which locates effects of poverty and oppression in the psyches and family relations of the poor and oppressed. The rational individual who is self-regulating and imbued with feelings, who has adapted to reality, exists in a personalised world not trammelled by power and desire. Yet it is not sufficient simply to point to such effects. This itself encourages a voluntarism which assumes that change can follow from subjects' recognising and choosing to stand outside the conditions of their own regulation. As the last chapter suggested, because modern social apparatuses both define and delimit normality, they also operate through the regulation of desire. Hence the workings of subjectivity enter into the production of the illusion of choice and fulfilment. But this subjectivity is not unitary. It is multiple and contradictory. Here, I suggest, it is precisely in the failure of the processes aimed at producing rational individuals, those aspects which are pathologised, that we might find a starting point in understanding multiple and contradictory subjectivity. For this enterprise I suggest that we might utilise certain concepts from Freudian psychoanalysis, but in a rather different way.

In the following section I shall sketch out some possible aspects of an analytic framework which uses both aspects of psychoanalysis and ideas developed from post-structuralism. I shall then go on to illustrate this through some examples from my own research. My aim here is less to provide a fully-fledged analysis than to point to a direction in which work might proceed.

Psychoanalysis, power and desire

Along with other work in the tradition of post-structuralism,[25] I have implicated psychoanalysis in the production of norms crucial to modern apparatuses of social regulation. Here, however, I shall be drawing on aspects of psychoanalysis which exist outside the framework of normative models and social welfare agencies, a body of work which, in principle at least, does not maintain an absolute distinction between the normal and pathological. Nevertheless, since psychoanalysis is implicated in those apparatuses of regulation as well as particular practices of child rearing and schooling, it helps create the very subject-positions I wish to deconstruct. Here I want to draw attention to two features of the regulation of practices and the constitution of subject-positions within them which are integral to my framework, discussed more fully elsewhere.[26] Firstly, following Foucault, power is implicated in the power/knowledge relations investigated in the creation and regulation of practices. Here, power is not a single possession of an individual, nor is it located in a unitary, static sense. Rather, power is shifting and fragmentary, relating to positionings given in the apparatuses of regulation themselves. Thus adults, mothers, for example, do not possess power by virtue of simply being in authority as in the Newsons' account. Nor can power be eradicated by personal harmony. Power exists in the apparatuses of regulation themselves.

From this it follows that women have power only in so far as they are positioned as mothers in relation to certain practices concerning the regulation of children. In this sense, although the effects of the regulation of a child are to be understood as real, they are not to be caused in any simple sense by the mother but by the very regulation and constitution of mothering in modern practices of child rearing. From this perspective, we might thus examine a child's experience of regulation not as an essential effect of the mother, but an effectivity produced in practices of mothering. However there is every reason to suppose a child may understand or experience a mother as the source of power and not its effect. Secondly, as I have argued, the practices which produce subject-positions are of necessity multiple, and those positions themselves are often diverse and contradictory. From here we can understand the mother-child relation as only one of a diversity of sites in which positions are created. This means that we can examine what happens, at the intersection of practices. Obvious examples of such intersections discussed already would be the relation of the position of ideal rational and active 'child' on the one hand and passive, nurturant femininity on the other. From here we may ask, what is the effectivity of such positionings for the lives of particular girls and women? Similarly, what is the relationship between child-rearing practices stressing that 'you cannot have what you want' and a pedagogy based on an illusion of choice for working-class children? In each practice an acceptable response in one will be the target of negative evaluation in the other. What I am suggesting is that the very contradictory nature of such positionings produces effects likely to result in anxiety states. It is to examine these effects that I wish to invoke certain insights from psychoanalysis.

I want to begin by making reference to a paper by Cathy Urwin[27] in which she re-worked certain concepts taken from Lacanian psychoanalysis utilising insights from post-structuralism. This enabled her to include and interrelate the concepts of power and desire in the workings of regulatory practices. Using an examination of recent studies in child language development, Urwin presents a re-working of Lacan's Mirror Stage to encompass a post-structuralist engagement with regulatory practices. This re-working emphasises the Mirror in Lacan's account as a metaphor for the illusion of perfect control. She exemplifies how discursive relations enter into the imaginary activity of the Mirror by suggesting that the production of meaning through ritualised communication procedures positions the mother as the one who to the infant is apparently the source of power. This is achieved as she offers the infant an illusion of perfect control, by enabling the infant to control her within particular practices through the use of idiosyncratic but meaningful activity. None the less her participation is governed by her own positioning within discursive practices. Later the infant must negotiate separation and attempt to deal with the painful consequences of giving up its illusory control, itself produced through the entry into discursive relations. This is achieved through the introduction of a third term and processes of identification, enabling the infant to take the place of Other within the regulation of practices. Urwin argues that the crucial relation of power and desire may be understood through the infant's taking, in a ritualistic way, the position of that Other, switching both position and power, moving from dependent to dominant and vice versa.

As in Lacan's account, Freud's analysis of narcissism is taken as central. The affirmation contained in the Mirror provides the infant with a narcissistic sense of omnipotence. The Other and regulation confirm the infant's fragile sense of self. However, the infant's relations with others can also be experienced as extremely persecuting. That is, relations and positions which do not permit the power/desire relations, giving the infant narcissistic control, may be experienced as destructive and annihilating. Urwin remarks,

> It is not simply a question of distorted feedback from a strange adult who fails to understand the baby's messages. . . . Rather, like the mirror in Lacan's account, which is as controlling as it is controllable, here the illusion of control has its counterpart in the illusion of total subjugation. (It is for this reason that narcissism and paranoia are juxtaposed in Lacan's reading of Freud.)[28]

Separation from the mother in this account is understood in terms of the uptake of positions within practices themselves. It is therefore no simple move away from dependence on the mother's presence (as in the work of Bowlby, for example). The effect of the illusion of control is to provide a sense of affirmation and power which has real effects within the practices in which it is inscribed. This means that separation becomes understood in terms of relations within and between practices. That is, the move from something is always a move to something else, and the move from one practice regulated in one way to another differentially regulated provides for the infant a sense of power or powerlessness, affirmation or persecution. Moreover since, as in Lacan's approach, identification with the Other is to be the object she most desires, it follows that the experience of annihilation or persecution will relate to the experience of lack of continuity or resources in being the object of the Other's desire within the new practice. Either the subject will experience this as the necessity for her/him to change (and therefore risk loss of total control or positive identities), or the Other will have to change, so that the subject becomes the object of desire. But, the projects for wished-for transformation in each case are shaky and highly likely to produce forms of anxiety, overt conflict or other modes of defence.

I want to argue that the production of narcissism and paranoia relates to the effectivity of identification with the Other who apparently regulates a practice. This is not a unitary quality of the person, as I have already stressed. Subjects are created as and in positions, not alone, but in practices and specific relational dynamics. In Urwin's as in Lacan's accounts, the Other of identification is not reducible to the nurturant mother. There are many Others who exist in practices, affording the possibility for multiple and contradictory subject-positions. It is this multiplicity which produces the totality of shifting relations of power and powerlessness which is subjectivity. Hence the very apparatuses of regulation and the practices themselves provide the possibility of the multiplicity of subjectivity and the experience of incoherence or fragmentation as it exists across practices.

It is by means of such an account that it might be possible to explore the effects upon, for example, working-class children and girls on entering into new practices. However, further conceptual tools are necessary. A valuable psychoanalytic concept, first put forward by Freud, suggests itself. This is the defence mechanism of splitting.[30] Freud initially developed the concept of the splitting of the ego. The basis of this splitting is a disavowal of castration. That is, the subject denies in consciousness the reality of castration – that females do not possess a penis. This produces neurotic and phobic symptoms. What is here is a denial of difference: its effects precisely are those of desire. To invest the woman with a penis in fantasy (most particularly in fetishism) is a denial that she does not possess it. Thus fantasy and reality exist side by side, so that Freud was led to describe the ego as split. The effects of this denial are ultimately a delusional reality.

Lacan uses this paper as central to his concept of a fundamental splitting of the subject and the delusional reality created in the fantasies of ideology, of the Imaginary. In this analysis, castration is a marker of a power difference. I am therefore suggesting that we might understand the effects of such a denial in terms of the effectivity of the positioning of a subject within a diversity of practices.

In conjunction with Urwin's analysis, it might be possible, firstly, to examine the effects of the transposition from one practice to another, and possible experience of persecution produced by this shift in relations. Different practices may produce different effects. In this case, the differences which concern me are those of class and gender. However, the shift from one practice to another, the effectivity of castration as a marker of power, relates centrally to the breaking of the mother-child dyad and the move from one set of discursive practices to another. This is in contrast to a simple move from dependence to independence, as I have stressed. That is, any shift is a move both out of and into another set of discursive relations and therefore involves a complex of positionings.

The production of persecution

As I have shown, present practices assume a universal class and gender neutral 'child', who, in development, passes from one 'environment' or 'context' to another through the utilisation and facilitation of cognitive and linguistic capacities. Basic to these practices is a reduction of difference to an add-on effect. There is also a denial of power and desire, the latter being reduced to the meeting of needs which hinge on the presence/absence of the mother. I am arguing for specific effects of a move from one practice to another in a discourse which does not recognise the effects of that transition. That is, current practices operate on a system of disavowals and denials, of castration, for example – girls can be like boys – or of class – mental labour is achieved through 'doing' or manual activity. This reduces the traumatic effects of the experience of difference to a lack or failure in the subject or the mother. In consequence, through operating on the basis of denials, the very practices themselves help to create and read back the effects as pathology. Given extreme feelings of persecution, the stages of transition will relate to attempts to deal with the loss of identification. Such effects may be open hostility, conflict, neurotic withdrawal as silence (and therefore accepting the regulation while covertly being hostile) and, later, apparent quiescence which none the less involves a disavowal. For example, our education system in its most liberal form treats girls 'as if' they were boys. Equal opportunities and much work on sex-role stereotyping deny difference in a most punitive and harmful way. Operating in these practices is a partial and shaky denial of castration. The 'clever girl' is positioned as though she could and can possess the phallus, while she has to negotiate other practices in which her femininity is what is validated.[31]

In this sense the 'delusional reality' consequent upon psychic defences is produced in those very practices which deny differences by failing to engage with the contradiction and pain produced through the act of splitting – of being positioned like a boy and like a girl and having to remain 'sane'. A denial of the reality of difference means that the girl must bear the burden of her anxiety herself. It is literally not spoken. She is told that she can be successful and yet the painful recognition that is actually likely to result from the fear of loss of one or the other (her femininity, her success, or both) is a failure to be either, producing neurotic anxiety, depression or worse. At best we might hope for the disavowal of the career girl. For, in fact, it is virtually impossible, in our times at least, for the girl to maintain positive identifications in both dimensions, both of which are necessary to the maintenance of her sense of coherence or identity. Yet the deleterious effects of non-acknowledged contradictions depend upon a circulation of denials – of difference, power and desire – within the very practices which regulate and position subjects. In a sense, then, rather than perpetuating the denial operating in the spurious circulation of needs, fulfilment and happiness, a recognition of struggle, conflict, difficulty and pain might actually serve to aid such girls.

At each intersection of practices, each site of difference, exists a boundary to be negotiated. As new identifications are created, so too is the potential for loss, annihilation and disavowal. Indeed we might argue that, within our present system of schooling, the success of working-class children and girls depends upon the effectivity of disavowal and therefore upon intense and persecutory pain experienced by such children. They have been chosen to succeed and yet the very possibility of their success depends upon a splitting – the negotiation of an impossible array of identifications in which they, becoming what the school wants, can no longer be what their family wants, and vice versa. Feeling desperate that they can exist in neither, that everything is lost in terrible and painful isolation, that nobody understands, neither home nor school, we might predict a terrifying experience consequent upon effects of simultaneous desire for identification and fear of total loss and annihilation.

In a recent series of interviews which I conducted with male and female academics, many women experienced such anxiety. Central features of such effects are silence, lack of confidence, the suppression of anger and hostility, contributing to the apparent docility of the person who believes that if they open their mouth they will 'say the wrong thing', and be thrown out of paradise – the longed-for resolution of the bourgeois dream. Sennett and Cobb[32] discuss similar effects with respect to class. In describing the experience of male manual workers and those with working-class backgrounds who became white-collar workers, they provide powerful evidence in support of the thesis I have set out. Indeed, they use the term 'splitting' although their reference point is the work of Laing on the politics of schizophrenia.[33] In describing the pain of becoming bourgeois, Sennett and Cobb point to the central experiences: of passivity, of the fear of letting go of work, the necessity to learn a new set of rules, yet constantly fearing forcible exclusions from the desired location, thus an enforced docility and passivity. They point to the apparatus of bourgeois individualism, of autonomy, choice, of 'being somebody', counterposing this with ways in which working-class people get through or make sense of their lives. These relate particularly to the idea of 'self-sacrifice', the displacement of one's own desires on to the fulfilment of and through others, and argue that 'splitting', the putting up of boundaries, is a necessary condition of survival for most people in 'getting from day to day'. It is therefore not insane, but the basis of sanity. As they put it, 'Society imposes the necessity for defensiveness.'[34]

What is highly significant in their analysis is the way in which they demonstrate the practical necessity of boundarisation within particular practices. This is a very different reading from one which would understand such coping strategies as pathological, the product of an unstable family, inadequate nurturance and so on. But my analysis would go further to suggest that not only are the effects of such practices deeply persecuting and deleterious, but their pathologisation renders these effects as experiences of abnormality. It also suggests that a denial of power in the creation of individuals does not serve to remove such effects (and here, the humanist concept of the happy factory mirrors the happy school and the happy family) but rather serves to strengthen their effectivity through the pathologising of those who do not display the qualities appropriate to natural, normal and healthy adjustment. But, since such defences might provide strategies for survival within existing practices, they provide important gains as well as losses. They have positive effectivity.

Here I suggest that Urwin's modifications to Lacan's account provide important insights in relation to the crossing of boundaries and to the potential for the constitution of subjectivity in schooling. Important to this analysis of power and desire is the positioning of the subject within practices. Identification with a powerful Other within the practice and the crossing of boundaries between practices is therefore central. However, since Freud's splitting related primarily to castration it must locate as formatory the practices in which the relations of the family are played out. In that sense, then, a variety of potentially conflictual and contradictory identifications is possible, relating to the others in the family constellation, parents, siblings, other caretakers, suggesting multiple sites for identification splitting. From the present perspective what is important is that, while the Other of identification is apparently the source of power, experienced as a possession, in practice the power is an effect of the positioning of the Other within a particular practice. This power is therefore constantly mobile and shifting and cannot be understood outside power/knowledge relations and therefore apparatuses of regulation. This allows the coherence of fantasy, fact and fiction, and goes beyond Lacan's structuralist appropriation of the imaginary and symbolic. Possession is a fiction, which is lived as fact through the veridicality of the practices themselves.

I would suggest that it is precisely the circulation of terms and positions and practices which allows the slippage from one position to another. That is, while the insertion of the subject into a variety of practices in which the phallus is, differentially, invested may have different effectivities, it may well be that it is the relations within and between them which is one of the conditions for psychic life. A girl who is positioned as clever in school while also the subject of masculine desire in another practice is still relating to the phallus. However, one practice assures her that she can be it, while another only ensures its possession through her being the object of sexual desire, and therefore the assumption of femininity. In each case we may assume actual men and boys involved, and yet a myriad of other places sediment the position. The girl may want to have a relationship with a boy as one source of affirmation[35] but there are many others, circulating in a variety of practices and cultural forms. Similarly and conversely, we do not have to assume (as some feminist arguments for single-sex schools have done) that the absence of male teachers for girls is equivalent to the removal of the phallus since in schooling the inscription of the phallus is in the very academy itself.

A bid for power

In stressing the productive potential of the power/knowledge relations of schooling and the multiplicity of positions for children to enter, the issue is now the relationship between those positions and the effectivity of their content. As I have argued, practices aim to produce learners who are active, discovering, autonomous and capable of rational argument. This does not mean that they will be effective, but it does mean that difference becomes pathologised. In attempting to understand how particular children live the effects of those multiple positionings, a first step is to explore the effectivity of different solutions. In this way we might examine the issues of conflict and silence. That is, how might a girl's docility in school produce both losses and gains? She might be denied the status of 'active learner' and yet at the same time be enabled to maintain another site of power, for example by taking the position of the Mother. Yet she must experience pain and anxiety if the contradiction between those positions is not recognised and understood as an effect of the pathologising process. What, too, if that pathology operates in relation to different and contradictory assumptions of the normal? How then are these resultant splittings lived?

In this respect it is important to recognise that if rational argument is taken to be the pinnacle of intellectual achievement, itself produced through an active and enquiring learner, certain behaviours are not only experienced within the workings of the pedagogy but they are validated. Let us follow this through with respect to conflict. We have seen that through the transformation of overt to covert self-regulation, conflict is displaced on to personal feelings and rational argument. Although some frustration is inevitable it must be allowed to be personalised and rationalised. Thus, the school provides a facilitating and nurturant environment in which an illusion of choice and control is presented to children. In this pedagogy, conflict is expected, choice is essential and some aggression inevitable. It is presented and understood as children's reactions to frustration, which must become rational argument. Hence displays of conflict are tolerated if they are understood as relating to frustration and activity. Naughtiness in young children, for example, is to be expected, validated and associated with masculinity. Furthermore, conflict is positively sought after and validated if it is understood as rational argument, the guarantor of 'brilliance' or 'real learning'.[36]

Conflict therefore is permitted only if it follows specific paths, otherwise conflict is pathologised. In this case the crucial distinction is between 'rational argument' and 'antisocial behaviour' (associated with delinquency). I want to give some examples of how this might work for particular children, beginning by examining a brief extract from a recording, made in a fourth-year secondary mathematics lesson. The girl in question, Charlotte, displays open conflict in her attacking of the teacher's 'claim to know', yet it is precisely this move which, while it threatens his power, leads him in an interview afterwards to evaluate her as 'brilliant'.

In a lesson on braille, the teacher begins by asking how many combinations of dots they can find given that they

> can use any combination up to six dots. Charlotte volunteers an answer, as does a boy, but the latter's answer depends on leaving one block blank with no dots on it. The teacher agrees with this and is immediately challenged by Charlotte: 'You said count the dots.' The teacher replies . . . 'I think it's just as good maths if you count this one or you don't as long as it is made clear what you're doing.' But she persists, 'we were talking about dots.' He says, 'I'm quite happy for you to take that attitude. I'm not arguing with you.'[37]

Girls like Charlotte who challenge in this way are 'active' – they act like boys – they are 'real children', have 'real understanding'. They come across as supremely confident. I suggest that their confidence lies in their claim to the phallus. That is, Charlotte resists the teacher, but it is simultaneously a bid for his power, an identification with him and the powerful other within her practice. But not just Charlotte's desire is involved. The teacher's judgment of her is also to place her as the object of his gaze, as an example of the kind of pupil he desires to produce. She is the object then of his desire, the 'Other of her Other' in the classroom. He says of her:

> '[She is] the one with the keenest brain in the sense of ideas. And she's the great problem-solver. . . . She's a tremendous abstract thinker, she's great at the kind of Maths that, perhaps, we don't recognise enough.'

No wonder, then, that there is simultaneously for both the teacher and Charlotte a narcissistic bid for position and a threat of annihilation which both must face. The teacher has to deal with her bid to oust him, which is presented in his response as a fear of loss of control of the class. He 'will not argue with her.' Charlotte also takes a risk – she could be laughed out of court. Yet something allows her to make that bid which would keep others totally and definitively silent. While they are silent they will never be able to stake out their claim to brilliance, which must exist as a secret fantasy desired as much as they fear its loss. I would suggest that what gives Charlotte the confidence to take the risk is that she has been affirmed in such a position in other practices especially in the bourgeois practices of her family and their similarity with the practices of the school.

Nevertheless, it may be important that the fear of power, of taking the position of the Other through narcissistic identification, carries this threat of annihilating or being annihilated. In this sense the investment in the Other as a source or site of safety might make such a risk too difficult to bear. Passivity and silence never bring that threat to the surface. The good girl never has to face an overt attack on the Other. Given the pejorative as well as positive evaluations of 'good' and 'hard-working' within the practices,[38] such a girl will never be positioned as 'brilliant' like Charlotte. However, in certain academic practices the relatively privatised act of writing allows the display of such bids for power without the necessity of facing the threat of annihilation within the social relations themselves. Yet this has particular effects. It produces attainment which is correct and therefore validated, but it is denied at the same time. The right answer produced in the 'wrong' way, by hard work and not brilliance.

Good performance combined with docility and helpfulness presents a striking picture not unlike that expected of primary schoolteachers themselves, who must possess capacities of nurturance to be 'amplified', yet must reach a standard of attainment necessary for teacher training. Conversely, girls who are 'nice, kind and helpful' are most suited to facilitating nurturance itself. It is perhaps important then that many young girls do not understand high attainment and femininity as antithetical. Girls who 'possess' both characteristics are highly validated. Yet, in a recent study an overwhelming number of girls of all ages gave descriptions of their ideal girls which included the terms 'nice, kind and helpful'.[39] Moreover, many girls expressly mentioned 'naughtiness' and 'horridness' as pejorative categories. They strove to be 'good', to not require 'telling off'. To not need 'telling off' seems to indicate a different discourse from that of 'being cross' and the personalisation of feelings. These girls respond to the power invested in the positioning of the teacher as necessitating either an active suppression and/or its conversion into helpfulness. Here then is no reaction to frustration, no rational argument, but a painful suppression of conflict which appears in the girls' accounts in two ways. Firstly, it is displaced on to boys who are 'horrid', 'naughty', 'annoying' 'bullies', and 'bad', and secondly, it is the object of masochistic self-mutilation.[40] Some girls whom I interviewed expressed such intence self-hatred that they could attribute to themselves no good qualities at all. It seems to me that a ceaseless array of ensnaring positions circulate here. For example, a girl who is desperate to suppress her 'horridness' can never become 'brilliant': she is constantly caught, not simply as a puppet at the mercy of different positionings, but by the grip of her refractory desires fixed in those practices themselves. Girls who gain power through becoming like the teacher[41] cannot possibly challenge the rules for which they are responsible as guardian. Such a move would bring that threat of powerlessness or annihilation, a threat to the desired position.

Three 6-year-old girls from the above study present some idea of a range of positions.

Janie, a working-class 6-year-old, at the top of her class, was almost totally silent both at school and home. She was well-behaved and polite and reserved her unacceptable comments for whispering. During one home recording she spent an hour and a half in silent work activity, not uttering a single word.

Janie's silence helps legitimate a position of good behaviour, which, since she says nothing, means she can say nothing wrong. If you cannot be clever at least there are rewards for being 'nice, kind and helpful', and no pejorative evaluations of horridness. Horridness is hidden, subverted. Let me give two further examples of 6-year-old girls.

Emily is a poor girl. She is classically passive and helpless. She cries on entering the classroom, refusing to leave her mother. The teacher comforts her. Whenever she tries to do work she gives up, asks for help, or, more often, sucks a thumb, has a pain and is let off further work. All her negative feelings are apparently displaced into hysterical symptoms such as bodily aches and pains. She is rarely, if ever, overtly naughty. Yet she is also comforted, cuddled, looked after. The teacher frequently worries about her and so comforts and never forces her to do any work.

Eleana is also extremely passive and very poor. She appears unable to follow simple instructions and the teacher has difficulty in getting her to do anything. She appears as a classic victim and has two categories for the children in her class – those who 'tell on' her (girls) and those who 'tell her off' (boys). She is thus positioned as the passive recipient of a brutal authority. Here is no personalised 'being cross'. However, Eleana commits secret and silent acts of destruction: she breaks the heads off dolls.

Here then is no natural passivity. Where Emily receives the teacher's nurturance, Eleana's passivity is desperate, erupting secretly into active destruction. While these girls seem precluded from engaging actively with rational argument, on the other hand, in the interviews with academics which I referred to earlier, it was quite common, especially in those women and men who came from upper-middle-class families, to describe their facility with rational argument as a sham. They could win over anybody and yet they saw it as too easy in its effect. Secretly, they felt 'hollow', that they were not really clever, that it was simply an elaborate theatre. Yet, since this cleverness was associated with 'hard work', itself a feature of working-class life (as opposed to symbolic activity viewed as 'play'),[42] they found it extremely difficult to do and had often made working-class students at university the target of their abuse. The following two interviews with male academics from different class backgrounds reveal different strategies and experiences of the negotiation of boundaries. The first, a memory of working-class schooldays, reveals the difficulty of negotiation of boundaries and the problems of 'being made visible' as itself a threat and source of terror:

> 'It goes back to the instance I described in primary school, made to stand in front of the class and do up my shoe laces, stand up in front of the class and do up my tie and secondly, the, this school was, as I would not put it, in class terms, completely removed from the kind of experience I'd had in what had been a very localised primary school and so I didn't want to be drawn to attention in front of these people about whom I felt very edgy . . . in case I couldn't keep up that standard.'

Another male academic, with a middle-class background, also

discusses the negotiation of boundaries. But his resistance is active and engages directly with the bid for power and simultaneous annihilation of the teacher:

> 'Being an intellectual was a act of fucking defiance by the time I was 15 or 16. . . . I remember things like, I remember realising that a very good strategy for throwing people – the authorities, fixing them, tricking them, was to just mix boundaries. . . . I remember going into a physics lesson one day with a copy of Joyce's *Ulysses*. . . . I realised that by being an intellectual you could even gain the support of the anti-school people, because the teacher came in and he said, "What are you doing bringing this filth into the classroom?", and I said, "I got it from the school library." '

In this example there is a deliberate play on the boundaries, open conflict, and yet it is intellectually powerful. Here is intellectuality, rational argument. Yet there is also considerable anger. Unsurprisingly, in these interviews there was also a huge array of anxieties about the public display of rational argument and the private expression of irrationality and emotionality. One may then ask, polemically, where is women's denied anger? It seems to be located in 'man'. And where is men's denied irrationality? It seems to have been invested in 'woman'. The Logos itself, then, must be deconstructed.

Woman, guardian and container of the irrational

Using the kind of analysis I have set out here, we can understand the Logos, and the pedagogic production of 'rational argument' itself, as an historically specific phenomenon. The investment of reason in the sexed-body, as the foundation of modern western scientific rationality, not only locates self-control in rational argument, but also places it at the centre of an omnipotent fantasy of control over the workings of the universe. Mastery and control of the 'real' are centrally located in claims to truth and therefore to possess knowledge. In this sense mastery, control and bourgeois masculinity are conjoined in that uncertain pursuit of truth. And yet, the very uncertainty provides the conditions for an ever-elusive and therefore incessantly sought-after masculinity. Rationality and rational argument become, in relation to their centrality in particular academic and public practices, aspects of individuality to be attained and regulated. In this sense such aspects of masculinity are not possessions of biological males. Females may cross over on to the side of masculinity, insofar as they are permitted entry into those practices. Similarly, since it is bourgeois individuality, possessed of rationality, which is taken as the key to normality, the working class can in principle become 'bourgeois individuals' by dint of those liberal practices which provide that possibility. However, such individuality and autonomy is produced at a price. Playful rationality is made possible through work, the hidden work of servicing, manual labour and nurturance. Here, the ultimate irony is to be found in the position of the middle-class male, whose powerful position is guaranteed by the trap of reasoned argument.

But if the truth of individuality can be deconstructed, we can then also simultaneously deconstruct its Others, those opposites which render it possible. Here I have tried to show how women, endowed with a natural capacity for nurturance, become the same place where rationality is assured. Our current pedagogy and child-rearing practices which celebrate the Logos are made possible by the facticity of the nurturant mother, the helpful teacher. Yet this capacity of nurturance occludes women's sexuality. This is the point of fear for it contains the irrational which permits rationality, constantly threatening to erupt through its surface. It may be important, therefore, to explore the possibility that the production of autonomy, of rational argument and the Logos itself, rather than breaking the mother-child dyad, actually depends upon the maintenance of a fantasy of omnipotence, of control over the Other. The practices pointed to by the Newsons, Turner, etc. discussed earlier make clear that autonomy depends on an 'illusion of choice', which is simultaneously an illusion of control. It is therefore vital to recognise that the truth-effects of that positioning of women actually make possible the fantasy of complementarity in which mothering assumes that needs can actually be met, that rationality is not ruptured by the constant play of the irrational on its surface. This fiction of fulfilment, of nurturance, of the bourgeois individual is at the expense of the positioning of women as the mother, who contains, soaks up, allows, facilitates the rationality of the child. She is therefore, in being the guardian, the safeguard for the production of the autonomous and rational knower; also its opposite.

In this the fraudulence of the Logos is that it holds masculinity not in an assurance of control but in a desperate terror of its loss. It is important, then, that we, as women, should not also be caught in an attempt to master the Logos, to take it as our guarantee and arbiter of truth, and of the possibility of change and transformation. As I have tried to indicate, its very production and reproduction depends upon a denial of desire and a displacement of the irrational on to women. However, the history of the Logos, and of scientific rationality, builds upon an even longer history, that of religion. In displacing religion, science sought to remove the soul. The Logos provided a mastery over, the regulation of, natural forces, rather than a supreme Other, God, whose power controlled the universe. The soul was that which existed beyond the materiality of the body, its excess. The displacement of the soul became also the displacement of the outside, represented to some extent by women's-power-with-nature, rather than the control over nature.[43] Women, the site of the terror, had to become imbued only with a passive receptivity which facilitated rationality in others. In this respect Lacan's examination of female mysticism and paranoia[44] is relevant here. It hinges particularly on the notion of the soul and of a fantasy of a good and perfect Other, God, who holds the power to liberate, to allow the subject to endure the chains of subjugation in order to be freed on death. The soul thus represents an excess, that which resists subjugation, is 'let out', only to make possible the docility required for the enduring of servitude. The passive, docile subject endures subjugation by means of this excess. It is displaced and stifles the possibility of rising up against the oppressor. This subjugation is endured by the splitting of rationality from its excess. In paranoia, a 'delusional reality' exists alongside that which resists subjugation. Passivity and docility might permit the subjugation in relation to an oppressive order, which allows it to be endured in the hope of release into the gaze of the good and perfect Other. Since helpful, kind, nurturant femininity assumes a giving, containing, then it also suggests the necessity of containing rage and desire – the desire for a place where one day the soul will be free, where the girl, the worker too, can bask in the light of the all-loving and accepting gaze – to have made it on to the side of the empowered.

The fantasy of the all-loving, all-giving Other, then, is created in the very practices which reward that docility, good behaviour, good performance. But if the Supreme Other is a fraud, the docile child, worker, is set up. Set up to want, to desire the excess of that *jouissance*, which is here and yet constantly out of reach and which permits the most punitive and harmful self-mutilation.

By no means concluded

Bourgeois democracy operates in relation to a nexus of practices which aim at the production of a self-regulatory citizen, who has integrated love and hate, and for whom no fantasy perfect good or evil Other exists. The displacement of religion into science displaces that perfect Other, God, that safe place in the sky, on to an 'adjustment to reality', to the existing social order. The human sciences, having first been concerned with 'docile bodies', felt the resistance inherent in an enforced docility. Self-regulation, the apparent freedom of activity, permitted that rational subject endowed with free will and free choice. The self-regulating citizen depends upon the facilitating nurturance, caring and servicing, of femininity. I have explored the possibility of an alternative analysis which might understand the effect of such a history in the production of subjects. Subjectivity as multiple, produced in contradictory and shifting positions, through power and desire, has specific and harmful effects upon those whose lack of fit is rendered pathological. In examining the creation of normalisation I have sought to deconstruct an absolute distinction between the normal and the pathological and the truth of a rational and universal subject. If practices and positions themselves are historically specific, not timeless truths, we can deconstruct the power of their obviousness.

The Logos seeks knowledge through rational argument, split from the irrational. Yet, other discourses, other practices are possible which do not recognise this splitting, nor reduce it to feelings. Although it is that side associated with the 'feminine' and the 'mad', such conditions remain essentialised only so long as we assume a complementarity and an absolute distinction rather than see these as sites of splitting and disavowal. However, in so far as those practices exist, they produce the effectivity of those knowledges and positions. There may be other knowledges, other truths which resist a reduction to a simple and logical coherence. As long as we fail to engage with those, we are prohibited from examining the effectivity of our positionings and workings for transformation. Change is not a matter simply of deconstruction. A new reading permits the possibility of struggle to work for transformation of that sociality, those practices and of the subject-positions produced within them. An ahistorical account of human subjectivity fails to engage with the very spatial and temporal specificity of truths and practices. There can be no truth which stands outside the condition of its production. In this pursuit, analysis of these conditions and exploration of our own historicity are inextricably intertwined.

There is, in this account, no lone individual, no single point of causality, but subjects created in multiple causality, shifting, at relay points of dynamic intersection. We can take apart the facts of complementarity, of male and female, rational and irrational, active and passive, mental and manual, which form the sites and possibility of our subjugation and of our resistance. We might then adopt a double strategy; one which recognises and examines the effects of normative models, whilst producing the possibility of other accounts and other sites for identification. Current accounts of the family and schooling which deny power and desire in a humanistic conception of nurturance serve to help keep us locked inside a powerful fiction of autonomy and possibility, which is not to be countered by a total pessimism but rather a working with and through an exploration of both our own formation in all its historical specificity and the formation of other possibilities of practice, as well as locations from which to struggle within existing ones. Thus, a working within those apparatuses of our present means not only our attempts at deconstruction but the possibilities for explorations which do not seek a knowledge which claims itself as true for all people, places, times.[45]

Notes

1 See J. Lacan (1977); Freud (1940).
2 See for example psychoanalytic studies, particularly approaches to Freud's 'Dora' case (Moi, 1981; Rose, 1978).
3 Michael Foucault, (1977).
4 Walkerdine (1984); Foucault (1979); Jones and Williamson (1979).
5 I have argued elsewhere (Walkerdine, 1984) that the displacement of passion in favour of a medicalised hygienic, dispassionate nurturance in mothers is an important aspect of the regulation of female sexuality. Passion (particularly in the family) was considered quite unhealthy. Weeks (1981) and Foucault (1979) point to the preponderance of incestuous practices in the working-class families at the time. For further detail about the moral regulation of female sexuality as its hygienisation and medicalisation see Bland (1981).
6 Walkerdine (1984) discusses in some detail the emergence of such a pedagogy and its strategic relation to developmental psychology. I shall not rehearse that argument or that history here.
7 See for example, Walkerdine (1983a).
8 Sayers (1982); Le Doeff (1981/2); Dyhouse (1977).
9 See also previous chapter.
10 There is a large body of work on this debate. See for example, articles in Williams (1970), Labov's (1970) famous 'The Logic of Non-standard English' and debates in Basil Bernstein's (1975) work.
11 Davin (1978); Widdowson (1983); Steedman (1982); Dyhouse (1977).
12 See discussion in Walkerdine (1984).
13 Walden and Walkerdine (1983).
14 In particular, activity and passivity represent normality in one and pathology in the other. See for example, the classic study

from psychiatric practice, Broverman *et al.* (1970).

15 Examples of such curriculum interventions would be Leila Berg's 'Nipper' reading books, which were to show the reality of urban working-class life, and Halliday's 'Breakthrough to Literacy' in which there were no reading books. Children made their own texts with word and sentence makers.

16 See quotation at the beginning of this chapter.

17 Hess and Shipman (1965), p. 173.

18 Turner (1973).

19 Becker (1964).

20 Quoted in Turner (1973), p. 136.

21 Turner (1973), p. 136.

22 Newson and Newson (1976).

23 Newson and Newson (1976), pp. 331–2.

24 Foucault (1979); Walkerdine (1981).

25 Foucault (1979); Donzelot (1979).

26 I have argued elsewhere that high attainment in girls combined with passivity is important to the maintenance of the 'caring professions' in which the women are good enough to go on to tertiary education, but not good enough to be 'brilliant' as in the ranks of the 'real understanders'. See Walkerdine (1983a).

27 Urwin (1984).

28 Urwin (1984), p. 301.

29 Urwin (1984), p. 301.

30 Freud (1940).

31 In a recent report (Walden and Walkerdine 1985a), we discuss such positionings with respect to a study of girls and boys in the fourth year of primary school and the first and fourth years of secondary school. It is important that such positionings are conscious and can be specified by the pupils, but the child who actually manages to exist positively at the nexus of contradictory positionings is rare.

32 Sennett and Cobb (1972).

33 See also Denise Riley (1983), who criticises Laing's view of the family. Importantly, of course, Laing was also making use of the psychoanalytic concept of splitting, but accuses the family, particularly the mother, in the foundation of its oppression.

34 Sennett and Cobb (1972), pp. 304–5.

35 See Wendy Hollway (1984b) for examples of this.

36 Walden and Walkerdine (1983); Walkerdine (1985).

37 Walden and Walkerdine (1983).

38 Walkerdine (1983a).

39 Walkerdine (1983a).

40 Recently, following an examination of girls' comics in which

slavery, and the silent acceptance of oppression in order to secure the longed-for happy ending, are the norm, I began to ask people about their fantasies. Fantasies of mutilation amongst women and working-class men abound; of crippled orphans, sickly children, cancer, and anorexia, as though only mutilation ensured the possibility of keeping one's place through self-control and docility produced in the most dangerous and punitive of forms.

41 Walkerdine (1981).

42 Play as a pedagogic device as opposed to work is worthy of examination in its own right. I have argued elsewhere that its utilisation is both gender- and class-specific (Walkerdine, 1983a).

43 Easlea (1980).

44 Lacan (1983).

45 I have explored some of these issues in relation to my own formation in Walkerdine (1985b). My courage to speak of these things, having felt so long trapped by silence, comes from many Others in a diversity of practices. I want to thank especially Jenny Dunn, Wendy Hollway, Philip Corrigan, Cathy Urwin and Carolyn Steedman. I did not always heed their lessons but they gave me courage to face conflict and struggle and to celebrate its possibility.

Bibliography

Note: The abbreviation *PP* stands for Parliamentary Papers series.

Adams, P. (1982), 'Family Affairs', *m/f*, no. 7, pp.3–14.

Adams, R. (1972), *Watership Down*, London, Collins.

Allen, S., Sanders, L. and Wallis, J. (1974), *Conditions of Illusion; Papers from the Women's Movement*. Leeds, Feminist Books.

Anstey, F. (Thomas Anstey Curthrie) (1982), *Vice Versa, or, A Lesson to Fathers*, London, Smith, Elder & Co.

Aries, P. (1960), *L'enfant et la vie familiale sous l'ancien régime*, Paris, Plon. Translated as *Centuries of Childhood* (1962) by Robert Baldick, London, Jonathan Cape.

Arnold, M. (1864), *A French Eton, or, Middle Class Education and the State*, London, Macmillan.

Arnold, M. (1869), *Culture and Anarchy*, London, Smith, Elder & Co.

Arnold, M. (1889), *Reports on the Elementary Schools 1852–1882*, edited by Sir Francis Sandford, London, Macmillan.

Ashton, T. S. (1951), *Iron and Steel in the Industrial Revolution*, Manchester, Manchester University Press.

Atkinson, P. (1977), 'The reproduction of medical knowledge', in R. Dingwall, C. Meath, M. Reid and M. Stacey (eds), *Health Care and Health Knowledge*, London, Croom Helm.

Bairne, G. (1975), *Pregnancy*, London, Pan.

Balibar, R. (1974), *Les Français Fictifs*, with the collaboration of G. Merlin and G. Tret, Paris, Hachette.

Balogh, J. (1927), 'Voces Paginarum', *Philologus*, vol. 82, pp.84–109, 202–40.

Banks, O. (1981), *Faces of Feminism*, Oxford, Martin Robertson.

Barrett, M. and MacIntosh, M. (1982), *The Anti-social Family*, London, Verso.

Barrie, J. M. (1902), *The Little White Bird*, London, Hodder & Stoughton.

Barrie, J. M. (1906), *Peter Pan in Kensington Gardens*, with drawings by Arthur Rackham, London, Hodder & Stoughton.

Barrie, J. M. (1911), *Peter and Wendy*, illustrated by F. D. Bedford, London, Hodder & Stoughton.

Barrie, J. M. (1915), *Peter Pan and Wendy*, the story of *Peter Pan* extracted from *Peter and Wendy*, illustrated by F. D. Bedford, authorised school edition, London, Henry Frowde, Hodder & Stoughton.

Barrie, J. M. (1926), 'Neil and Tintinnabulum', in Cynthia Asquith (ed.), *The Flying Carpet*, London, Partridge.

Barrie, J. M. (1927a), 'Captain Hook at Eton', *The Times*, London, 8 July 1927.

Barrie, J. M. (1927b), *Capt. Hook at Eton*, autograph manuscript, New Haven, Conn., Reinke Rare Books and Manuscript Library.

Barrie, J. M. (1928), *Peter Pan* in *The Plays of J. M. Barrie*, London, Hodder & Stoughton.

Barrington, M.R. (1972), *Crookes and the Spirit World*, London, Souvenir Press.

Barrow, L. (1980), 'Socialism in eternity: the ideology of plebeian spiritualists, 1853–1913', *History Workshop Journal*, vol. 9, pp. 37–69.

Becker, W. C. (1964), 'Consequences of different kinds of parental discipline', in M. L. Hoffman and L. W. Hoffman (eds), *Review of Child Development Research*, New York, Russell Sage.

Benson, R. and Constable, G. (1982) (eds), *Renaissance and Renewal in the Twelfth Century*, Oxford, Clarendon Press

Benstock, S. (1983), 'At the margin of discourse: footnotes in the fictional text', *Publications of the Modern Language Association of America*, vol. 98, no. 2, pp. 204–25.

Berg, L. (1977), *Reading and Loving*, London, Routledge & Kegan Paul.

Bernstein, B. (1975), *Class, Codes and Control*, vol. 3, London, Routledge & Kegan Paul.

Bisset, J. (1904), *Memoir of James Bisset*, ed. T.B. Dudley, Leamington Spa, Glover.

Bland, L. (1981), 'The domain of the sexual: a response', *Screen Education*, no. 39.

Blyton, E. (1941), the 'St Clare's' series, *The Twins at St Clare's*, London, Methuen.

Blyton, E. (1942), the 'St Clare's' series, *The O'Sullivan Twins*, London, Methuen.

Blyton, E. (1943), the 'St Clare's' series, *Summer Term at St Clare's*, London, Methuen.

Blyton, E. (1944a), the 'St Clare's' series, *Second Form at St Clare's*, London, Methuen.

Blyton, E. (1944b), the 'St Clare's' series, *Claudine at St Clare's*, London, Methuen.

Blyton, E. (1945), the 'St Clare's' series, *Fifth Former at St Clare's*, London, Methuen.

Blyton, E. (1946), the 'Malory Towers' series, *First Term at Malory Towers*, London, Methuen.

Blyton, E. (1947), the 'Malory Towers' series, *Second Form at Malory Towers*, London, Methuen.

Blyton, E. (1948), the 'Malory Towers' series, *Third Year at Malory Towers*, London, Methuen.

Blyton, E. (1949), the 'Malory Towers' series, *Upper Fourth at Malory Towers*, London, Methuen.

Blyton, E. (1950), the 'Malory Towers' series, *In the Fifth at Malory Towers*, London, Methuen.

Blyton, E. (1951), the 'Malory Towers' series, *Last Term at Malory Towers*, London, Methuen.

Board of Education (1910), *The Teaching of English in Secondary Schools*, Circular 753, London, Board of Education.

Board of Education (1912), *Suggestions for the Consideration of Teachers and Others Concerned in the Work of Public Elementary Schools*, Circular 808, London, Board of Education.

Boas, G. (1966), *The Cult of Childhood*, London, Warburg Institute.

Bolgar, R. R. (1954), *The Classical Heritage and its Beneficiaries*, Cambridge, Cambridge University Press.

Bolgar, R. R. (1976), *Classical Influences on European Literature, 1500–1700*, Cambridge, Cambridge University Press.

Bradley, B. (no date), *The Neglect of Hatefulness in Psychological Studies of Early Infancy*, mimeo, Cambridge, University of Cambridge.

Bratton, J. S. (1981), *The Impact of Victorian Children's Fiction*, London, Croom Helm.

Brazil, A. (1918), *A Patriotic Schoolgirl*, London, Blackie.

Brazil, A. (1921), *Loyal to the School*, London, Blackie.

Brazil, A. (1925), *My Own Schooldays*, London, Blackie.

Broverman, I. *et al.* (1970), 'Sex-role stereotypes and clinical adjustments of mental health', *Journal of Consulting and Clinical Psychology*, no. 34, pp.1–7.

Brown, G. and Harris, T. (1978), *Social Origins of Depression: A Study of Psychiatric Disorder in Women*, London, Tavistock.

Brown, P. *et al.*, (1981), 'A daughter: a thing to be given away', in Cambridge Women's Studies Group (ed.), *Women in Society*, London, Virago.

Bruce, D. F. (1921), *Dimsie Moves Up*, London, Oxford University Press.

Bruner, J. S. (1978), 'Learning how to do things with words', in J. S. Bruner and A. Garbon (eds), *Human Growth and Development*,

Wolfson College Lectures, 1976, Oxford, Oxford University Press.

Bullock, A. (1974), *A Language for Life*, report of the Committee of Inquiry appointed by the Secretary of State for Education and Science under the Chairmanship of Sir Alan Bullock, London, HMSO.

Burman, S. (1979)(ed.), *Fit Work for Women*, London, Croom Helm.

Burstyn, J. (1980), *Victorian Education and the Ideal of Womanhood*, London, Croom Helm.

Burt, C. (1937), *The Backward Child*, London, University of London Press.

Byron, M. (1925a), *J. M. Barrie's Peter Pan and Wendy*, re-told for little people, pictures by Mabel Lucie Atwell, London, Hodder & Stoughton.

Byron, M. (1925b), *J. M. Barrie's Peter Pan and Wendy*, re-told for boys and girls, pictures by Mabel Lucie Atwell, London, Hodder & Stoughton.

Byron, M. (1930), *The Littlest Ones' Peter Pan and Wendy*, re-told for the nursery, illustrated by Kathleen Atkins, London, Hodder & Stoughton.

Cadogan, M. and Craig, P. (1976), *You're a Brick Angela!: A New Look at Girls' Fiction from 1839 to 1975*, London, Gollancz.

Calhoun, D. (1973), *The Intelligence of a People*, Princeton, New Jersey, Princeton University Press.

Carby, H. (1980), 'Multi-culture', *Screen Education*, vol. 34, p. 62–70.

Chalmers, G. S. (1976), *Reading Easy, 1800–1850*, London, Broadsheet King.

Christian Mothers Magazine, 1844 onwards.

Christian Observer, 1801 onwards.

Cixous, H. (1976), 'The laugh of the Medusa', *Signs*, vol. 1, no. 4, pp. 875–93.

Clanchy, M. (1979), *From Memory to Written Record*, London, Arnold.

Clement, C. (1983), *The Lives and Legends of Jacques Lacan*, New York, Columbia University Press.

Clement, C. and Cixous, H. (1975), *La jeune née*, Paris, Union General d'Editions.

Cohen, L. and Manion, L. (1983), *Multicultural Classrooms*, London, Croom Helm.

Cohen, M. (1978), *Sensible Words: Linguistic Practice in England 1640–1785*, Baltimore, Johns Hopkins Press.

Cohen, P. (1983), *A Calculating People*, Chicago, University of Chicago Press.

Cole, W. O. and Sambi, P. S. (1978), *The Sikhs: Their Religious Beliefs and Practices*, London, Routledge & Kegan Paul.

Connell, R. W. (1983), *Which Way is Up?*, Sydney, George Allen & Unwin.

Cooter, R. (1984), *Cultural Meanings of Popular Science: Phrenology of Consent in Nineteenth Century Britain*, Cambridge, Cambridge University Press.

Copasetic, J. (1979), 'Rude boys don't argue', *Melody Maker*, 19 May.

Corran, G. and Walkerdine, V. (1981), *The Practice of Reason: Volume 1: Reading the Signs of Mathematics*, mimeo, London, University of London, Institute of Education.

Corrigan, P. R. D. (1984), *In/forming Schooling: Space/Time/ Textuality as Regulative Features of the Historical Construction and Contemporary Policies, Practices and Outcomes of Compulsory State provided 'Mass' Schooling Systems*, mimeo, Ontario, Ontario Institute for Studies in Education.

Crookes, W. (1874), 'The last of Katy King', *Spiritualist*, 5 June 1984, reprinted in full M.R. Barrington (ed.), *Crookes and the Spirit World*, London, Souvenir Press, 1972, pp. 137–41.

Curtis, A. and Blatchford, P. (1981), *Meeting the Needs of Socially Handicapped Children*, Walton-on-Thames, Nelson.

Dane, C. (1917), *Regiment of Women*, London, Heinemann.

Dane, C. (1926), *The Women's Side*, London, Herbert Jenkins.

Darwin, B. (1929), *The English Public School*, London, Longman.

Davidoff, L. (1973), *The Best Circles: Society, Etiquette and the Season*, London, Croom Helm.

Davie, R., Butler, N. and Goldstein, H. (1972), *From Birth to Seven*, London, Longman.

Davies, Charles Maurice (1875), *Mystic London, or, Phases of Occult Life in the Metropolis*, London, Tinsley Bros.

Davies, Charles Maurice (1874), *Heterodox London, or, Phases of Freethought in the Metropolis*, London, Tinsley Bros.

Davies, W.J.F. (1973), *Teaching Reading in Early England*, London, Pitman.

Davin, A. (1978), 'Imperialism and motherhood', *History Workshop Journal*, vol. 5, pp. 9–65.

De La Salle, F. (1935), *The Conduct of the Schools*, English translation, New York, McGraw-Hill.

Department of Education and Science (1967), *Children and Their Primary Schools* (Plowden report), London, HMSO.

Department of Education and Science (1967), *Children and Their Primary Schools*, London, Arnold.

Derrida, J. (1974), *Writing and Difference*, London, Routledge & Kegan Paul.

D'Esperance, Elizabeth (1897), *Shadow Land, Or, Light from the Other Side*, London, George Redway.

Digby, Anne (1978), *First Term at Trebizon*, London, Granada, 1980.

Digby, Anne (1979), *Second Term at Trebizon*, London, Granada, 1980.

Digby, Anne (1979), *Summer Term at Trebizon*, London, Granada, 1980.

Dixon, B. (1977), *Catching Them Young: Volume 1: Sex, Race and Class in Children's Fiction: Volume 2: Political Ideas in Children's Fiction*, London, Pluto Press.

Donaldson, M. (1978), *Children's Minds*, London, Fontana.

Donnison, Jean (1977), *Midwives and Medical Men*, London, Heinemann.

Donzelot, J. (1979), *The Policing of Families*, London, Hutchinson.

Doudney, Sarah (1878), *Monksbury College: A Tale of Schoolgirl Life*, London, Sunday School Union.

Doudney, Sarah (1886), *When We Were Girls Together*, London, Hodder.

Douglas, J.W.B. (1964), *The Home and the School*, Glasgow, MacGibbon & Kee.

Drennan, G.D. (1909), *Peter Pan, His Books, His Pictures, His Career, His Friends*, re-told in story form from J.M. Barrie's dramatic fantasy, London, Mills & Boon.

Dudley, T.B. (ed.) (1904), *Memoir of James Bisset*, Leamington Spa, Glover.

Durkheim, E. (1938), *The Evolution of Educational Thought*, London, Routledge & Kegan Paul, 1977, original published in Paris.

Dyhouse, C. (1977), 'Social Darwinistic ideas and the development of women's education in England, 1800–1920', *History of Education*, vol.3, no.1.

Easlea, B. (1980), *Witch Hunting, Magic and the New Philosophy*, Hassocks, Sussex, Harvester.

Eden, Emily (1979), *The Semi-Attached Couple*, London, Virago.

Edwards, E. (1879), *The Old Taverns of Birmingham*, Birmingham, Buckler Bros.

Edwards, John R. (1979), *Language and Disadvantage*, London, Arnold.

Eliot, George (1964), *Felix Holt, the Radical*, London, Dent.

Ellis, Havelock (1879), *Sexual Inversion: Studies in the Psychology of Sex*, vol. 2, London, Macmillan; revised edn, Philadelphia, Davis, 1928.

Ellis, Mrs Sarah Stickney (n.d.), *The Daughters of England*, London, London Printing and Publicity Co.

Ellis, Mrs Sarah Stickney (n.d.), *Mothers of England*, London, Peter Jackson, Son & Co.

Ellis, Mrs Sarah Stickney (n.d.), *The Women of England*, London, London Printing and Publishing Company.

Elshtain, J.B. (1981), *Public Man, Private Woman*, Oxford, Martin Robertson.

Emsley, C. (1979), *British Society and the French Wars 1793–1815*, London, Macmillan.

Essen, J. and Ghodsian, M. (1979), 'Children of immigrants: school performance', *New Community*, vol. 7, no. 3, pp. 422–9.

Faderman, Lillian (1981), *Surpassing the Love of Men: Romantic Friendships and Love Between Women from the Renaissance to the Present*, London, Junction Books.

Farmer, Penelope (1969), *Charlotte Sometimes*, Harmondsworth, Penguin, 1972.

Fildes, Sarah (1983), 'The inevitability of theory', *Feminist Review*, vol. 14, pp. 66–8.

F.J.T. [Florence J. Theobald] (1870), *Heaven Opened, or, Messages for the Bereaved From Our Little Ones in Glory*, London, J. Burns.

Flaubert, Gustave (1877), 'Un coeur simple', in *Trois Contes*, Paris, Charpentier.

Flavell, Roger H. (1983), *Language Users and Their Errors*, London, Macmillan.

Fletcher, J. (1846), *Report on Infant Schools run on the Principles of the British and Foreign School Society*, Committee of Council on Education.

Flick, C. (1978), *The Birmingham Political Union*, Connecticut, Archon Books.

Fogelman, K. (1976), *Britain's Sixteen Year Olds*, London, National Children's Bureau.

Forest, Antonia (1948), *Autumn Term*, Harmondsworth, Penguin, 1977.

Foucault, M. (1970), *The Order of Things*, London, Tavistock.

Foucault, M. (1973), *The Birth of the Clinic* (translated by A. Sheridan), London, Tavistock.

Foucault, M. (1977), *Discipline and Punish*, London, Allen Lane.

Foucault, M. (1979), *The History of Sexuality*, London, Allen Lane.

Foucault, M. (1980), *Power/Knowledge: Selected Interviews and Other Writings 1972–1977*, edited by Colin Gordon, Hassocks, Sussex, Harvester.

Fox-Genovese, E. (1977), 'Property and patriarchy in classical bourgeois political theory', *Radical History Review*, vol.4, nos. 2–3, Spring-Summer.

Freud, Sigmund (1905, 1908), 'Fragment of an analysis of a case of hysteria', *Pelican Freud Library*, vol. 8, Harmondsworth, Penguin. 1980.

Freud, S. (1951), 'The splitting of the ego in the process of defence', *Standard Edition of the Complete Psychological Works of Sigmund Freud, vol. 23*, London, Hogarth Press (first published 1940).

Freud, Sigmund (1977), 'Case histories I: Dora and Little Hans', *Pelican Freud Library*, vol. 8, Harmondsworth, Penguin.

Fulford, R. (1976), *Votes for Women*, London, White Lion.

Furet, F. and Ozouf, J. (1982), *Reading and Writing*, Cambridge, Cambridge University Press.

Gallop, Jane (1982), *Feminism and Psychoanalysis: The Daughter's Seduction*, London, Macmillan.

Galton, Maurice, Simon, Brian and Croll, Paul (1980), *Inside the Primary Classroom*, London, Routledge & Kegan Paul.

Gaskell, Elizabeth Cleghorn (1960), *The Life of Charlotte Brontë*, London, Dent.

Gavron, H., (1965), *The Captive Wife*, London, Routledge & Kegan Paul, new edition 1983.

Gegeo, Karen Ann Watson (1977), 'From verbal play to talk story', in Susan Ervin Tripp and Claudia Mitchell Kernan (eds), *Child Discourse*, New York, Academic Press.

Girouard, M. (1975), *Victorian Pubs*, London, Cassell & Collier Macmillan.

Glendinning, Victoria (1983), *Vita: The Life of V. Sackville-West*, London, Weidenfeld & Nicolson.

Gordon, C. (1980), 'The normal and the biological: a note on Georges Canguilhem', *Ideology and Consciousness*, no. 7, pp. 33–7.

Goyder, D.G. (1824), *A Manual Detailing the System of Instruction Pursued at the Infant School, Bristol*, London, Thomas Goyder (3rd edn).

Goyder, D.G. (1826), *A Treatise on the Management of Infant Schools*, London, Simpkin & Marshall.

Grafton, A. and Jardine, L. (1982), 'Humanism and the School of Guarino: a problem of evaluation', *Past and Present*, vol. 96, pp. 51–80.

Greater London Council Record Office and Library (1901) (SBL/188), *Minutes of the Special Committee on the Selection of School Books*, 1899–1901, Greater London Record Office and Library (1902), *School Board for London, Minutes, Proceedings*, 1899–1902.

Greater London Council Record Office and Library (1904) (SBL/

1350), *Final Report of the School Board for London 1870–1904*, Part I, Books and Apparatus, pp. 147–50.

Greater London Council Record Office and Library (1915), *London County Council Education Committee Minutes*, 1904–1911.

Green, R.L. (1954), *Fifty Years of Peter Pan*, London, Peter Davis.

Guttsman, W.L. (1954), 'Aristocracy and middle class in the British political elite 1886–1916', *British Journal of Sociology*, vol. 5, no. 1, pp. 12–32.

Halévy, E. (1926), *Les Impérialistes au Pouvoir 1895–1905*, Part 1 of Volume 4, *Epilogue 1895–1914*, of *Histoire du peuple anglais au XIXe siecle*, 5 vols, Paris, Hachette, 1912–32.

Hall, Catherine (1979), 'The early formation of Victorian domestic ideology', in S. Burman (ed.), *Fit Work for Women*, London, Croom Helm, pp. 15–32.

Hall, Robert A. (1972), 'Elgar and the intonation of British English', in Bolinger, Dwight (ed.), *Intonation*, Harmondsworth, Penguin.

Hall, Stuart (1977), 'Education and the crisis of the urban school', in John Raynor and Elizabeth Harris, *Schooling in the City*, London, Ward Lock.

Hall, S. and Jefferson, T. (eds), *Resistance through Ritual*, London, Hutchinson, 1976.

Hall, Trevor H. (1962), *The Spiritualists: The Story of Florence Cook and William Crookes*, New York, Helix Press, Garrett Publications.

Halsey, A.H. (1971), *EPA Problems and Policies*, London, HMSO.

Hamilton, D. (1978), 'The changing disciplines of schooling', unpublished paper, Glasgow University.

Hamilton, D. (1981), 'Of simultaneous instruction and the early evolution of class teaching', unpublished paper, Glasgow University.

Hardinge, Emma (1859), *The Place and Mission of Woman – An Inspirational Discourse*, Boston, Hubbard W. Swett.

Hammond, William A. (1879), *Fasting Girls: Their Physiology and Pathology*, New York, G.P. Putnam's Sons.

Harris, Mary K. (1963), *Penny's Way*, Harmondsworth, Penguin, 1979.

Harris, R. (1980), *The Language Makers*, London, Duckworth.

Harrison, J.F.C., *The Second Coming: Popular Millennarianism, 1780–1850*, London, Routledge & Kegan Paul.

Hartman, M. and Banner, L.W. (eds) (1974), *Clio's Consciousness Raised*, New York, Harper Torchbacks.

Hayashi, T. (1978), *The Theory of English Lexicography, 1530–1791*, Amsterdam, John Benjamins.

Hebdidge, D. (1979), *Subculture, The Meaning of Style*, London, Methuen.

Hendrickson, G. (1929), 'Ancient reading', *Classical Journal*, vol. 25, pp. 182–96.

Henriques, J., Hollway, W., Urwin, C., Venn, C. and Walkerdine, V. (1984), *Changing the Subject: Psychology, Social Regulation and Subjectivity*, London, Methuen.

Hess, R.D. and Shipman, V. (1965), 'Early experience and the socialisation of cognitive modes in children', *Child Development*, vol. 36, no. 3, pp. 869–86.

Higginson, J.H. (1974), 'Dame schools', *British Journal of Educational Studies*, vol. 22, pp. 166–81.

Hill, F. (1893), *An Autobiography of Fifty Years in Time of Reform*, London, Richard Bentley & Son.

Hobsbawm, E.J. (1977), *The Age of Capital*, London, Abacus.

Hollingsworth, B. (1974), 'The mother tongue and public schools in the 1860's, *British Journal of Educational Studies*, vol. 22, no. 3, October, pp. 312–24.

Hollway, W. (1984a), 'Fitting work', in Henriques *et al.* (eds), *Changing the Subject.*

Hollway, W. (1984b), 'Gender identity in adult social relations', in Henriques *et al.* (eds), *Changing the Subject.*

Horowitz, F.G. and Paden, L.Y. (1976), 'The effectiveness of environmental intervention programmes', in B. Caldwell and L. Ricciuti (eds), *Review of Child Development Research*, vol. 4, Chicago, University of Chicago Press.

Hoskin, K. (1979), 'The examination, disciplinary power and rational schooling', *History of Education*, vol. 8, no. 2, pp. 135–46.

Houghton, Georgiana (1881), *Evenings at Home in Spiritualist Seance*, London, Trubner & Co.

Hubert, J. (1974) 'Belief and reality: social factors in pregnancy and childbirth', in M.P.M. Richards (ed.), *The Integration of a Child into a Social World*, Cambridge, Cambridge University Press.

Jackson, Brian (1979), *Starting School*, London, Croom Helm.

Jaeger, W. (1936–45), *Paideia: the Ideals of Greek Culture* (3 vols) Oxford, Blackwell.

James, Alan (1974), *Sikh Children in Britain*, London, Oxford University Press.

James, Alan (1981), 'The "multicultural" curriculum', in Alan James and Robert Jeffcoate (eds), *The School in the Multicultural Society*, London, Harper & Row.

James,Henry(1886);*The Bostonians*,London,Sidgwick&Jackson,1948.

James, J.A. (1856), *Female Piety, or, the Young Woman's Friend and Guide through Life to Immortality*, London, Hamilton Adams & Co.

Jeffcoate, R. (1979), 'A multicultural curriculum: beyond the orthodoxy', *Trends in Education*, vol. 4.

Jolly, H. (1981), *Book of Child Care: The Complete Guide for Today's Parents*, London, Sphere.

Jones, K. and Williamson, K. (1979), 'The birth of the schoolroom', in *Ideology and Consciousness*, no. 6, Autumn.

Kellogg, S.H. (1938), *A Grammar of the Hindi Language*, London, Kegan Paul.

King, Ronald (1978), *All Things Bright and Beautiful*, Chichester, Wiley.

Knox, B. (1968), 'Silent reading in antiquity', *Greek, Roman and Byzantine Studies*, vol. 9, pp. 421–35.

Krouse, R.W. (1984), 'Patriarchal Liberalism and beyond: from John Stuart Mill to Harriet Taylor', in J.B. Elstain (ed.), *The Family in Political Thought*, Brighton, Harvester.

Labov, W. (1970), 'The logic of non-standard English', in F. Williams (ed.), *Language and Poverty*, Chicago, Markham.

Lacan, J. (1977), *Ecrits: A Selection*, London, Tavistock.

Lacan, J. (1983), 'God and the jouissance of the woman', in J. Mitchell and J. Rose (eds), *Jacques Lacan and the Ecole Fruedienne: Feminine Sexuality*, London, Macmillan.

Lambert, Wallace E. (1977), 'The effects of bilingualism on the individual', in Peter A. Hornby (ed.), *Bilingualism: Psychological Social and Educational Implications*, New York, Academic Press.

Land, Hilary (1981), 'Who cares for the family?', in R. Dale *et al.* (eds), *Education and the State, Vol. 2: Politics, Patriarchy and Practice*, Lewes, Sussex, Falmer Press.

Lasch, C. (1978), *Haven in a Heartless World: The Family Besieged*, New York, Basic Books.

Latham, R. (1981), *Dictionary of Medieval Latin from British Sources, Fasc. II*, London, Oxford University Press.

Laycock, Thomas (1840), *A Treatise on the Nervous Diseases of Women*, London, Longman, Orme, Brown, Green & Longman.

Leach, P. (1977), *Baby and Child*, London, Michael Joseph.

Le Doeff (1981/2), 'Pierre Roussel's Chiasmus', *Screen Education*, vol. 34, pp. 37–50.

Leibowitz, A. (1975), 'Women's work in the home', in C. Lloyd (ed.), *Sex Discrimination and the Division of Labour*, New York, Columbia University Press.

Leinster-Mackay, D.P. (1976), 'Dame schools: a need for review', *British Journal of Educational Studies*, vol. 24, pp. 33–48.

Lewis, I.M. (1978), *Ecstatic Religion – An Anthropological Study of Spiritual Possession and Shamanism*, Harmondsworth, Penguin.

Lyons, John (1968), *Introduction to Theoretical Linguistics*, Cambridge, Cambridge University Press.

McCann, J. (ed. and tr.) (1952), *The Rule of St Benedict*, London, Burns Oates.

McCann, Philip and Young, Francis (1982), *Samuel Wilderspin and the Infant School Movement*, London, Croom Helm.

McCann, W.P. (1966), 'Samuel Wilderspin and the early infant schools', *British Journal of Educational Studies*, vol. 14, pp. 188–204.

McCord, N. (1958), *The Anti-Corn Law League 1838–46*, London, Allen & Unwin.

McCullagh, Sheila (1976), *The Green Man and the Golden Bird*, St Albans, Hart-Davis.

Mack, E.C. (1941), *Public Schools and British Opinion since 1860*, London, Methuen.

Mackail, D. (1941), *The Story of J.M.B.*, London, Peter Davies.

McKendrick, N., Brewer, J. and Plumb, J.H. (1982), *The Birth of a Consumer Society: The Commercialization of Eighteenth Century England*, London, Europa.

MacLeod, Sheila (1981), *The Art of Starvation*, London, Virago.

McRobbie, Angela (1978), *Jackie: An Ideology of Adolescent Femininity*, Birmingham, Centre for Contemporary Cultural Studies, Occasional Paper.

McRobbie, Angela (1980), 'Settling accounts with subcultures', *Screen Education*, vol. 34, pp. 37–50.

Manchester Statistical Society (1837), *Report of a Committee on the State of Education in the Borough of Manchester in 1884* (2nd edn), London, James Ridgway & Son.

Manton, Jo (1976), *Mary Carpenter and the Children of the Streets*, London, Heinemann.

Marenholtz-Buelow, Bertha Maria (1855), *Women's Educational Mission Being an Explanation of Friedrich Froebel's System of Infant Gardens*, London, Darton.

Marrou, H. (1956), *A History of Education in Antiquity*, London, Sheed & Ward.

Martineau, H. (1983), *Deerbrook*, London, Virago.

Mathews, M. (1966), *Teaching to Read; Historically Considered*, Chicago, University of Chicago Press.

Mayo, Charles and Elizabeth (1837), *Practical Remarks on Infant Education*, London, Seeley & Burnside.

Mayo, Charles (1827), *Observations on the Establishment and Direction of Infant Schools*, London, Seeley & Sons.

Mayo, Elizabeth (1838), *Model Lessons for Infant School Teachers*, London, Seeley & Burnside.

Meade, L.T. (1886), *A World of Girls*, London, Cassell.

Meade, L.T. (1891), *A Sweet Girl Graduate*, London, Cassell.

Meade, L.T. (1894), *Betty, A Schoolgirl*, London, Chambers.

Meade, L.T. (1898), *The Girls of St Wode's*, London, Chambers.

Meade, L.T. (1911), *The Girls of Merton College*, London, Chambers.

Medhurst, R.G. and Goldney, K.M. (1964), 'William Crookes and the physical phenomena of mediumship', in *Proceedings of the Society for Psychical Research*, vol. 54, pp. 25–157.

Middleton, N. (1970), 'The Education Act of 1870 as the start of the modern conception of the child', *British Journal of Educational Studies*, vol. 18, no.2, June 1970, pp. 166–79.

Miller, Jane (1980), 'How do you spell Gujerati, Sir?', in L. Michaels and Christopher Ricks (eds), *The State of the Language*, Berkeley, University of California Press.

Miller, Jane (1983), *Many Voices*, London, Routledge & Kegan Paul.

Mitchell, J. and Oakley, A. (eds) (1976), *The Rights and Wrongs of Women*, Harmondsworth, Penguin.

Mitchell, J. and Rose, J. (1983a), *Jacques Lacan and the Ecole Freudienne: Feminine Sexuality*, London, Macmillan.

Mitchell, J. and Rose, J. (1983b), Interview in *m/f*, no. 8.

Moers, Ellen (1978), *Literary Women*, London, The Women's Press.

Moi, T. (1981), 'Representation of patriarchy: sexuality and epistemology in Freud's Dora', *Feminist Review*, no. 4.

Money, J. (1977), *Experience and Identity: Birmingham and the West Midlands, 1760–1800*, Manchester, Manchester University Press.

Moore, Laurence R. (1977), *In Search of White Crows: Spiritualism, Parapsychology and American Culture*, New York, Oxford University Press.

Moore, Laurence R. (1980), 'The spiritualist medium: a study of female professionalism in America', in Esther Katz and Anita Rapone (eds), *Women's Experience in America: An Historical Account*, New Brunswick, New Jersey, Transaction Books.

Murdoch, J. and Sylla, E. (1975), *The Cultural Context of Medieval Learning*, Dordrecht, Reidel.

Nash, B. (ed.) (1980), *The Complete Book of Babycare*, London, St Michael.

Nelson, Geoffrey, K. (1969), *Spiritualism and Society*, London, Routledge & Kegan Paul.

Newcastle Commission, PP. 1861 XXI, Volume I, Part 1.

Newson, John and Elizabeth (1965), *Patterns of Infant Care in an Urban Community*, Harmondsworth, Penguin.

Newson, J. and Newson, E. (1974), 'Aspects of Childrearing in the English-speaking world', in M. Richards (ed.), *The Integration of a Child into a Social World*, Cambridge, Cambridge University Press.

Newson, J. and Newson, E. (1976), *Seven Years Old in an Urban Community*, Harmondsworth, Penguin.

Oakley, A. (1980), *Women Confined*, London, Martin Robertson.
O'Connor, D.S. (ed.) (1907), *Peter Pan Keepsake*, the story of *Peter Pan* re-told from Mr Barrie's fantasy, foreword by W.T. Stead, London, Chatto & Windus.
O'Connor, D.S. (1912), *The Story of Peter Pan*, a reading book for use in schools, with illustrations by Alice B. Woodward, London, Bell.
O'Day, R. (1982), *Education and Society, 1500–1800*, London, Longman.
Okin, S.M. (1980), *Women in Western Political Thought*, London, Virago.
Ong, W. (1972), *Rhetoric, Romance and Technology*, Ithaca, New York, Cornell University Press.
Orbach, Susie and Eichenbaum, Luise (1983), *What do Women Want?*, London, Michael Joseph.
Orwell, George (1970), 'Shooting an elephant', in *The Collected Essays, Letters and Journalism of George Orwell: An Age Like This*, Harmondsworth, Penguin.
Owen, Alex (forthcoming), 'Women and nineteenth-century spiritualism: strategies in the subversion of femininity', in J. Obelkevitch, L. Roper and R. Samuel (eds), *Religion and Society*, London, Routledge & Kegan Paul.
Pascoe, C.E. (ed.) (1881), *Everyday Life in Our Public Schools*, London, Griffith & Farran.
Peck, Sabrina (1978), 'Child discourse in second language acquisition', in Hatch, Evelyn (ed.), *Second Language Acquisition*, Rowley, Mass., Newbury House.
Piaget, Jean (1954), *Play, Dreams and Imitation*, London, Routledge & Kegan Paul.
Pitcairn, E.H. (ed.) (1899), *Unwritten Laws and Ideals of Active Careers*, London, Smith, Elder & Co.
Plumb, J.H. (1975), 'The new world of children in the eighteenth century', *Past and Present*, vol. 67, pp. 64–93.
Podmore, Frank (1902), *Modern Spiritualism: A History and a Criticism*, vol. 2, London, Methuen.
Pole, Thomas (1823), *Observations Relative to Infant Schools*, Bristol.
Porter, R. (1982), *English Society in the Eighteenth Century*, Harmondsworth, Penguin.
Prochaska, F.K. (1980), *Women and Philanthropy in Nineteenth Century England*, Oxford, Oxford University Press.
Public Schools from Within (1906), a collection of essays on public school education written chiefly by schoolmasters, London, Low & Marston.
Quigly, Isabel (1982), *The Heirs of Tom Brown: The English School Story*, London, Chatto & Windus.

Report of the Commission Appointed to Inquire into Popular Education (1866), PP 1866, Volume 21, Part I.

Resnick, D. and Resnick, L.C. (1977), 'The nature of literacy: an historical exploration', *Harvard Educational Review*, vol. 47, no. 3, pp. 370–85.

Rich, A. (1980), *On Lies, Secrets and Silences*, London, Virago.

Riley, D. (1979), 'War in the Nursery', *Feminist Review*, vol. 2.

Riley, D. (1983), *War in the Nursery*, London, Virago.

Roberts, A.F.B. (1972), 'A new view of the infant school movement', *British Journal of Educational Studies*, vol. 20, pp. 154–64.

Rogers, A. (1959), 'Churches and children – a study in the controversy over the 1902 education act', *British Journal of Education Studies*, vol. 8, no. 1, November, pp. 29–51.

Ronjat, Jules (1913), *Le Developpment du langage observé chez un enfant bilingue*, Paris, Champion.

Rosaldo, M.Z. and Lamphere, L. (1974), *Women, Culture and Society*, Stanford, California, Stanford University Press.

Rose, J. (1978), 'Dora – fragment of an analysis', *m/f*, no. 2.

Rose, N. (1979), 'The psychological complex: mental measurement and social administration', *Ideology and Consciousness*, no. 5, pp. 5–68.

Ross, E. (1983), 'Survival networks: women's neighbourhood sharing in London before World War One', *History Workshop Journal*, no. 15, pp. 4–27.

Rouse, R. and Rouse, D. (1979), *Preachers, Florilegia and Sermons*, Toronto, Institute of Pontifical Studies.

Rover, Constance (1970), *Love, Morals and the Feminists*, London, Routledge & Kegan Paul.

Russell, Dora (1925), *Hypatia, or, Woman and Knowledge*, London, Kegan Paul.

Rutter, M. (1972), *Maternal Deprivation Reassessed*, Harmondsworth, Penguin.

Saenger, P. (1982), 'Silent reading: its impact on late medieval script and society', *Viator*, vol. 13, pp. 367–414.

Sanches, Mary and Kirshenblatt Gimblett, Barbara (1976), 'Children's traditional speech play and child language', in Kirshenblatt Gimblett, Barbara (ed.), *Speech Play*, Philadelphia, University of Pennsylvania Press.

Sayers, J. (1982), *Biological Politics*, London, Methuen.

Schellenberger, John (1982), 'Fiction and the first women students', *New University Quarterly*, vol. 36, no. 4, Autumn, pp. 352–8.

Schochet, G.J. (1975), *Patriarchalism in Political Thought*, Oxford, Blackwell.

Segal, L., Rowbotham, S. and Wainwright, H. (1979), *Beyond the Fragments*, London, Merlin Press.

Select Committee on Education in England and Wales, (1835), PP. 1835, vol. VII.

Sennett, R. and Cobb, R. (1977), *Hidden Injuries of Class*, Cambridge, Cambridge University Press.

Sharp, Evelyn (1897), *The Making of a School Girl*, London, Marshall & Russell.

Sharp, Evelyn (1933), *Unfinished Adventure*, London, John Lane.

Sharp, Rachel and Green, Anthony (1975), *Education and Social Control*, London, Routledge & Kegan Paul.

Shuard, H. (1981), 'Mathematics and the ten-year-old girl', *Times Educational Supplement*.

Silver, Harold (1965), *The Concept of Popular Education*, London, MacGibbon & Kee.

Simon, B. (1960), *Studies in the History of Education, Volume 1, 1780–1870*, London, Lawrence & Wishart.

Simon, Brian (1974), *The Two Nations and the Educational Structure 1780–1870*, London, Lawrence & Wishart.

Sixth Report of the Children's Employment Commission of 1862 (1867), PP. 1867, vol. 16.

Skultans, Vieda (1983), 'Mediums, controls and eminent men', in Pat Holden (ed.), *Women's Religious Experience*, London, Croom Helm.

Smith, A. (1759), *The Theory of Moral Sentiments*. Published Oxford, Oxford University Press, 1976.

Smith, Brian Sutton (1972), *The Folkgames of Children*, Austin, University of Texas Press, for the American Folklore Society.

Smout, T. (1982), 'Who was born again at Cambuslang? New evidence on popular religion and literacy in eighteenth-century Scotland', *Past and Present*, vol. 97, pp. 114–27.

Southgate, Vera, *et al.* (1981), *Extending Beginning Reading*, London, Heinemann.

Spencer, Margaret (1980), 'Handing down the magic', in Phillida Salmon (ed.), *Coming to Know*, London, Routledge & Kegan Paul.

Spender, Dale (1980), *Man Made Language*, London, Routledge & Kegan Paul.

Spock, B. (1969), *Dr Benjamin Spock's Baby and Childcare*, London, New English Library.

Stacey, M. and Price, M. (1981), *Women, Power and Politics*, London, Tavistock.

Steedman, C. (1982), *The Tidy House: Little Girls Writing*, London, Virago.

Steedman, C. (1985), 'The mother made conscious', *History Workshop Journal*, vol. 20.

Stewart, W.A.C. and McCann, W.P. (1967), *The Educational Innovators, Volume 1, 1750–1880*, London, Macmillan.

Stock, B. (1983), *The Implications of Literacy*, Princeton, New Jersey, Princeton University Press.

Stone, Maureen (1981), *The Education of the Black Child In Britain*, London, Fontana.

Stow, David (1938), *Supplement to Moral Training and the Training System*, Glasgow.

Stowe, Charles Edward (1889), *The Life of Harriet Beecher Stowe*, London, Sampson Low, Marston, Searle & Rivington.

Strauss G. (1978), *Luther's House of Learning*, Baltimore, Johns Hopkins Press.

Stronach, Alice (1901), *A Newnham Friendship*, London, Blackie.

Tanner, L.B. (ed.) (1970), *Voices from Women's Liberation*, New York, Signet.

Taylor, Barbara (1978), 'The woman-power: religious heresy and feminism in early English socialism', in Susan Lipshitz (ed.), *Tearing the Veil: Essays on Femininity*, London, Routledge & Kegan Paul.

Taylor, Barbara (1983), *Eve and the New Jerusalem*, London, Virago.

Taylor, William (1969), *Society and the Education of Teachers*, London, Faber & Faber.

Theobald, Morrell (1887), *Spirit Workers in the Home Circle*, London, T. Fisher Unwin.

Tolson, A. (1977), *Limits of Masculinity*, London, Tavistock.

Tough, Joan (1977), 'How shall we educate the young child?', in Alan Davies (ed.), *Language and Learning in Early Childhood*, London, Heinemann.

Townsend, John Rowe (1965), *Written for Children*, revised edn, Harmondsworth, Penguin, 1976.

Trinder, B. (1973), *The Industrial Revolution in Shropshire*, London, Phillimore.

Tripp, Susan Ervin (1974), 'Is second language learning like the first?', *TESOL Quarterly*, vol. 8, no. 2.

Troyna, Barry (1982), 'The ideological and policy responses to black pupils in British schools', in Anthony Hartnett (ed.), *The Social Sciences in Educational Studies*, London, Heinemann.

Turner, D.A. (1970), '1870: the state and the infant school system', *British Journal of Educational Studies*, vol. 18, pp. 151–65.

Turner, G.J. (1973), 'Social class and children's language of control at age 5 and 7', in B. Bernstein (ed.), *Class, Codes and Control*, vol. 2, London, Routledge & Kegan Paul.

Urwin, C. (1984), 'Power relations and the emergence of language', in Henriques *et al.* (eds), *Changing the Subject*.

Vaizey, Mrs G. De Horne (1913), *A College Girl*, London, Religious Tract Society.

Van der Post, Laurens (1977), *Jung and The Story of Our Time*, New York, Vintage Books.

Venn, C. (1984), 'The subject of psychology', in Henriques *et al.* (eds), *Changing the Subject.*

Vincent, David (1982), *Bread, Knowledge and Freedom*, London, Methuen.

Vygotsky, L.S. (1978), *Mind in Society*, Cambridge, Mass., Harvard University Press.

Walden, R. and Walkerdine, V. (1983), 'A for Effort, E for Ability: the case of girls and maths', *Primary Education Review*, Summer.

Walden, R. and Walkerdine, V. (1985, a), *Girls and Mathematics: From Primary to Secondary Schooling*, Bedford Way Papers, London, Heinemann.

Walden, R. and Walkerdine, V. (1985, b), *Gender and Education: Psychology's Construction of the Feminine*, Milton Keynes, Open University.

Walkerdine, V. (1981), 'Sex, power and pedagogy', *Screen Education*, no. 38.

Walkerdine, V. (1983a), 'Girls and mathematics: reflections on theories of cognitive development', paper given at the ISSBD Conference, Munich.

Walkerdine, V. (1983b), Final Report to the Social Science Research Council.

Walkerdine, V. (1983c), ' "She's a good little worker": femininity in the early mathematics classroom', *GAMMA newsletter.*

Walkerdine, V. (1983d), 'It's only natural: rethinking child-centred pedagogy', in A.M. Wolpe and J. Donald (eds), *Is There Anyone Here from Education*?, London, Pluto.

Walkerdine, V. (1984), 'Development psychology and the child-centred pedagogy: the insertion of Piaget's theory into primary school practice', in Henriques *et al.* (eds), *Changing the Subject.*

Walkerdine, V. (1985), 'Dreams from an ordinary childhood', in E. Heron (ed.), *Truth, Dare or Promise: Girls Growing Up in the 1950s*, London, Virago.

Walkerdine, V., Walden, R. and Own, C. (1982), 'Some methodological problems in the interpretation of statistical data relating to girls' performance in mathematics', British Psychological Society Education Section Conference, Durham.

Weeks, J. (1981), *Sex, Politics and Society*, Harlow, Essex, Longman.

Weir, Ruth (1970), *Language in the Crib*, The Hague, Mouton.

Wells, Gordon (1981), *Learning Through Interaction*, Cambridge, Cambridge University Press.

Whalley, J. (1969), *English Handwriting, 1540–1853*, London, HMSO.

Whitbread, Nanette (1972), *The Evolution of the Infant/Nursery School*, London, Routledge & Kegan Paul.

White, B.L. (1967), 'An experimental approach to the effects of experience on early human behaviour', in J.P. Mill (ed.), *Minnesota Symposium on Child Psychology*, vol. 1, pp. 201–26, Minneapolis, University of Minnesota Press.

Whiteman, M. (1983) (ed.), *Variations in Writing*, Baltimore, Erlbaum.

Widdowson, F. 1983 see p. 309.

Wilderspin, Samuel (1825), *Infant Education*, London, Simpkin & Marshall (3rd edn).

Wilkinson, Margaret (ed.) (1900), *Autobiography of Emma Hardinge Britten*, London, John Heywood.

Wilkinson, R. (1964), *The Prefects: British Leadership and the Public School Tradition*, London, Oxford University Press.

Williams, F. (ed.) (1970), *Language and Poverty*, Chicago, Markham.

Williams, Raymond (1975), *The Country and the City*, St Albans, Granada.

Williamson, Judith (1978), *Decoding Advertisements*, London, Marion Boyars.

Willis, P. (1978), *Learning to Labour*, London, Saxon House.

Wilson, Amrit (1982), 'You think we've got problems', *New Statesman*, 13 November.

Wilson, R. (1914), *Macmillan's Sentence Building*, a graduated course of lessons in synthetic English, 14 vols, London, Macmillan.

Wilson, William (1925), *The System of Infants' Schools*, London, George Wilson.

Winnicott, D.W. (1971), *Playing and Reality*, London, Tavistock, (Harmondsworth, Penguin, 1974).

Winslow, L.S. Forbes (1881), *Fasting and Feeding Psychologically Considered*, London, Balliere, Tindall & Cox.

Women's Studies Group (1978), *Women Take Issue: Aspects of Women's Subordination*, Birmingham, Centre for Contemporary Cultural Studies and London, Hutchinson.

Woodruff, P. (1954), *The Men who Ruled India: Volume 2, The Guardians*, London, Jonathan Cape.

Worpole, Ken and Morley, Dave (1982), *The Republic of Letters*, London, Comedia.

Wright, G.H. (1913), *Chronicles of the Birmingham Chamber of Commerce 1813–1913 and of the Birmingham Commercial Society 1983–1812*, Birmingham.

Wyld, H.C. (1906) *The Place of the Mother Tongue in the National Education*, London, John Murray.

Name index

Subject index